Beautiful
BATTLE

MARY E. DEMUTH

HARVEST HOUSE PUBLISHERS

EUGENE, OREGON

Cover by Koechel Peterson & Associates, Inc., Minneapolis, Minnesota

Cover photo © Thinkstock; Koechel Peterson & Associates

This book contains stories in which the author has changed people's names and some details of their situations in order to protect their privacy.

BEAUTIFUL BATTLE
Copyright © 2012 by Mary E. DeMuth
Published by Harvest House Publishers
Eugene, Oregon 97402
www.harvesthousepublishers.com

Library of Congress Cataloging-in-Publication Data
DeMuth, Mary E., 1967-
Beautiful battle / Mary E. DeMuth.
    p. cm.
Includes bibliographical references (p.   ).
ISBN 978-0-7369-4380-2 (pbk.)
ISBN 978-0-7369-4381-9 (eBook)
1. Spiritual warfare. 2. Christian women—Religious life. I. Title.
BV4509.5.D455 2012
235'.4082—dc23

                                                    2011018974

To Jodi Vinson and Kimberly Baker,
beautiful women who deliberately prayed me through

Acknowledgments

I'm particularly indebted to Dr. J. Scott Horrell for his class notes on angelology. Thank you, Scott, for your graciousness in letting me read through them.

Thanks, too, to Patrick, my theological hubby, who read through this book, offering helpful critique and a hefty dose of perspective and encouragement.

Thanks to my kids, Sophie, Aidan, and Julia, who allowed me to write bits and pieces of their stories here. I count it a privilege to battle alongside you.

I so appreciate Leslie Wilson and D'Ann Mateer, who took pains to read through this manuscript and offer critique.

Thanks to the great staff at Harvest House who shepherded this book to press. LaRae Weikert, thanks for jumping at this book. Your eagerness helped fuel the passion for it. Thanks to Kathleen Kerr for your much-needed cheerleading through the editing process. You lifted my heart.

Esther Fedorkevich, you've been an amazing agent, friend, and partner. Thank you.

Thanks to the readers who offered their stories so freely.

I am indebted to my prayer team as always, but particularly with this book. You kept the darkness at bay as I tried to write in the light. Thank you Twilla Fontenot, Ashley Weis, Kevin and Renee Bailey, Carla Smith, Caroline Coleman, Cheramy Mayfield, Colleen Eslinger, Jeanne Damoff, Darren and Holly Sapp, D'Ann Mateer, Dorian Coover-Cox, Erin Teske, Katy Gedney, Kimberly Baker, Ginger Vassar, Helen Graves, Holly Schmidt, Jan Winebrenner, Jen Powell, Kathy ONeall, Katy Raymond, Denise Willhite, Anita Curtis, Diane Klapper, Lesley Hamilton, Leslie Wilson, Lilli Brenchley, Liz Wolf, Marcia Robbins, Marcus Goodyear, Grace Bower, Marybeth Whalen, Pam Le Tourneau, Paula Moldenhauer, Rae McIlrath, Phyllis Yount, Becky Ochs, Sandi Glahn, Sarah Walker, Shawna Marie Bryant, Tim Riter, Tina Howard, Tracy Walker, Heidi Van Dyken, Paul Napari, Renee Mills, Stacey Tomisser, John Davis, Carla Williams, Nicole Baart, Tosca Lee, Marilyn Scholtz, TJ Wilson, Jim Rubart, Patrick DeMuth, Jody Capehart, Susan Meissner, Ariel Lawhon, Mary Vestal, Amy Sorrells, Lisa Shea, Dena Dyer, Kathryn Thomas, Carol Avery, Cyndi Kraweitz, Don Pape, Esther Fedorkevich, Susie Larson, Christy Tennant, Jodi Vinson, and Ericka Smiley.

Jesus, You are beautifully victorious. For that, I humbly thank You.

Contents

Introduction 7

Part One:
Foundations

1 Our Story:
The Gaping Hole and Freedom 13

2 Satan's Story:
Understanding the Enemy Who Towers *and* Cowers 21

3 The Right Story:
God's Sovereignty. The Wrong Story: Our Comfort. 37

4 Living the Right Story:
Balancing Between Ignorance and Overreaction 49

5 So What's the Story, Exactly? What Is Spiritual Warfare? 55

Part Two:
Proactive: How We Participate in the Beautiful Battle

6 Breathing Prayer 69

7 Loving Truth 85

8 Practicing Risk 91

9 Slaying Idols 97

10 Worshiping God 105

11 Living the Bible 111

12 Embracing Rest 119

13 Chasing Healing 125

Part Three:
Reactive: What We Do in the Midst of the Beautiful Battle

14 When Fear Rushes In 135

15 When Christians Hurt You 145

16 When Your Mind Attacks 155

17 When Your Family Faces a Battle 167

18 When Sin and Addictions Threaten 175

19 When the Mouth Becomes a Weapon 183

20 When Overt Attack Assails You 189

**Part Four:
Victory: We Can Live with Hope
When the Beautiful Battle Rages**

21 Overcoming in Community 197

22 Mountains and Valleys 203

23 Finding Abundance and Perspective 211

24 Go Forth! 223

    Notes 231

Introduction

I'm not much for war. I don't relish my son's seeming addiction to the History channel, a channel my husband renamed "The Hitler Channel." I can't shoot a gun, pull a bowstring taut, or comprehend tank warfare. I don't like conflict on a global scale, nor do I relish arguments in an interpersonal arena. Simply put, I'm warfare-avoidant.

So why in the world would I write a book about spiritual warfare?

Because whether I avoid it or not, the truth is we live in a battle zone. I can't put my fingers in my ears, sing la-la-la-la-la, and hope spiritual conflict will cease. I've seen enough of Satan's outright attacks against me and those I love to know a head-in-the-ground approach only makes for demonic victory. We can't hide. This war will not go away. And there are consequences if we shrink back.

I don't write this book to glorify Satan's tactics, but to point them out. I don't resort to histrionic fear as I unpack spiritual truth about demonic activity on this earth; instead, together, we'll discover the might and power and verve of our holy and amazing God, the Victorious One.

While it is true that we face battles aplenty in our personal lives, relationships, schools, churches, cities, and governments, it is truer still that Jesus came to this earth to bring abundance and victory. How can I be so sure? In a smaller-than-global scale, He's joyfully revolutionized my life.

I grew up oblivious to God's activity in the world. Surrounded by drug abuse, neglect, and sexual assault, I knew at a young age that this world wasn't safe. And if I cherished my own safety, I would have to provide it for myself. Problem was, I couldn't always protect myself. Bad things happened. Bad people acted cruelly. By the time I was thirteen, I despaired my life and wanted to end it.

But God would win the battle for my life and eventually my heart. His sovereign hand saw fit to send me to a school counselor who saved my life, then prompted my friend to invite me to Young Life in ninth grade. By tenth grade in the shelter of a Christian camp, I succumbed to His holy wooing and gave my tattered life to Him. In that moment, the darkness fled. Many of the doubts, suicidal thoughts, fears, and heartache God flung away. He tucked His powerful Holy Spirit into the crevasses of my heart, set my feet on a firm path, and instigated joy.

When I burst through the doorway of my home, I felt my heart would overflow. I spilled, leaked, and gushed the gospel to my unsuspecting mom, who grew visibly angry, then belligerent. She felt I'd joined a cult and warned me about my newfound faith. That conflict between us continues to this day.

Even with little support at home for my faith, God grew me. He provided Christian friends, a church, and good leaders who shored me up. He instigated this adventure I'm on, thrilling me on trips around the world—Malaysia, Singapore, Ghana, South Africa, Europe. In those adventures, and in the confines of my own home with three teenagers and a handsome husband, I have seen Him bring victory from heartache, power from weakness, beauty from failure, purpose from grief. That's the power of the God we serve, this Victorious One.

I can't help but spill, leak, and gush His capability to you. How can I not share what God's accomplished in me? How can I not pull back the veil of this crazy life and point to all the victory He's wrought in me? Because the power of God-breathed spiritual warfare is this: changed lives.

And mine's been changed, reshaped, renewed, rejuvenated, refined by the One who conquered death and Satan in one defiant, glorious crucifixion and resurrection. This is not a book about evil. It's a book about the outrageous victory God sends our way. It's about freedom and how God moves and trains us from glory to glory. It's about finding beauty where devastation seeps. It's about truth and authenticity. It's about the power of God to heal our hearts, to move situational mountains, to intercede when we're weary.

That's my heart in writing this book—to point you to the Victorious One.

To revel in His ability to move, not my ability to follow.

To elevate Him, praise Him, reveal Him.

Because Jesus Christ is the answer to every dark thought, attack, and evil scheme. The more I send you His way, the more victorious your soul will be. The more you rest in His power residing within you, the more peace you'll experience. And the bigger He is in your own life, the smaller your struggles seem.

Those of you who have read my other books will know I'm no Pollyanna. I'm never one to sugarcoat. So my verbiage about victory and the immense beauty of Jesus is genuine. I know we are in an epic war. I know we're battle-scarred. But more than that I know the One who battles before and behind us just as He did in Nehemiah's time: "At whatever place you hear the sound of the trumpet, rally to us there. Our God will fight for us" (Nehemiah 4:20).

In that beautiful battle, I know His light will obliterate the darkness.

If we will allow Him.

Part One

FOUNDATIONS

Before we get into the nitty-gritty of daily spiritual warfare, it's important that we establish a foundation for the beautiful battle. We must answer fundamental questions about who we are as warrior women, who God is, and how Satan came to be such a malevolent force in today's world. Apostle's Church pastor JR Vassar says, "You can trace all evil, error, and violence back to Satan. His ultimate desire is to deceive all people away from God into sin, misery, death, and eternal destruction."[1]

And yet we serve a triumphant, victorious God who sent His Son for the very purpose of destroying Satan's schemes. That one fact undergirds our confidence, gives us hope and joy, and enables us to overcome the trials and temptations Satan sends our way.

Because I believe in the importance of prayer as we engage in spiritual warfare, I'll offer a prayer at the end of each chapter.

Chapter 1

Our Story:
The Gaping Hole and Freedom

You stir man to take pleasure in praising you,
because you have made us for yourself,
and our heart is restless until it rests in you.[1]

St. Augustine

He sent me e-mails. He seemed to care. He engaged me in conversation, asked me questions, validated my dreams. Only he wasn't my husband.

I'd chastised myself once before for letting my heart bend toward another man. And I'd created boundaries to keep me safe. Yet this man persisted. By God's grace, I ran the other way.

I wish I didn't have to write words like this. I wish I didn't have to confess it so stark on the page, but as I started this book, the Lord reminded me of this story, of my own dabbling in emotionally inappropriate relationships with men.

For a long time, I wondered why I craved the attention of men, why I felt like a drooping flower in need of the watering can of male attention. But now I know.

The men who pursued me shared haunting similarities. Both older. Both in authority. Both tending toward narcissism. As I worked through these similarities, something clicked. God's gentle wooing and kindness exposed me to myself. Then came that painful *aha*. My sin, my giving the devil a stronghold, had everything to do with a gaping hole in my heart.

I grew up trying to fill that hole, but no one seemed to want to fill it. Teenage boys told me they liked me, but they stole my innocence. A

13

drug-filled home kept me insecure and afraid. Divorce, then death, took my father. In my mother's own pain she couldn't fill me, and in her penchant toward narcissism she couldn't see me. When I met Jesus at 15, that gaping hole brimmed with His living water, and for a long time the hole felt filled.

In retrospect, I see that there's still a part of Mary that needs affirmation. There's still a need in me to run after my father (authority figure, older) and my mother (narcissism) to fill me up. As long as I allow the gaping hole to remain, I will continue to struggle with this sin, this gnawing need.

What does this have to do with spiritual warfare?

Everything.

Because our raw woundedness is the primary opening the enemy uses to attack our souls. Our own bent toward filling the gaping hole will continue to lead us to darker and more insidious situations as we claw at significance. Obsessions form. Hiding becomes our way of life. Addictions flourish. If we do not deal with our deficits truthfully in the light, Satan's darkness may be our lot. And in that darkness, we start believing his terrible lies:

- You deserve every pain that comes your way.
- You can't have true victory in the Christian life.
- You will never change.
- You will never experience true joy.
- You are nothing.
- You are insignificant.
- All you can hope for is to struggle well (or not so well) in this life.

Have you entertained thoughts like those? Ever felt the stinging power of lies that sound so much like truth, you devour them? Have you tried to fill up a wound with people? Addictions? Money? Power? Pride?

Consider this: "For all that is in the world, the lust of the flesh and the lust of the eyes and the boastful pride of life, is not from the Father, but is from the world" (1 John 2:16 NASB). And who is temporarily prowling over this world system? Satan. "Be of sober spirit, be on the alert. Your adversary, the devil, prowls around like a roaring lion, seeking someone to devour" (1 Peter 5:8 NASB).

Satan devours us from the inside out by convincing us that something in this world will ultimately fill our hearts. And yet nothing will, which is why the first step in conquering Satan's lies and traps is filling our gaping hole with what truly satisfies.

In speaking to the nation of Israel, God also highlights our own tendency toward filling the hole. "For My people have committed two evils: They have forsaken Me, the fountain of living waters, to hew for themselves cisterns, broken cisterns that can hold no water" (Jeremiah 2:13 NASB). In our own injury (in my case a gaping mother and father hole), we seek to fill that hole with our own water instead of Living Water. What's the water? Other people, stuff, experiences, pleasure. Momentarily, our hole fills—only to leak out again. We believe that somehow, in our own effort, we can heal ourselves, fix ourselves, put our Humpty Dumpty selves back together. But we can't. Ever. That's why we're tired.

Psalm 39:6 sums up our lot: "We are merely moving shadows, and all our busy rushing ends in nothing."

Nothing.

All that digging and waiting to be filled equals nothing.

So how do we fill the gaping hole?

First, recognize that you have one.

Look over your life and see where you've fallen into sin, where you've rushed after that which doesn't satisfy. For me, that meant facing my desire for male attention and analyzing its roots. It meant praying, alone and with friends. It meant seeking counsel and advice. It meant sharing my embarrassing story with accountability partners who walked with me and asked me hard questions. It meant confessing my sin to my husband. It meant setting appropriate boundaries. But far more than all those good, important things, it meant asking Jesus to be the Living Water inside me.

> Living Water personified asks a broken cistern of
> a woman for water. He asks the same of us.

Second, understand Satan's counterfeiting tactics.

Satan is the guru of greener grass, the conniver who promises pleasure if only you'll slip a big toe through the fence. He brews dissatisfaction while you fight to maintain contentment. Be assured, his promises are empty. They are designed to enslave you. Though he promises kingdoms, he delivers slums. And he whispers all these things at your point of weakness, that place where you've tried to fill your gaping hole.

Third, remember Jesus.

He is the Living Water, the only One who satisfies. Consider from a new perspective the story of Jesus's encounter with the woman at the well. That woman has a gaping hole. She's felt unloved in her life, unwanted. She tries to fill the hole with men—several men. And still, she thirsts. But Jesus doesn't slake her thirst with the well water. He doesn't offer to pour her a cup. Instead, He works at exposing her thirst by asking her for a drink. Imagine! Living Water personified asks a broken cistern of a woman for water. He asks the same of us.

We Are the Woman at the Well

The woman marvels at His question, particularly because she knows Jews don't associate with Samaritans—yet here stands Jesus, a well-known Jewish teacher. Perhaps she's felt the sting of rejection before. Maybe His kindness exposes the wound.

Jesus responds to her words about being a Samaritan by telling her, "If you knew the generosity of God and who I am, you would be asking me for a drink, and I would give you fresh, living water."

Still, she doesn't understand His words. She's thinking about filling her soul with physical water. She replies, "Sir, you don't even have a bucket to draw with, and this well is deep. So how are you going to get this 'living water'? Are you a better man than our ancestor Jacob, who dug this well and drank from it, he and his sons and livestock, and passed it down to us?"

The patriarch Jacob dug a well; that is true. But the One who formed Jacob in the womb, the One who created the oceans, the One who fashioned the Samaritan woman's heart, stands before her. Living Water without a bucket. He doesn't chastise her ignorance, doesn't poke fun either. He simply tells her, "Everyone who drinks this water will get thirsty again and again. Anyone who drinks the water I give will never thirst—not ever. The water I give will be an artesian spring within, gushing fountains of endless life."

She tells Him to give her this water so she doesn't have to come back to the well. He could've done it. He could've given her His presence right there, pointing out the difference between His living water and the stagnant pool at the bottom of the well, but He doesn't. He wants to expose the way she has tried to fill herself. So He asks her to call her husband, to which she replies, "I have no husband."

He tells her she's spoken the truth, and then He reveals the truth of her situation—five husbands past, and one current live-in boyfriend. They talk about Samaritans and Jews and the proper way to worship God. Jesus tells her, "Your worship must engage your spirit in the pursuit of truth. That's the kind of people the Father is out looking for: those who are simply and honestly themselves before him in their worship. God is sheer being itself—Spirit. Those who worship him must do it out of their very being, their spirits, their true selves, in adoration."

For a woman who's spent her life coddling her own need, this language must have stupefied. Worship God from way down deep inside? Adore Him instead of wooing men? Trade that which seems to satisfy for that which truly, fully fills her? In her confusion, she says, "I don't know about that. I do know that the Messiah is coming. When he arrives, we'll get the whole story."

"I am he," Jesus says. "You don't have to wait any longer or look any further" (selections from John 4:7-26 MSG).

What life-altering words! The Samaritan woman's life stands in front of her. It's Jesus. His living water will satiate the thirst she tried to satisfy with the attention of men. She doesn't have to scheme and fret. Doesn't have to manipulate others to be filled. Look at her final act: "The woman took the hint and left. In her confusion she left her water pot."

She leaves the water pot behind—the one thing she'd used to physically quench her thirst, the security she once had for something altogether better: the Fountain of Living Water.

That's where spiritual warfare begins—leaving our own methods of filling our gaping holes at the well and allowing Jesus to fill every thirsty, needy place with His Living Water. Later, Jesus reiterates His invitation to all of us: "Let anyone who is thirsty come to me and drink. Whoever believes in me, as Scripture has said, rivers of living water will flow from within them" (John 7:37-38 NIV).

If rivers of Living Water flow from within us, very little can tempt us to fill our gaping holes from the outside. And if Jesus fills us, Satan will have a hard time distracting us.

And yet we struggle.

Like the woman at the well, I can attest that I thirsted for male attention again. And again. But as I've learned to let go of the water pot, to settle into Jesus's words, to let them permeate my heart, I feel the gushing, the welling up of the kind of water that ultimately, deeply satiates me. His infusion of Living Water drowns out my need to fill the hole. His presence makes me truly, fully satisfied.

Finding full satisfaction in Christ is the beginning of the spiritual warfare journey, but it's not the entirety of it.

The Dance

As I prayed about this chapter, the Lord reminded me of an awkward time in my life: seventh grade physical education. During that year, we learned several dances—the waltz, the fox-trot, and the swing—culminating in a demonstration in front of the entire school. If we learned our dances well, we'd be picked to be part of the program. For a scrawny, all-elbows-and-knees girl, this proved challenging. So I practiced. And stepped on my poor partner's feet. And tried to lead (confession: I still do). Even so, we improved. Miraculously, we won a spot in front of the school. And we danced our steps.

That same year, I attended my first junior high dance. I'm not sure why they were called dances, since most of the time people remained plastered to the four yellow walls of our cafeteria, insecure and needy. Standing next to a friend, twiddling my fingers, wondering if I'd ever get asked to dance, I felt about as small as the narrow width of my shoes. I watched the popular girls whirl and laugh. I noticed the way the boys looked at those girls, a hint of wanting in their eyes. I wanted to be wanted. That hole I shared earlier? It screamed then. In the context of that experience, I didn't dance.

So what made the difference? Why did I happily dance in one realm and shrink back in another? Two words: parameters and practice. Within the confines of a physical education class, dancing was commanded, normative. The teachers expected everyone to take a part. And for those of us who struggled and wanted to improve, they provided coaching and time to do so. They gave us the gift of parameters and practice.

That's what this book will do. I give you permission to learn about something that may frighten or bewilder you. Within the confines of this book, I share principles and techniques that will equip you to walk the spiritual warfare path. Your job is to practice freely, to stumble and try again, to be willing to try new steps. This is not the time to shrink back into the woodwork while the popular girls smile and flirt. It is, as Solomon wrote, "a time to dance" (Ecclesiastes 3:4).

> In His fullness we forget about ourselves, our wounds, and our needs, and we dance with Him unencumbered, free.

There's too much at stake to shrink back. Too many lives need to be touched. Too many people (including yourself) need to be set free, just as the woman at the well experienced freedom. Too many people walk around with gaping holes, filling them with trinkets while Jesus, the treasure of our souls, extends His hand in invitation. He invites us all to dance, and He particularly invites you who hold this book in your hands. Will you accept His invitation?

Spiritual warfare has more to do with the state of your heart before a holy God than a list of things to do or avoid. It involves interaction, sometimes confusion, falling down, getting back up. It involves your willingness to look foolish, to take crazy steps, to trust God's voice. While there are principles to know and practice, it's your ability to trust in God's power and authority that will bring about the victorious life.

A Life of Freedom

We've moved from gaping holes to wild dances. Isn't that what the life of freedom looks like? We try to fade into the outer walls of life, feeling the sting of being outcasts, only to realize the God of the Universe extends His hand, invites us to Him, and fills us up to overflowing. In that fullness we forget about ourselves, our wounds, and our needs, and we dance with Him unencumbered, free.

My own freedom has been won on many battlefields, one of which I've shared in this chapter—my need for love, acceptance. I'm reminded of this powerful, truth-filled verse in Revelation 12:11: "And they have defeated [the devil] by the blood of the Lamb and by their testimony. And they did not love their lives so much that they were afraid to die." How do we overcome the wily schemes of the devil? First by the precious, overflowing, beautiful blood of Jesus. And then by sharing what He's done with others. I rest in that as I write these stark words on a blank page. I rest in the power of the cross, the blood Jesus shed there. And I'm here to write stories of testimony—mine, others, maybe even yours—for the sake of finding an overcoming faith. The kind of faith that withstands assault, the kind that gives little worry about life or death. This book is my testimony. I pray it is yours.

Mind if I pray for you?

Lord, help my friend reading this chapter to see her holes, the places she determines to fill herself with that which does not satisfy. Help her to be willing to share those needy places with a trusted friend, to confess any sin that results from those holes, and to find freedom to receive Your living water. Fill her up, Jesus. To overflowing. May she find satisfaction today in You alone. Amen.

Chapter 2

Satan's Story:
Understanding the Enemy
Who Towers *and* Cowers

There are two equal and opposite errors into which our race can
fall about the devils. One is to disbelieve in their existence. The
other is to believe, and to feel an excessive and unhealthy interest
in them. They themselves are equally pleased by both errors,
and hail a materialist or magician with the same delight.[1]

C.S. LEWIS

C.S. Lewis succinctly captures the dilemma we face in thinking about Satan and his minions. My hope in this book is to be realistic. Not dismissive of the devil's schemes, but not glorying in them, either. To give you a sound scriptural understanding of him without inflating his over-wrought ego. Because it's this overly-inflamed ego that brought him to where we find him today. Permit me to tell the story.

Once upon a Time

God existed—and exists—in three persons: God the Father, God the Son, and God the Holy Spirit. They were together before time. In their fellowship among each other, they existed always, all sufficient, never lacking. God created angelic beings to serve Him. These angels loved serving Him, trusting every decision He made in the realm of His eternal kingdom. No jealousy or hatred or strife could be found among God's servants, content to serve. They understood their place in the kingdom, to point to God's great worth and renown. In light of God's supreme power and beauty, nothing else seemed to matter.

The seeming chief of the angels rejoiced in this contentment day by day. He enjoyed watching God walk, talk, and sing among Himself. God's power and knowledge dazzled the cherub.

But something shifted in a hiccup of a moment. A slight reorientation of the gaze from God's splendor to his own. Every day the amount of time spent gazing at God ebbed in light of Satan's newfound affection for himself, his beauty, his power. He may have reasoned, *Surely there is a place in this kingdom for more than one God.* He sowed discontent among other angelic servants, plotting to set up his own kingdom where the servants would follow him, revere him, extol his beauty.

Something shifted in a hiccup of a moment. A slight reorientation of the gaze from God's splendor to his own.

God warred against Satan and the angels he'd deceived. Satan must've resisted, but his resistance came against God like an ant against a bear. God banished Satan and his turncoat allies from His presence. The banishment only made Satan furious, determined to retaliate against the insolent God.

While scholars have debated whether the following two passages are about Satan or merely about the actual rulers (the king of Babylon and the prince of Tyre) to whom they are addressed, a great many affirm these are both/and passages—both about the kings discussed and Satan's fall from heaven. With that in mind, read:

Isaiah 14:4,12-15

You will taunt the king of Babylon. You will say,

"The mighty man has been destroyed.
Yes, your insolence is ended…
How you are fallen from heaven,
O shining star, son of the morning!
You have been thrown down to the earth,
you who destroyed the nations of the world.
For you said to yourself,
'I will ascend to heaven and set my throne
     above God's stars.
I will preside on the mountain of the gods
far away in the north.

I will climb to the highest heavens
and be like the Most High.'
Instead, you will be brought down to the place
of the dead,
down to its lowest depths."

Ezekiel 28:2,12-17

Son of man, give the prince of Tyre this message from the
Sovereign LORD:

"In your great pride you claim, 'I am a god!
I sit on a divine throne in the heart of the sea.'
But you are only a man and not a god,
though you boast that you are a god…"

Son of man, sing this funeral song for the king of Tyre. Give
him this message from the Sovereign LORD:

"You were the model of perfection,
full of wisdom and exquisite in beauty.
You were in Eden,
the garden of God.
Your clothing was adorned with every precious stone—
red carnelian, pale-green peridot, white moonstone,
blue-green beryl, onyx, green jasper,
blue lapis lazuli, turquoise, and emerald—
all beautifully crafted for you
and set in the finest gold.
They were given to you
on the day you were created.
I ordained and anointed you
as the mighty angelic guardian.
You had access to the holy mountain of God
and walked among the stones of fire.

"You were blameless in all you did
from the day you were created
until the day evil was found in you.
Your rich commerce led you to violence,
and you sinned.

So I banished you in disgrace
from the mountain of God.
I expelled you, O mighty guardian,
from your place among the stones of fire.
Your heart was filled with pride
because of all your beauty.
Your wisdom was corrupted
by your love of splendor.
So I threw you to the ground
and exposed you to the curious gaze of kings."

Centuries later the apostle John writes, "For the world offers only a craving for physical pleasure, a craving for everything we see, and pride in our achievements and possessions. These are not from the Father, but are from this world" (1 John 2:16).

Pleasure.

Stuff.

Achievement.

Satan craved pleasure outside of what God provided. He saw himself as worthy of worship, and he prided himself on his ability to be like God. Since there can be only one true God, and because Satan is merely a created being incapable of creation, God's loving act was to banish him and his cohorts. Which brings us back to the story.

God Fashions the Earth

In six days, God breathed a new, physical kingdom into existence. Matter from non-matter. Time from eternity. Dirt from the proclamation of His mouth. Animals, water, mountains, birds, oxygen, life itself— and then His crowning achievement—a creature made in the very image of God. Man, woman, He called them. His smile shone over the two. He proclaimed them "very good."

When Satan saw God's deep affection for this man, this woman, his anger ignited. He might not be able to compete with this all-powerful Creator God, but he could maim and mar the Creator's new love. So he shape-shifted into one of the snakes he'd come to admire in his exile, only he kept his voice. Satan spied the two there, naked and unashamed, gazing at a tree from which they weren't supposed to eat. In his exile, Satan's heart had darkened, grown more intelligent, conniving. He knew he couldn't persuade the terrible creatures to rebel outright as he had. But he could woo, entice, deceive. His tactic became deception and lies and his three fallbacks.

Pleasure.

Stuff.

Achievement.

So he slithered to the woman, whispered in her ear that God withheld pleasure from her by limiting her fruit intake. He made her crave something outside of God's stated provision. He portrayed God's goodness as restriction, practically parading the fruit before her as evidence that God had no intention of making her happy, taunting her with achievement-oriented words, words about being like God, understanding the nature of good and evil.

Through skillful words, he deceived her until she not only *wanted* the forbidden fruit, but also believed she *needed* it. His voice was smooth, taunting, tantalizing, seductive even. "If you take it, you'll find out what it's like to be God's equal. You'll finally understand the kingdom He's created. You'll be just like Him." Satan paused and refrained from saying, "... just as I have found."

To his delight, the woman and the man took happy, crunchy, wet bites. In that moment, he heard God's groan—an agony that made Satan smile. *So that's all it takes*, he thought. Mess with God's crowning achievement, and you hurt Him.

Satan could woo, entice, deceive. His tactic became deception and lies and his three fallbacks: Pleasure. Stuff. Achievement.

The man and woman hid from God. Where there had never been bloodshed, wet, sticky blood spilled to the earth to cover their nakedness with fur and skins. God cursed the woman, multiplying her pain in childbirth. No longer would she be an equal with her husband, but under his authority. He caused thorns to erupt from the garden, multiplying the man's toil in work. And to Satan, God spoke of the future, of how one day He would right every wrong, punish his rebellion completely. But for now Satan faced life crawling forever on his belly under the foot of mankind, tasting the dust of earth.

Years and years and years Satan sucked dust as he tormented and bothered the man and woman's offspring. Unchecked, he puffed up with pride, no longer banished to the outer regions, but given free roaming privileges around the kingdom of earth and even the throne of the triune God. It seemed God had forgotten His mandate to once and for all punish Satan for his pride and evildoing.

God Sends His Son

The cry heard from Bethlehem shattered Satan's complacency, inciting him to scream into King Herod's royal ear to kill all the baby boys in the region. It squealed into rage when Satan led the God-man into the wilderness to tempt Him as he had the man and woman in the garden so many years ago. He used the same appeal, the same tactic as from old:

Pleasure.

Stuff.

Achievement.

With these three words in mind, notice how Satan tries to tempt Jesus in the desert.

Pleasure.

"Then Jesus, full of the Holy Spirit, returned from the Jordan River. He was led by the Spirit in the wilderness, where he was tempted by the devil for forty days. Jesus ate nothing all that time and became very hungry. Then the devil said to him, 'If you are the Son of God, tell this stone to become a loaf of bread.' But Jesus told him, 'No! The Scriptures say, "People do not live by bread alone."'"

Stuff.

"Then the devil took him up and revealed to him all the kingdoms of the world in a moment of time. 'I will give you the glory of these kingdoms and authority over them,' the devil said, 'because they are mine to give to anyone I please. I will give it all to you if you will worship me.' Jesus replied, 'The Scriptures say, "You must worship the LORD your God and serve only him."'"

Achievement.

"Then the devil took him to Jerusalem, to the highest point of the Temple, and said, 'If you are the Son of God, jump off! For the Scriptures say, "He will order his angels to protect and guard you. And they will hold you up with their hands so you won't even hurt your foot on a stone."' Jesus responded, 'The Scriptures also say, "You must not test the LORD your

God.'" When the devil had finished tempting Jesus, he left him until the next opportunity came" (Luke 4:1-13).

Satan threw his entire arsenal at Christ during his foray on earth. In recorded history to that point, no one engaged and cast out as many demons as Jesus did during His three years of ministry on the earth. Yet He employed no tactics or gimmicks in doing so. Jesus's exorcisms were swift and clean. It's fascinating to study the words of demons in response to Jesus. They present the most astute, compelling theology, forced to tell the truth about Jesus every time He calls them out. "The Christology of demons in their exclamations before Jesus is one of the most extraordinary witnesses recorded in the Synoptics," writes Dr. Scott Horrell.[2]

Satan felt he'd scored the ultimate victory when he enticed Judas to betray his Friend with a kiss. He must've felt elation and glee when the very people Jesus hailed from turned on Him and pushed for crucifixion. And what a histrionic song Satan must've sung as Jesus let out His last, sacred breath. Not only had Satan victoriously attacked God's creation, he'd instigated the killing of part of the Trinity. A surefire, heady victory.

But...

But three days later in the womb of earth, life quaked. To the horror of the one bent on theft, murder, and destruction, Jesus, the Son of God, resurrected, victorious over the grave. Satan, the destroyer, the speaker of lies, shrieked, cowered, and knew. His time roaming the earth was simply a numbered abacus of days and nights.

In this in-between time after Jesus's resurrection and His second coming, Satan continues his fight as a defeated enemy. I love what author Sydney Page says about Satan's current state: "The Christian who takes the demonological teaching of the Bible seriously can confront temptation and evil with confidence, knowing that Christ has already defeated the forces of evil and their ultimate doom is assured."[3]

Someday, Satan will be destroyed in what the Bible calls the lake of fire. But until then, what is his role? What does he do?

He is the god of this world.

The god of this world seeks to subvert the message of God. "If the Good News we preach is hidden behind a veil," says Paul, "it is hidden only from people who are perishing. Satan, who is the god of this world, has blinded the minds of those who don't believe. They are unable to see the glorious light of the Good News. They don't understand this message about the glory of Christ, who is the exact likeness of God" (2 Corinthians 4:3-4).

<blockquote>
Satan cannot stand beneath the power
of the cross of the risen Christ.
</blockquote>

In that controlling of this world, he incites those who don't yet believe in Jesus, enticing them to live in sin, to revel in their broken nature. "Once you were dead because of your disobedience and your many sins. You used to live in sin, just like the rest of the world, obeying the devil—the commander of the powers in the unseen world. He is the spirit at work in the hearts of those who refuse to obey God. All of us used to live that way, following the passionate desires and inclinations of our sinful nature. By our very nature we were subject to God's anger, just like everyone else" (Ephesians 2:1-3).

Though he prowls, Satan's effectiveness against God's chosen children is thwarted. "We know that God's children do not make a practice of sinning, for God's Son holds them securely, and the evil one cannot touch them. We know that we are children of God and that the world around us is under the control of the evil one" (1 John 5:18-19).

He rules over demons.

In addition to ruling this world, Satan controls and commands an army of demons. When speaking of the final judgment, Jesus said, "Then the King will turn to those on the left and say, 'Away with you, you cursed ones, into the eternal fire prepared for *the devil and his demons*" (Matthew 25:41, emphasis mine). It's important to note that Satan is in no way God's equal. He is finite. He is created. He is uncreative. He can't be everywhere; therefore it's important not to say "Satan's tempting me," as he can only be in one physical place at a time. His agents of evil, or malignant spirits, do his bidding in some sort of hierarchical command. He is not all-knowing. He is not all-powerful. Though he roars a huge show, his ultimate position is below the blood of Jesus. He cannot stand beneath the power of the cross of the risen Christ.

The story's been told of Martin Luther waking from sleep one night. There at the end of his bed apparently sat Satan. Luther roused himself, then said, "Oh, it's only you," and went back to sleep. His is the proper response when we consider Satan as the defeated Enemy. We should not disbelieve his existence. If we do, we do so to our peril. But neither should we assign godlike characteristics to him.

He has access to God.

Even in his defeat, Scripture clearly reveals that Satan continues to have access to God's throne. In the book of Job, which we will explore further in the next chapter, Satan approaches God regarding an upstanding follower of God. We see him in other portions of Scripture with the same kind of access. "Then the angel showed me Jeshua the high priest standing before the angel of the LORD. The Accuser, Satan, was there at the angel's right hand, making accusations against Jeshua. And the LORD said to Satan, 'I, the LORD, reject your accusations, Satan. Yes, the LORD, who has chosen Jerusalem, rebukes you. This man is like a burning stick that has been snatched from the fire'" (Zechariah 3:1-2). In the book of Luke we see Jesus declaring this reality to Simon Peter: "Simon, Simon, Satan has asked to sift each of you like wheat" (Luke 22:31).

It's important to note that although Satan has access to God, this does not make him co-equal in standing with God. He is not equal in strength. He is not omniscient or omnipresent. He is a created being. C.S. Lewis elaborates in his introduction to *The Screwtape Letters*: "The commonest question is whether I really 'believe in the Devil.' Now, if by 'the Devil' you mean a power opposite to God and, like God, self-existent from all eternity, the answer is certainly No. There is no uncreated being except God. God has no opposite. No being could attain a 'perfect badness' opposite to the perfect goodness of God; for when you have taken away every kind of good thing (intelligence, will, memory, energy, and existence itself) there would be none of him left."[4]

These are Satan's roles here on earth today. But what does he do? How does he attack us? How does he influence the world? Four ways.

He tempts and seduces.

We first see his ability to tempt and seduce through his successful contact with Adam and Eve. And we see those same enticements of pleasure, stuff, and achievement when he tempts Jesus in the wilderness. He is seen in the sin of Ananias, having tempted him to lie to the Holy Spirit. And he loves to tackle new believers with his seeming favorite sin: pride. "An elder must not be a new believer," Paul cautioned in his letter to Timothy, "because he might become proud, and the devil would cause him to fall" (1 Timothy 3:6).

He deceives, lies, and counterfeits.

Satan's fame comes from his ability to twist truth and masquerade. He is, as the Scripture says, "a murderer from the beginning, and does not stand in the truth, because there is no truth in him. Whenever he speaks a lie, he speaks from his own nature, for he is a liar, and the father of lies" (John 8:44 NASB). Not only does he whisper lies to pontiffs and paupers alike, he connives to deceive those who, in turn, will actively deceive the church. Until I lived in France as a missionary, I'd read verses like these and think they didn't apply to the church today: "These people are false apostles. They are deceitful workers who disguise themselves as apostles of Christ. But I am not surprised! Even Satan disguises himself as an angel of light. So it is no wonder that his servants also disguise themselves as servants of righteousness. In the end they will get the punishment their wicked deeds deserve" (2 Corinthians 11:13-15). Perhaps one of the most painful realizations I've had in my years of ministry is that Satan infiltrates our churches through deceiving the people there—sometimes those in leadership. And we often fail to recognize these folks. When they wreak havoc, it shakes our faith because we can't understand why Christ-followers would act in such deceptive and anti-Christian ways.

Beyond deception in our churches, there will come a time when Satan directly influences the Antichrist. "This man will come to do the work of Satan with counterfeit power and signs and miracles. He will use every kind of evil deception to fool those on their way to destruction, because they refuse to love and accept the truth that would save them" (2 Thessalonians 2:9-10). After this, during the end of days, more deceiving spirits will be unleashed. "And I saw three evil spirits that looked like frogs leap from the mouths of the dragon, the beast, and the false prophet. They are demonic spirits who work miracles and go out to all the rulers of the world to gather them for battle against the Lord on that great judgment day of God the Almighty" (Revelation 16:13-14).

Thankfully, Satan's deception will end with a mighty push. "The angel threw him into the bottomless pit, which he then shut and locked so Satan could not deceive the nations anymore until the thousand years were finished. Afterward he must be released for a little while" (Revelation 20:3).

These Scriptures highlight Satan's schemes, his keen ability to deceive and lie. Since he creates nothing and can only counterfeit or destroy what God creates, his best weapons are to tell lies about God's creation and incite you to believe those lies.

He destroys and kills.

One of Satan's names is Destroyer. When we lived in France, we saw lives completely ravaged through his and his subordinates' tactics. Ministries were destroyed, killed. God's name was trashed as a result. Nothing delights Satan more than tearing down what God builds.

Jesus's desire is to bring ultimate abundance to our stories by bringing good of all the attacks and evil that comes our way.

He also loves snatching away the words we share with others about Jesus. "The seeds that fell on the footpath represent those who hear the message, only to have the devil come and take it away from their hearts and prevent them from believing and being saved" (Luke 8:12).

Satan is no mealymouthed foe. He prowls and hungers for destruction. He is no kitty cat. His bite has saber teeth. His words roar. "Stay alert!" warns Peter. "Watch out for your great enemy, the devil. He prowls around like a roaring lion, looking for someone to devour. Stand firm against him, and be strong in your faith. Remember that your Christian brothers and sisters all over the world are going through the same kind of suffering you are" (1 Peter 5:8-9).

In the midst of his destruction, he steals like a thief. Jesus equates him to a robber. "The thief's purpose is to steal and kill and destroy. My purpose is to give them a rich and satisfying life" (John 10:10).

Jesus's desire is to bring ultimate abundance to our stories by bringing good of all the attacks and evil that comes our way. He is the master scriptwriter of our lives. Satan does destroy. And one way he does that is to *destory* us (to rework the letters a bit). He wants to rob us of the victorious story we long to share with a sin-weary world. My friend Malcolm puts it: "We insult Jesus when we live defeated lives."[5] And we cower to Satan when we allow him to write our stories.

He has hordes of demons placed strategically around the earth.

You may have heard the term "territorial spirits" in conjunction with spiritual warfare. That's the idea that Satan has physical places on earth where he has either higher concentrations of demons or demons of greater evil in specific areas. While we should not let the idea of this sideline us or make us afraid, the truth is Satan does command an army of evil spirits. They do his bidding. They seem to be restless, and some are more evil than others, as evidenced by this Scripture passage:

> When a defiling evil spirit is expelled from someone, it drifts along through the desert looking for an oasis, some unsuspecting soul it can bedevil. When it doesn't find anyone, it says, "I'll go back to my old haunt." On return it finds the person spotlessly clean, but vacant. It then runs out and *rounds up seven other spirits more evil than itself* and they all move in, whooping it up. That person ends up far worse off than if he'd never gotten cleaned up in the first place. That's what this generation is like: You may think you have cleaned out the junk from your lives and gotten ready for God, but you weren't hospitable to my kingdom message, and now all the devils are moving back in (Matthew 12:43-45 MSG, emphasis mine).

These verses show the mobility of demons as well, how they roam and seek people and places to inhabit.

In Mark 5, we see Jesus in the Gerasene region where He met the man of the tombs. This man was so tormented and wild that chains couldn't contain him. He cut himself with sharp stones and took to howling and roaming. Here's where we pick up the story. Notice what the demon says in relation to physical places in the text.

> When Jesus was still some distance away, the man saw him, ran to meet him, and bowed low before him. With a shriek, he screamed, "Why are you interfering with me, Jesus, Son of the Most High God? In the name of God, I beg you, don't torture me!" For Jesus had already said to the spirit, "Come out of the man, you evil spirit."
>
> Then Jesus demanded, "What is your name?"
>
> And he replied, "My name is Legion, because there are many of

us inside this man." Then the evil spirits begged him again and again not to send them to some distant place. There happened to be a large herd of pigs feeding on the hillside nearby. "Send us into those pigs," the spirits begged. "Let us enter them."

So Jesus gave them permission. The evil spirits came out of the man and entered the pigs, and the entire herd of 2,000 pigs plunged down the steep hillside into the lake and drowned in the water (Mark 5:6-13).

Again, demons can roam freely, though they are subject to the voice of Jesus. They must obey and go where He sends them. Note, too, how evil their intent is. They'd spent years torturing and destroying the man of the tombs, and when they entered the substantial herd of pigs they incited mass porcine suicide.

Perhaps the most intriguing text about demons being in particular places comes from Daniel 10, where Daniel prays and then receives a belated answer in the form of an angel. When the angel finally comes he says, "Don't be afraid, Daniel. Since the first day you began to pray for understanding and to humble yourself before your God, your request has been heard in heaven. I have come in answer to your prayer. But for twenty-one days the spirit prince of the kingdom of Persia blocked my way. Then Michael, one of the archangels, came to help me, and I left him there with the spirit prince of the kingdom of Persia. Now I am here to explain what will happen to your people in the future, for this vision concerns a time yet to come" (Daniel 10:12-14). This shows that Satan has a hierarchy (princes) of demons, and they seem to be able to control certain territories on earth.

Have you ever traveled somewhere and felt instantly that the spiritual climate was different? When I would travel to the United States when I lived in France, I could palpably feel a difference. Once when I landed in Dallas, an overwhelming sense of peace settled into me, along with this thought: *There are many Christians here.* On that same trip home to Nice, the moment I landed I felt a wet blanket of doom descend over me. I could explain in human terms, of course, that I felt homesick and those feelings influenced how I experienced both places. But I'm convinced the spiritual strongholds in France were different. When the wet blanket fell on me, I started crying. I couldn't stop for several hours, even at home. Finally, we had friends come over and pray for the darkness to lift.

One of the people I met in France relayed a chilling story. She and a friend were in Gourdon, a hilltop village where you could see the Côte d'Azur in the distance. The Mediterranean Sea sparkled that day. In a hiccup of a moment, both friends saw a vision of an octopus enveloping the entire sea (obviously as they were a good 20 miles away this couldn't have been a real octopus). Neither spoke to each other about the vision until later, when they both confirmed they'd seen the same thing. Months passed. My friend didn't share this vision with a soul. One day her mother asked her, "What comes to mind when you think of Satan in this area?"

Without thinking, she blurted out, "An octopus."

Her mom, surprised, said, "Why would you say that?"

She relayed the story. Her mother, who had been an active intercessor for the south of France, said, "Whenever intercessors get together to pray, that's what they perceive over this area: an octopus."

Lest you believe that only some countries have dark forces, a more lighthearted illustration is in order. When we came home on furlough from France, we'd spent two years there not really struggling with materialism. As missionaries, of course, we didn't have much to begin with, but still, our family hadn't been obsessed with things and having more. We touched down in Dallas, then drove down the freeway toward our home church. Our children started chirping from the back of the van. "Look, there's Target! Let's go to Target." "Wow, Costco! I want to go." Our children, in an instant, had turned into happy little materialists. When one of them said, "Look, let's go to Mattress Giant," Patrick and I laughed. Two minutes in America trumped two years of contentment.

Which all goes to show that we have a conniving, intelligent enemy. He knows when to be subtle and when to be overt. He knows which lies will deceive each culture. He disperses his troops to different locales to perform specific acts of espionage and coercion. Not only does Satan roam to and fro throughout the earth, but he sends his demons to do the same.

He wages war against the church.

Satan's biggest foe is not necessarily you or me by ourselves; it's our collective body as the church. We are the hands and feet of Jesus as the Body of Christ. If Satan can immobilize or discredit the church, he wins significant victories. The Bible shows him as an enemy sowing weeds among us. "Then, leaving the crowds outside, Jesus went into the house. His disciples said, 'Please explain to us the story of the weeds in the field.' Jesus replied, 'The Son of Man is the farmer who plants the good seed. The field is the world, and the good seed represents the people of the Kingdom. The weeds are the people who belong to the evil one. The enemy who planted the weeds among the wheat is the devil. The harvest is the end of the world, and the harvesters are the angels'" (Matthew 13:36-39).

Satan works to prevent God's redemption work from being spread across the nations. In one instance, he directly prevented Paul from doing ministry. "We wanted very much to come to you, and I, Paul, tried again and again, but Satan prevented us" (1 Thessalonians 2:18). He also gives believers thorns—difficult situations, health issues, discouragement—to keep us defeated. Thankfully, God uses these very weaknesses to strengthen us. "So to keep me from becoming proud," says Paul in his letter to the Corinthians, "I was given a thorn in my flesh, a messenger from Satan to torment me and keep me from becoming proud. Three different times I begged the Lord to take it away. Each time he said, 'My grace is all you need. My power works best in weakness.' So now I am glad to boast about my weaknesses, so that the power of Christ can work through me. That's why I take pleasure in my weaknesses, and in the insults, hardships, persecutions, and troubles that I suffer for Christ. For when I am weak, then I am strong" (2 Corinthians 12:7-10).

Beyond sowing weeds and poking us with thorns, Satan accuses the church day and night. If you've ever felt condemned, unworthy, shamed, dirty, stupid, or deeply embarrassed, chances are Satan had some sort of hand in it. Thankfully, his voice will not always be spouting condemnation our way. In the apostle John's vision of the end of time, he writes, "Then I heard a loud voice shouting across the heavens, 'It has come at last— salvation and power and the Kingdom of our God, and the authority of his Christ. For the accuser of our brothers and sisters has been thrown down to earth—the one who accuses them before our God day and night'" (Revelation 12:10).

Looking around the world today, we can see Satan's animosity and rage against the church. Persecuted Christians abound. Martyrdoms have increased. Satan's attacks involve both persecution and death. Even so, God encourages us to stand strong, to not lose heart. "Don't be afraid of what you are about to suffer. The devil will throw some of you into prison to test you. You will suffer for ten days. But if you remain faithful even when facing death, I will give you the crown of life…I know that you live in the city where Satan has his throne, yet you have remained loyal to me. You refused to deny me even when Antipas, my faithful witness, was martyred among you there in Satan's city" (Revelation 2:10,13).

Satan is certainly alive, but he is not well. He is a defeated destroyer. He thrives on our disobedience. And he glories when we slip into his pet sin, pride. I love what the writer Timothy Warner says. He synthesizes the story of Satan with our stories today. "The principle tactic of Satan in his conflict with God from the very beginning, therefore, has been to deceive God's children into believing that the tremendous potential which resides within them can be realized by living life under their own control, rather than under God's control, and to believe that there is a legitimate source of power other than Yahweh."[6]

Satan is a defeated destroyer.

The true source of rejuvenating life and power is Jesus Christ. But before we get to His story, we need to take a long look at one of the most righteous persons who ever lived and how he found that rejuvenating life after debilitating loss.

—

Mind if I pray for you?

Lord, I pray You would show Yourself strong in the midst of the beautiful battle. Help us see You as victorious and conquering and able and stronger than our Enemy. Thank You that You have already won the battle. Thank You that from the cross You said, "It is finished." Help us rest in that finished work of victory. Amen.

Chapter 3

The Right Story: God's Sovereignty.
The Wrong Story: Our Comfort.

Suffering keeps swelling our feet so that earth's shoes won't fit.[1]

JONI EARECKSON TADA

W hen our family ventured to southern France to be missionaries, we lived wide-eyed, expectant. We knew that God would take care of us, bring us meaningful work, and reward our faithfulness. And yet within months, our team struggled to stay together, our house in Texas had been hijacked by a conman, and our children cried frequently before, during, and after school.

In a book about spiritual warfare, you might expect me to talk about God wanting us all to be healthy, wealthy, and perfectly happy—with favorable circumstances awaiting us around every bend of obedience. That the goal of our ardent prayers should be happiness. And that anything that prevents us from having what we perceive as an abundant life should be attacked. But sometimes life is plain messy. And Satan isn't behind every annoyance. It's simplistic to think that Satan is our only obstacle on this earth, that he throws away our money, attacks us with illnesses, and revokes our prosperity. We forget the devil's greatest schemes, tempting us to want pleasure, stuff, and achievement more than we want God.

The truth is we serve a sovereign Lord. A God who sees everything. A God who filters everything—even Satan's activities—through His holy hands. God allows pain. God allows awful circumstances. He allows suffering. He allows financial ruin. Why? I wish I could fully answer that. But I do know this: I grow the most through adversity. I can't honestly say

I've grown in prosperity. That's the beauty of God's surprising, paradoxical ways. He gives and takes away. And yet when things are taken from us (health, wealth, standing, sanity), He uses those detriments for our good. The beauty of the cross is not that Jesus relinquished all suffering there, but that He opened the door to redemption through our suffering. Oswald Chambers wrote, "If God has made your cup sweet, drink it with grace; if He has made it bitter, drink it in communion with Him."[2]

With Chambers's words echoing in our mind, let's take a look at a man who did everything right and had everything taken away. Job was godly. According to some health and wealth perspectives, Job's formula should've read:

**Job's holiness + God's requirements for blessing =
material wealth, abundant health, and prosperous living.**

Instead the formula is much more problematic (and biblical):

**Job's holiness + God's sovereignty =
testing and trials that ultimately bring Job closer to God.**

Isn't that the gist of the oft-quoted Romans 8:28? Reading it along with the verse that follows brings this to stunning light: "And we know that in all things God works for the good of those who love him, who have been called according to his purpose. For those God foreknew he also predestined to be conformed to the image of his Son, that he might be the firstborn among many brothers and sisters" (NIV). Yes, He works all things for the good, even for Job. Why? That He might conform him to the image of Christ. The purpose of our suffering isn't to have a great testimony. It isn't to point the finger of accusation at ourselves and say we brought on our calamity by our lack of faith. No, trials and struggles and distresses simply help us become more like Jesus. More selfless. More giving. More hope-filled. More forgiving. More abundant.

Life in the spirit, in the realm of spiritual warfare, is not about a simple formula of you being good, God rewarding you with a happy life, and you then telling everyone else to do the same. It's a holy interaction with a not-so-easy-to-understand God. It's being near to Him even when it looks like He's forsaken you. It's discipleship. It's learning to have joy in pain. That's the kind of life that stands out in a crazy, needy world. Not the kind of faith that guarantees benefit, but one that shines brightly even when life knocks it down.

Life in the spirit is a holy interaction with a
not-so-easy-to-understand God.

I love how Eugene Peterson introduces the book of Job in his seminal translation of the Bible, *The Message*. He writes, "Job gives voice to his sufferings so well, so accurately and honestly, that anyone who has ever suffered—which includes every last one of us—can recognize his or her personal pain in the voice of Job. Job says boldly what some of us are too timid to say. He makes poetry out of what in many of us is only a tangle of confused whispers. He shouts out to God what a lot of us mutter behind our sleeves. He refuses to accept the role of a defeated victim."[3]

For a simple recap, the story of Job is one of God's sovereignty, of Satan's ability to attack, of well-meaning friends' misplaced advice, and of a man who asks questions. In the beginning of the book of Job, we're reminded that Satan has access to God's throne. "Now there was a day when the sons of God came to present themselves before the Lord, and Satan also came among them. The Lord said to Satan, 'From where have you come?' Satan answered the Lord and said, 'From going to and fro on the earth and from walking up and down on it'" (Job 1:6-7 ESV). Here we see Satan's dominion over the earth, his roaming ways.

The Lord asks Satan if he's seen Job, how blameless and righteous he is. Satan counters, "Does Job fear God for no reason?" (verse 9). He details all the ways God has blessed and protected Job. God allows Satan to take family and friends from Job, but does not allow him to touch Job with sickness.

When Job continues to respond righteously to adversity, Satan asks permission to touch him with sickness, which God allows. It's in this terrible state that Job's friends find him, picking at his boils and scabs, utterly bereft, with his wife encouraging him to curse God and die. In the balance of the book Job's friends try to blame his sin for his pain, insisting that he somehow brought it upon himself. And it culminates with Job honestly railing against God, only to find out that God is God and Job is not. Job ends his discourse with God by saying, "I had heard of you by the hearing of the ear, but now my eye sees you" (Job 42:5 ESV). Job went from hearing to seeing God—but it took a horrific set of trials to bring him across that wide space.

If we suffer patiently and with faith,
we'll begin to catch the fringes of His ways.

So what does a woman do when cowering under painful circumstances? How does she endure like Job? How does she frame the suffering theologically? How is "suffering well" an integral part of spiritual warfare? What happens if we suffer alone? Does it matter? Make a difference? Indicate a tinge of our own significance?

Job suffered alone. And sometimes, so do we.

Yes, Job had his wife and his well-meaning friends, but in the depth of his pain, he felt abandoned. Not one soul seemed to understand. Not one person shouldered his grief fully. We live in a world in which, at any moment of the day, we can be surrounded by virtual "friends." Still, we are a lonely people. We crave community. None of us wants to suffer alone. And yet, sometimes God calls us to a Job-like journey that feels scary and isolated. Why? I'm not intelligent enough to understand the heart or mind of the Almighty. But I know I've grown deep roots during loneliness. And I've found more and more of Jesus in those forsaken places. In Job 26, Job recounts the greatness of God, how unlike us He is. He rebukes and the world trembles. He quiets the waters with a word. Look at the way this chapter ends: "By His breath the heavens are cleared; His hand has pierced the fleeing serpent. Behold these are the fringes of His ways; and how faint a word we hear of Him! But His mighty thunder, who can understand?" (13-14 NASB).

We serve a powerful, surprising God. And if we suffer patiently and with faith, we'll begin to catch the fringes of His ways.

But what's the point of suffering? Are we like Job, suffering to prove our integrity? Why go through all that? Why alone?

To worship God in the silence.

One answer comes from a favorite book, *When God Weeps,* by Joni Eareckson Tada. She writes of her good friend John who suffers from a debilitating illness. And mostly, he suffers alone. Joni says:

God's purpose is to teach millions of unseen beings about Himself, and we are a blackboard upon which God is drawing lessons about Himself for the benefit of angels and demons. God gets glory every time the spirit world learns how powerful His everlasting arms are in upholding the weak. They learn it is God who permeates every fiber of John's being with perseverance. My friend's life is not a waste. Although not many people seem to care, someone—a great many someones—care more than John can imagine. John's life does something else. It disgusts Satan. The trust John shows God drives the Devil up a wall.[4]

I gain perspective when I read and reread this passage. Our suffering, even if it's endured completely alone, matters. Our praise in the midst of pain means something. It deals a blow to the Enemy of our souls. It testifies to the angels that God is strong when we are weak and needy. That is the crux of spiritual warfare, to declare to the Enemy and his demons that God is God and we are not. Even if we feel bewildered. Even if we long for relief. Even if we lack strong relationships, if we are friendless or some sort of pariah. Even then, He knows. He suffered in a like manner on the cross. Disrobed, disgraced, and bloodied, He cried the agonizing cry, forsaken by friends, lost to the Father in a holy moment. He's been there. He'll meet you in the lonely, shattered places.

Our suffering, even if it's endured completely alone, matters.

Suffering in solitude like Job changes our vision. We may have heard God in the past, but through the crucible of suffering we see Him! And suddenly the crying in the dark feels like a part of the journey toward knowing Him in an entirely new way. Not only do we shake the heavens when we praise Him through our trials, we move from hearing to seeing the Almighty. If you suffer alone today, take heart. Praise Him in the midst of the darkness. Praising God while the tumult swirls is true spiritual warfare. And wait in anticipation for the day you see God more clearly.

I've lived in the counterintuitive place where I've felt the vise of Job-like circumstances. It happened when we church planted in France, where I felt like Satan had carved a bull's-eye on our foreheads. We couldn't claim any victories. Though we'd followed God to France and followed His direction back to the United States, we found very little to say about victory or wealth or emotional health. Most of that was stripped from us in the crucible of our obedience.

I wrote the following in the aftermath of those years, raw from the pain, still bewildered:

> This will be my last post from France. It's hard to even write that. So much is roiling inside me, my emotions glaring from frustration to grief to elation to sadness. But I'd like to commemorate our two-plus years here by thanking Jesus for all the lessons He's taught me:
>
> • Dependence. Leaving everything familiar either makes you paranoid that the world is going to fall apart or dependent on the One who holds the world together.
>
> • Trust. When your income comes from the generosity of others and not from some corporate entity, you realize how little your trust in God was. I learned God was truly my provider.
>
> • Stability. I've learned how much of a drama-queen I can be. Without many friends nearby, I've had to learn to talk myself down and give my rantings to Jesus. It's one of the most refreshing gifts God has given me: the knowledge that I can and should always run to Him first.
>
> • Spiritual warfare. Oh man. I could go on and on. It's thick here. And dark. But we've learned to discern and battle and trust.
>
> • Stripping. Much of who I thought I was has been stripped away, down to the bare bones of me. And yet I still love Jesus with a passion, even when I feel small or naked or needy or tired or broken. He's still there.
>
> • Family. God has knit our family together in amazing ways through some very difficult times as well as lighthearted moments. We saw our youngest daughter, Julia, come to Jesus this year and be baptized.
>
> • Impact. "You came here just for me," she said when we had lunch together. "It was not a waste. Don't you dare

think that. You saved my life." I needed to hear those words, that my friendship meant something to someone here. Thank You, Jesus.

- Remembering. "I have a word from the Lord," another friend said. "You know how hard it is here. You please tell the American church how hard it is. Pray for us. Please, pray for us." How can we not? God has engraved these French believers deep into our hearts.

- Perseverance. It was one foot in front of the other. Step. Step. Step. Dogged obedience. But we persevered, and we found Jesus faithful with each step.

- Rest. This last year, we've celebrated Sabbath. I thank God for that. My heart is better, more renewed, more alive, more joyful, more free because of it. I will fight for it when we get back to the busy U.S.

- Contentment. We've lived in a small house with one car and have learned the secret of being content.

There is so much more I could say, but it's late, and I have to get to sleep. The packers come tomorrow, the movers on Tuesday. They'll pack up our lives in France, send our things on a container across the Atlantic. But they can't pack our hearts. Part of us will always live here, thankful for Jesus who met us one thousand upon one thousand times in a land in desperate need of His grace, joy, peace, freedom, and salvation.

Rereading what God did in that painful place pauses my heart. God does not call us to manipulate Him into giving us happy lives. No, like Dietrich Bonhoeffer writes, "When Christ calls a man, He bids him come and die."[5] Like Job, we had to die to what looked like worldly success. We had to equate the blessing of God with God's ability to fill us in the lack, not fill us with stuff or health. As a woman who longs for and adores stability and peace, this kind of holy embracing of chaos shattered me. But it shattered me in the best possible way. It made me realize a sad truth about myself: I'm a happiness addict.

I long for financial ease, for traffic to cease, for my children to volunteer to do the dishes. Though I know God isn't the vendor of a perfectly stress-free life, deep down I believe He owes me. Isn't that what the abundant life is all about? My happiness?

Though I'm not one to subscribe to the prosperity gospel, I realize I have a smidgen of that theology resting dormant in my heart. When the stress level in France reached a pinnacle, my reasoning went something like this: *Lord, we followed You around the world to serve You. Why is this happening? Can't You fix this?* But heaven fell silent.

Following Jesus doesn't guarantee we'll have lives of ease or we'll be immune from trials. In many cases, trials increase. The Scripture is clear. "Indeed, all who desire to live godly in Christ Jesus will be persecuted" (2 Timothy 3:12 NASB). Perhaps that's the greatest measure of our Christian life. Perhaps we can take our true spiritual temperature by the number of trials heaped upon us. Perhaps the abundant life is less about the absence of trial than finding joy in the midst of the trials that come. J.B. Phillips translates James 1:2 this way: "Don't resent [trials] as intruders, but welcome them as friends."

What about you? Are you a happiness addict? Are you more interested in receiving God's gifts than His presence? Answer the following questions, asking God to sift your heart as you respond.

1. Do you avoid painful situations, even though you know God might be leading you through them?

2. Do you make daily decisions based solely on your wants?

3. What does your prayer life look like? Do you regularly ask God to remove the trials you face?

4. What is more important to you—maintaining or upgrading your lifestyle or making decisions based on God's upside-down kingdom?

5. What brings you the greatest joy in this life? Getting what you dreamed of or sacrificing for the sake of the gospel?

These are not easy questions. So often, I seek my personal happiness over God's smile. I live for my reputation rather than His. I get caught up in the materialism of life, always wanting more-more-more and forgetting that He is my provider. Being addicted to personal happiness may sound normal, but really, it's tyranny. Because when will we ever have enough?

How do we measure it? Chasing after happiness puts us on one of those hamster wheels, forever running, getting nowhere.

What can we do to free ourselves from this addiction? Here are 12 ideas:

1. Serve somebody.

Jesus said, "For even the Son of Man did not come to be served, but to serve and to give His life as a ransom for many" (Mark 10:45 NASB). Jesus set for us an example of service. He washed feet. He healed folks. He gave and gave and gave. He poured out His life. He was about the business of His Father, always obeying His will—and that will was often service. Every time He served, Satan shuddered.

2. Addict yourself to heaven.

Become intoxicated with the reality of heaven, where God hands out rewards for faithful service. Know that the trials of life are often sent by God to produce bits and pieces of glory, both in our hearts and in the life hereafter. "For momentary, light affliction is producing for us an eternal weight of glory far beyond all comparison, while we look not at the things which are seen, but at the things which are not seen; for the things which are seen are temporal, but the things which are not seen are eternal" (2 Corinthians 4:17-18 NASB).

3. Practice being uncomfortable.

If your addiction to happiness bends toward a need for comfort, try being uncomfortable. Walk instead of driving. Stop to help a homeless person, realizing your hands may be the hands of Jesus for him or her. Make an inconvenient choice for the sake of blessing others.

4. Take a kingdom risk.

Dare to take a mission trip. In those times where I'm battling culture shock, loneliness, and disorientation, I sense the presence of Jesus like never before. Risking for the sake of the kingdom of God has helped me loosen my need for happiness and increased my faith in God's available strength.

5. Give away your stuff.

Jesus said, "Beware, and be on your guard against every form of greed; for not even when one has an abundance does his life consist of his possessions" (Luke 12:15 NASB). There is more to life than clutter. True abundance never comes from getting more. Instead, give away something you love. It will break the hold greed has on your heart.

6. Actively rejoice when something is amiss.

Paul tells us to rejoice always (1 Thessalonians 5:16). Always. Not just when things go your way, but particularly when things don't. The next time circumstances don't cooperate, make a choice to rejoice in the goodness of God.

7. Step outside your comfort zone.

Afraid to initiate prayer for a grieving friend? Do it anyway. Too bitter to forgive that family member? Make a choice to forgive them in person. Whenever you step out to do the things Jesus is challenging you to do, God stretches and grows your faith. You'll never grow if you settle for ease.

8. Practice self-denial.

Breaking an addiction often means denying ourselves. Choose today to forgo something you crave.

9. Study the countercultural beatitudes.

Next time you're longing for life to fit into your own personal nirvana, open the Bible to the fifth chapter of Matthew and meditate on Jesus's words. You'll see an upside-down kingdom where the poor are rich and the persecuted are rewarded.

10. Live the American dream in reverse.

Instead of upgrading to new appliances, rejoice in what you have. In lieu of a bigger, newer car, buy an older model. Save money in order to joyfully give it away.

11. Practice contentment.

Learn the art of having enough. Fast from advertising—in magazines, the Internet, TV. You'll be surprised how high your contentment level will rise when you're not constantly bombarded with the command to "buy this, buy that." Instead, investigate poverty in your city or the world and actively choose to meet a legitimate need.

12. Rekindle your belief in God's sovereignty.

God is sovereign. He sees everything that happens in our lives. Every trial and perturbation sifts through His hands. Remembering this will help when you encounter potholes in the road of life. The beauty of His sovereignty is that He helps us through each unhappy event, giving us strength when we're weak (see 2 Corinthians 12:9-10).

The longer I walk with Jesus, the more I realize that His calling and His kingdom are not at all about my ease and comfort, my health and wealth. My addiction should first be to Him, not to happiness. Walking through this 12-step process, I understand afresh that life's not all about my life, or my happiness. It's about joyfully walking in His footsteps. It's about seeing God, about walking through trials—even if I suffer alone—for the sake of His renown. It's about living counterculturally in a way that angers the god of this world, who throws distraction and vice our way. It's about giving up on happiness for the sake of developing counterintuitive joy.

If we as women live lives like this, you can bet the kingdom of darkness will quake in fear. If we can take note of Job's life, how his trials brought him closer to God, how he learned contentment, we will develop into steadfast, immovable warrior women, unable to be shaken or distracted.

—

Mind if I pray for you?

Lord, help us to keep in mind that most of our growth happens in the trials that come our way. May today be the day we welcome trials as friends. Lift our heads from despair. Keep us close to You because we know Your nearness is our good. Rescue us from thinking that the good life is about power or things or a perfectly ordered life. Release us from the tyranny of our own control. Amen.

Chapter 4

Living the Right Story: Balancing Between Ignorance and Overreaction

Devil is the opposite of angel only as Bad Man is the opposite of Good Man. Satan, the leader or dictator of devils, is the opposite, not of God, but of Michael.[1]

C.S. LEWIS

When our youngest daughter started acting out of character, we chalked it up to living in France, attending a new school, and battling a language barrier. When she argued back—not normal for her—we assumed she was struggling emotionally with the move. Only later did we find out she was hearing voices. We'd been ignorant of Satan's schemes.

Years earlier, in college, a freshman girl on my wing pulled me into her room. "Satan is living in my stuffed animals." She pointed to a stuffed bear, a plush cat. As her Resident Assistant and a Christian, I didn't know the proper way to respond to demonic toys, so I prayed. I asked Jesus to please protect her. She interrupted me. "They're mocking you," she said. But the mouths of the bear and the cat remained mute. Eventually, I brought my pastor in to pray for her, and we found her some psychological help.

We run the risk of both extremes as women. We can become so busy in our frenetic lives that we live as if there is no spiritual battle. Or we can lose ourselves in unhealthy speculation about the powers of darkness, unconsciously assigning more power to such forces than is biblical. Balancing the two perspectives is the heartbeat of this chapter.

One way to achieve this balance is to look at the names of Satan, contrasting them with the many names of God.

49

Satan actually means *adversary*, deriving from the Hebrew word meaning "to hide in ambush." Think of him as a wolf preying on a herd of lambs. Then remember that we serve *Jehovah-Rohi*, the Lord is our shepherd. God protects us from those who prey.

Devil, *diabolas*, is a synonym for Satan, which means slanderer, accuser, defamer, false accuser. And yet God is *Jehovah-M'Kaddesh*, the Lord who sanctifies. He is the one who makes us clean. He is also *Jehovah-Tsidkenu*, the Lord our righteousness. No matter how much Satan and his horde throw slander and accusations our way, we can rest on God being our righteousness. This belief alone can silence Satan's defamations forever.

Satan is also called the tempter. And yet we know this truth from James 1:13: "And remember, when you are being tempted, do not say, 'God is tempting me.' God is never tempted to do wrong, and he never tempts anyone else." Not only does God not tempt us, but He provides a way of escape. "The temptations in your life are no different from what others experience," says Paul. "And God is faithful. He will not allow the temptation to be more than you can stand. When you are tempted, he will show you a way out so that you can endure" (1 Corinthians 10:13). We may feel alone when we're tempted, but God is *Jehovah-Shammah*, the Lord is there. He is with us everywhere.

Jesus called Satan the evil one. But we serve a God who sent His perfect, sinless Son to conquer the evil in our hearts and combat the evil plaguing this world. Jesus, the sinless Messiah, dealt a crushing blow to Satan's plans. We serve *Jehovah-Shalom*, the Lord is our peace. Peace, in this instance, not only means finished, fulfilled, and whole, but also perfected. Where Satan prowls and longs for us to follow in his footsteps, littering our lives with sin, heartache, and shame, God enters in, forgives our sin, and gives us the Holy Spirit who perfects us.

Satan is also called *Beelzebub*, which literally means "lord of the flies" or "prince of demons." He commands his horde of demons to wreak mischief in our lives. Yet God is also known as *Jehovah-Sabaoth*, the Lord of hosts. He commands the angelic host on our behalf.

Jesus called Satan a murderer and destroyer because he can only kill and maim and tear apart. God is simply *Jehovah*, or *Yahweh*. That name occurs 6,823 times in the Old Testament. It means He is the Great I Am, the self-existing one. He existed prior to Satan. He created Satan. And He created everything you see today, even the laundry in your hamper. Because of that, we must remember that God is the God of life, of creation, of creativity. He builds; Satan perverts. He is also *Jehovah-Jireh*, the Lord will provide. When we lost our home to a conman while on the mission field, we learned that although things can be stolen from us, God is greater still. He provided beautifully for our family—more than material things. He built our faith stronger, wider, deeper because of the trial.

Satan is also known as the father of lies. As I mentioned earlier, he cannot speak the truth. If you've ever known someone who constantly lies, remember that she probably didn't start off that way. But years and years of lying have convinced her that her lies are the truth. Imagine Satan's thousands of years of lying. He cannot help but spew untruth everywhere he goes. We know that Jesus is truth with skin on. He declared "I am the way, the truth, and the life" in John 14:6. We serve a God who embodies truth. I love how Eugene Peterson translates Psalm 51:6: "What you're after is truth from the inside out. Enter me, then; conceive a new, true life." Our ability to be truth-tellers in a lying-centric culture depends wholly on drawing near to the God of truth.

Satan is deemed the ruler of this world, the god of this age, the prince of the air. He prowls and snarls. He roams the dust of earth, continually bent on destroying Christians. Yet God rules everything. He is the sovereign one. He is *El-Elyon,* the most high God. He is *El-Roi*, the strong one who sees. He is *El-olam*, the everlasting God.

We see Satan as the serpent in the garden—a slick, sly, dangerous foe. And yet God is *Jehovah-Rophe*, the Lord who heals. We may be bitten by sin's deceit, but Jesus defeated that wound and, through the Holy Spirit, heals us, renews us, changes us, gives us a future and a hope.

Satan can disguise himself as an angel of light, as a good entity, with smooth words and cunning tactics. He appears righteous though he is full of dead man's bones. He inspires Pharisees. He loves to deceive believers into following those who pretend to be followers of Jesus. But we must not forget that God is light. He created light. First John 1:5 declares, "This is the message we have heard from him and declare to you: God is light; in him there is no darkness at all" (NIV).

We examine the names of Satan versus the names of God to provide a balanced perspective. Yes, Satan is a powerful, conniving foe. But he is not as big as God by any stretch. We need to see him as he really is: a sniveling, defeated enemy. Yes, Satan exists, but God has always existed, outside the parameters of time and space, and He will put an end to Satan. Yes, we should take Satan seriously, but more than that, we cannot afford to take God lightly. He is the everlasting, everexisting, everpowerful, ever-beautiful one.

We need to see Satan as he really is:
a sniveling, defeated enemy.

Sometimes our thoughts on spiritual warfare dance dangerously close to giving Satan more power than he actually has. Exodus 34:6-7 says, "And he passed in front of Moses, proclaiming, 'The LORD, the LORD, the compassionate and gracious God, slow to anger, abounding in love and faithfulness, maintaining love to thousands, and forgiving wickedness, rebellion and sin. Yet he does not leave the guilty unpunished; he punishes the children and their children for the sin of the parents to the third and fourth generation'" (NIV). We might be tempted to believe there is such a thing as a generational curse that must be broken in a person's life. Are demons passed down from parents to children? While I agree that any one of us may be affected by demonic activity, this idea of needing extra prayer for generational curses seems to place Satan's ability to oppress higher than God's ability to atone. A high view of Jesus's atonement on the cross and His ultimate defeat of evil there renders "extra prayer" unnecessary.

It's important to note that the above verse says nothing about demonic activity. It is God who punishes, not Satan. Contrast that with the blessings God grants the righteous in Exodus 20:6. "But I lavish unfailing love for a thousand generations on those who love me and obey my commands."

Colossians 2:10 should give believers a huge sigh of relief: "So you also are complete through your union with Christ, who is the head over every ruler and authority." Christ has already taken care of the sin in your life. He has authority over Satan and his activities. His death and resurrection have already conquered Satan's activity. Believing that, rather than trying to figure out what sins your father committed and saying a prayer to combat a supposed generational curse, will set you free. We must think rightly about God, His power, and His ability to conquer our already-defeated foe.

We follow a gospel plus nothing. We don't need Jesus plus special prayers. Or Jesus plus our knowledge of our ancestors' sins. These were the sins of the Colossian and Galatian churches, believing there was more to the gospel than simple, earth-shattering belief.

We follow a gospel plus nothing.

Here's the truth: we are all under a generational curse—the original sin of Adam and Eve in the Garden of Eden. Yet Jesus's outrageous act on the cross once and for all frees us from the worst of all curses: sin and death. "For as in Adam all die, so in Christ all will be made alive" (1 Corinthians 15:22 NIV). Jesus conquered original sin, which trumped all other generational curses. Do we put more emphasis on the sin of others than the power of the cross? If Christ conquered original sin, then past familial sin pales. And we give sin more power when we name it, focus on it, and forget about Jesus's power to overcome it.

Personally, I could cite all sorts of shenanigans by my relatives as reasons for feeling defeated. I could blame them for all my current problems. In my lineage are criminals, sex offenders, child abusers, and hypocrites. But the moment Jesus beautifully invaded my life, He took my sin. He healed me. He delivered me. He made me new. He pointed me to the great future. My life, then, is not a scary adventure of trying to discover and bind the sins of my parents and grandparents and great-grandparents. It's a joyful journey of thanking God for what He's done already and what He continues to do through me. This running toward God assures me of a godly legacy for generations to come.

Having a high view of God and a proper theology of Satan helps us live victoriously, not overly scared of Satan's traps, but living in proper fear of a holy, powerful God who loves us and has already secured our deliverance. Author and speaker Neil T. Anderson presents an interesting metaphor: people are like houses. He writes, "Suppose a family hasn't taken the garbage out of their house for months, and they have spilled food and beverages without cleaning up. That will attract a lot of flies. To resolve this problem, I don't think it is necessary to study the flight patterns of the flies and determine their names and rank structure in the insect hierarchy... To 'focus on the flies' in our lives is to allow the devil to set the agenda for us and distract us from the real issue—which is to get rid of the garbage."[2] It's far better for us to concentrate on the Owner of the house and do what we can control (repent of sin, cease ungodly habits) than to overemphasize our study of Satan and his "flies."

We have a real enemy, yes, but an even stronger God who empowers us daily to deal with our garbage and walk in the light.

Mind if I pray for you?

Lord, I lift my friend to You, the author and perfecter of her faith. Please show Yourself strong on her behalf. Be the God who sees, heals, hears, lives, empowers, and delivers. Lift her eyes above the enemy's tactics in her life to You, the true victor. May she not discount evil, dismissing it as nonexistent, but neither let her bathe in it. Give her a healthy balance of fear and faith. Amen.

Chapter 5

So What's the Story, Exactly?
What Is Spiritual Warfare?

This is the broader picture: Two kingdoms in conflict.
One of a usurper king who has captured people and is
keeping them in bondage to sin, inflicting suffering, and
leading them to eternal alienation from God. The other
king is Jesus who triumphs over the evil king and liberates
the captives, reconciling them to God and freeing them to
live a new life that beforehand has not been possible.[1]

JR VASSAR

The Chinese woman— small as an American fifth grader—writhed and growled, fending off several men who uttered strongly worded prayers. I stepped back from the scene roaring before me, terrified at the woman's ferocious anger, the voice that didn't sound like hers, the uncanny ability to fend off all those men. Prayer erupted all around the woman in the semi-underground church in Malaysia. Crying. Intercession. More flailing. The name of Jesus spoken hundreds of times in English and Mandarin and Malay. As a twenty-two-year-old single missionary, I watched as the woman eased into her right mind under the influence of prayers and sweet singing, how her face smoothed from contortion to placidity. She stood on wobbling legs, then smiled—tired, but set free.

Back in the states three years later, in the midst of our first church-planting meeting, a woman pointed at my newly-pregnant belly. My husband, Patrick, and I, zealous to spread the gospel to our community, had anticipated this first meeting for weeks, preparing for the launch of a new Jesus endeavor. But when the woman pointed and screamed, "You better get that pregnant lady out of here! I'm coming for her child!" my zeal for doing something new and risky for God turned to naked fear. Members of our little group prayed for the woman, but we were never quite sure of her freedom.

Later as a mother of three, I doubled over, unable to speak my discomfort to my family in the minivan. We headed to some new friends' home, but the nausea wouldn't abate. I clutched at the seatbelt, telling myself to not vomit, praying I wouldn't. When we arrived, our friends showed our family their Hindu gods preening from their closet on a shelf created just for them—empty, piercing eyes emanating from tiny figurines, incense smoldering in praise. Some days later, I experienced a strangling dream, my breath stolen by the scene before me—our Indian friends wrestling sexual sin. I begged God to remove me from the dream. When I awakened, I felt a strong need to pray for them. When I shared the nightmare with a Christian friend of theirs, he asked, "Mary, how did you know they struggled with pornography?" I didn't. But God did.

Planting another church, this time on the other side of the world in France, my seven-year-old daughter wept. "Mommy," she told me, "I'm hearing voices in my head. Mean voices. Telling me to do bad things."

"Like what?" Her face did not contort. I did not throw up. Nor did I dream. But my heart felt ripped in half.

"Like kicking my brother."

The voices woke her up at night, tormenting her, frightening her, changing her happy-go-lucky personality to a somber, scaredy-cat mess.

I share these sporadic sensational stories not to titillate, but to show that spiritual warfare happens to ordinary people. As women, friends, sisters, daughters, mothers, we will encounter the powers of darkness along our journey. Note, however, the period of time between each "out there" occurrence. Years passed within the margins. Significant life bloomed between the bookends of overt spiritual attack. Does that mean demonic influence is only spectacular and spooky? No. The vast majority of our interactions with the dark side happen in the mundane, shouldered in the small decisions we women make.

We are a unique lot, women. Gifted with uncanny discernment and a propensity toward fear, we often face spiritual warfare in halted ways— sometimes with bold confidence, other times with dismissal. Some cower just thinking about the one Jesus calls the Thief, the one who comes to steal, kill and destroy us, our families. But few will debate the tangible presence of the Evil One in this world, how palpable, how real he is.

I conducted a poll as I started this book, soliciting advice and direction from a wide variety of women. Of all the advice readers gave me, the most popular piece was this: Be sure you have people praying you through. I agree. This book has incubated inside me quite some time, but the fear of really putting words on the screen has kept me quiet. I've felt the weight of spiritual attack. I know how personal and painful the devil's schemes are. I'm well aware he won't be happy about me stepping into this arena. Even today, I received a stressful (though untrue) correspondence from the IRS, and I shook my head.

And so it begins.

As women, we don't like to think about warfare. I remember cowering when a bully wanted to fight me in the eighth grade. I made every effort to make peace with her so I wouldn't have to fight. Basically, I'm a wimp. But I've learned throughout the years as a Christian that God doesn't call us to be wimps. He's called us to be fearless. Strong. Many times during my family's two-and-a-half-year church plant in France, I felt like I'd been in a war, as the spiritual battle swirled thick. I didn't always feel strong. I felt a bit like David engulfed in King Saul's armor: ill-equipped and small.

Some of us tend to shy away from warfare talk—shields, swords, helmets, armor—arguing that warfare is man's work. But that's completely wrong. Sandra Glahn, a professor at Dallas Theological Seminary, has spent many years studying women in Scripture and the cultures surrounding the biblical narrative. Consider what she has to say about women and warfare: "One of the challenges of the gender talk in the church over the last decade is the association of 'warrior' with 'male.' Yet all believers, male or female, are called to engage in battle. Courage and firmness and singleness of mind are human traits, not male traits. Interestingly the imagery throughout Proverbs 31, describing the ideal woman, is that of battle. It begins 'An excellent wife, who can find…' And the word for 'excellent' is the same word we translate 'valor' when referring to David's mighty men. Throughout this acrostic poem, translators have tended to find female-associated words—a noble wife—and in doing so have failed to help all believers see that Lady Wisdom is clothed for warfare and battles on the offensive."[2]

Likewise, Ephesians chapter 6 doesn't just apply to half of the human race; it's for the redeemed race of people, men and women, fighting shoulder to shoulder—not against each other, but against evil personified. A war waged in the heavens. It makes sense to think of women as warriors if you think about it in terms of motherhood. What mother wouldn't sacrifice herself to protect a child? True, not all will protect, but most will. If an intruder attacks your children, you will intervene. God also has maternal imagery in the Bible—a hen gathering and protecting her chicks under her wings, a mother nursing and coddling her young. If God created us male and female in His image, then women, too, are a beautiful, completing picture of God. And yet God is a warrior.

I had the privilege of attending a Veteran's Day assembly at my daughter's school. I didn't expect to cry, but as those veterans struggled to stand and be recognized, something in me broke. Seeing their lives and imagining what acts of heroism defined them startled me. It made me want to be a warrior like that, fit for uniform, able to sacrifice, to live selflessly. The keynote speaker spoke of his father-in-law, Billy, who saved lives in the Vietnam War and earned two purple hearts to prove it. When asked about his time there, he replied, "We did our jobs, nothing more. We did our best to make it back home."

What a perfect sentiment for all of us to follow in terms of our responsibility as Christians on this earth. It reminds me of Luke 17:10: "In the same way, when you obey me you should say, 'We are unworthy servants who have simply done our duty.'" When we battle as women warriors, we are simply doing our duty. And, like Billy, we are to do what it takes to get home. That means thinking eternally, always longing for the home for which we were created. With that view in mind, we are more apt to fight the good fight.

But this spiritual warfare quest is not something to battle through in our own feeble strength. When our daughter experienced demonic oppression, my wily ability did nothing to help. Only Jesus could deliver, pure and simple. Just speaking His name over her brought healing. And, ultimately, it was her young voice asking that name to save her that eventually freed her from the voices in her head. Battles may rage on this earth, but the weapons we use—which we will explore in future chapters—are divine. As Paul writes, "We are human, but we don't wage war as humans do. We use God's mighty weapons, not worldly weapons, to knock down the strongholds of human reasoning and to destroy false arguments. We destroy every proud obstacle that keeps people from knowing God. We capture their rebellious thoughts and teach them to obey Christ" (2 Corinthians 10:3-5).

So we wage a beautiful battle using spiritual weapons. But what does that mean, practically, in a woman's life? How do we fight?

It's not about us...

First, we must settle the fact that spiritual warfare isn't about us. It's about God exalting Himself. It's about His ability, not ours. It's about the bigness of God, the smallness of our enemy, and our resulting humility. We must put things in proper perspective. Many of us may have memorized Psalm 46:10 in Sunday school, but we neglected to remember the latter half of the verse. "Cease striving and know that I am God," it says. But then it continues, "I will be exalted among the nations, I will be exalted in the earth" (NASB). In our humility, we must cease striving. We must acknowledge that He is God and we are not. And we must remember that God doesn't need our help to carry out His kingdom plans. Yet because of His great mercy and love, He chooses to let us play a part.

So believe this: God is big. Satan is a defeated enemy. God opposes the proud, but He gives grace to the humble. So our role in spiritual warfare is to humbly seek God—believing in His power, and not shrinking away in fear.

...It's about God's absurd tactics.

In spiritual warfare, God sometimes uses absurd tactics to accomplish His victory. Consider the story of Jericho, where battle is waged by circumnavigating a city and hollering on the seventh day. Or the story of Gideon, where God whittles his army down to nearly nothing in order to route the enemy. Or the story of Deborah, where God uses a girl named Jael to kill an evil king with a tent peg. Or the story of Jesus, where God the Father sends His Son in human flesh to redeem the world. Counterintuitive! Absurd! God's ways are not our ways.

As 1 Corinthians 1:26-29 illustrates, God chooses weak and foolish and needy folks to accomplish His purposes: "Remember, dear brothers and sisters, that few of you were wise in the world's eyes or powerful or wealthy when God called you. Instead, God chose things the world considers foolish in order to shame those who think they are wise. And he chose things that are powerless to shame those who are powerful. God chose things despised by the world, things counted as nothing at all, and used them to bring to nothing what the world considers important. As a result, no one can ever boast in the presence of God."

During a difficult time in my marriage where I'd exhausted my prayer efforts and felt completely undone, the Lord told me to do a random thing—to confront a good friend about some issues in her life. I didn't want to do it, knowing how painful it would be for both of us. But God kept waking me up at night, pressing me to do it. So I did. And I suffered. But in that obedience, God turned my husband's heart back toward me. Now I'm not going to preach around the world that if you confront your friend God will restore your marriage. What I will say is this: whatever God asks you to do, do it, even if it's counterintuitive. Trust that His way, even if it seems unrelated, is the way He wants to work in your heart and the hearts of those for whom you battle.

The battle isn't about what we see...

With obedience in mind, we can then look at the weaponry God gives us to accomplish His purposes. We'll delve into these tools (the Word, prayer, authenticity, forsaking idols, etc.) in the next few chapters. Though we use these weapons in our everyday world, they have eternal and ethereal impact. It's important to note that when we're experiencing a painful trial, particularly if it involves people, our battle isn't against those people. It's against who or what influences them. Paul asserts, "For we are not fighting against flesh-and-blood enemies, but against evil rulers and authorities of the unseen world, against mighty powers in this dark world, and against evil spirits in the heavenly places" (Ephesians 6:12).

Frederick Buechner writes, "If we are to love our neighbors, before doing anything else we must see our neighbors. With our imagination as well as our eyes, that is to say like artists, we must see not just their faces, but the life behind and within their faces. Here it is love that is the frame we see them in."[3] Viewing people as enemies is not seeing them through God's eyes. He deemed mankind worthy of rescue. His love compelled Him to die for them. Therefore, when we see people only as combatants, we shrink in our love not only for them, but also for the God who made them. This battle isn't against people. It's against the forces of evil in this world.

...It's about hard work alongside vigilance.

Spiritual warfare is active, not passive. It takes hard work and vigilance. Even so, we cannot allow specific spiritual attack to render us useless in daily life. In France, I allowed the defeat and whispered torment to immobilize me. I spent many days making up excuses why I couldn't engage with new friends. I preferred my bed to getting up and walking the kids to school. I scared my husband. He watched his normally active, outgoing wife become a recluse. Only through much prayer (by others) and a gritty determination to move forward for the sake of my family did I start dipping my toe into the waters of life there. It was a daily choice I made to engage, a forcing, a begging of God to empower me despite the warfare swirling around us.

Spiritual warfare takes hard work and vigilance.

Nehemiah, one of the wisest leaders in the Bible, has some important lessons for us as we strive to strike the work/warfare balance. In charge of rebuilding the toppled walls of Jerusalem, Nehemiah faced attacks from outside as the work continued. Instead of cowering in fear and giving up the God-ordained work, he implemented a persevering plan. He kept half the folks working on the wall while he stationed the other half as sentries, guarding the city. But even the workers armed themselves at all times. "The laborers carried on their work with one hand supporting their load and one hand holding a weapon. All the builders had a sword belted to their side" (Nehemiah 4:17-18). It's no surprise that they built the wall in record time. Note how equipped they were both to work hard and defend themselves during the construction. "During this time, none of us—not I, nor my relatives, nor my servants, nor the guards who were with me—ever took off our clothes. We carried our weapons with us at all times, even when we went for water" (Nehemiah 4:23). This is what I had to learn to do in France, amid difficult ministry experiences, outward spiritual attack, and relational hardship. I learned to be more alert in my day-to-day life, to be braced for the battle. We are all part of the kingdom work. We must live in such a way that we expect opposition.

...It's about seeing things from God's perspective.

I love the story of Elisha and his servant as they faced an impossible battle. "When the servant of the man of God got up early the next morning and went outside, there were troops, horses, and chariots everywhere. 'Oh, sir, what will we do now?' the young man cried to Elisha. 'Don't be afraid!' Elisha told him. 'For there are more on our side than on theirs!' Then Elisha prayed, 'O LORD, open his eyes and let him see!' The LORD opened the young man's eyes, and when he looked up, he saw that the hillside around Elisha was filled with horses and chariots of fire" (2 Kings 6:15-17). I don't often see chariots of fire, unless you're referring to a 1980s movie, but these verses highlight something we must believe: God fights on our behalf even when we can't physically see the battle. He has trained warrior angels attentive to His call. When we feel overwhelmed and battle-weary, it's important that we ask God to open our eyes to His battle and how He is waging it.

The more we walk in wholeness, the more we learn to walk away from sin and toward love, the more God is glorified in us.

When I shared openly about our struggles in France with Brandilyn, a good friend of mine who loves to pray, she told me that as she prayed she saw demonic powers circling above our home in France. That resonated with me. Every time I walked in the house, I felt them. But she also said that she saw us being delivered from those dark forces—soon. She prayed that prayer in September, and by December we had moved away from that home, back to the States. I'd expected some sort of cosmic battle where those dark forces were forced to flee, but instead God chose to move us away from them.

…It's about God's renown.

Our job as women warriors is to make God's name known and famous throughout the earth. The battles we engage in aren't about us; they're about the glory of God. I love how God defends His renown even in our rebellion. "Our ancestors in Egypt were not impressed by the LORD's miraculous deeds. They soon forgot his many acts of kindness to them. Instead, they rebelled against him at the Red Sea. Even so, he saved them— to defend the honor of his name and to demonstrate his mighty power" (Psalm 106:7-8). God saved the Israelites for His sake, His renown. Sure, they got to experience deliverance, but God received the glory.

Even when we plead for God to rescue us, our heart should be bent toward His glory, not merely our rescue. Psalm 31:3 says, "You are my rock and my fortress. For the honor of your name, lead me out of this danger."

…It's about our personal restoration.

As women well-loved by God, we play an important, irreplaceable role in God's advancing kingdom. If we live believing lies about our worth, we will continue to live in defeat. We must ask for and live in restoration.

A few years ago, my friend Malcolm Thomas was a victim of a vicious home invasion in which his son was shot and paralyzed. One thing he said after the experience stuck with me. "We insult Jesus when we live defeated lives." Malcolm is a man who continues to train people to share Jesus wherever he goes. He doesn't allow the tragedy to define him. And in persevering, he retains his dignity.

Most of my adult life has been spent recovering from a difficult childhood. I can't imagine what my life would be like today had I not run to God for healing. My testimony points to the power of God to restore the most broken life. I see chasing healing as a part of warfare. The more we walk in wholeness, the more we learn to walk away from sin and toward love, the more God is glorified in us.

I'm not saying we must have it all together to be a part of God's redemptive plan on earth. On the contrary, God uses our weakness and vulnerability to change us and empower our weakness. But for those of you who fight a difficult past, rejoice in your weakness because the power of Christ cannot coexist with your strength. Your weakness is the doorway for His power to walk through.

...It's about the restoration of this world.

Spiritual warfare is about God restoring us individually, but it's also about God restoring all of us together. We engage in spiritual warfare when we work on behalf of justice issues. When one slave is freed, we participate in restoration, bringing God's heart to this broken world. When we defend the orphan or stick up for the oppressed, we represent God to the powers of darkness. Satan's greatest ploy is to enslave people, keeping them in darkness in the futility of their minds. As we actively seek to change that paradigm, we shake Satan's unstable kingdom.

But we don't seek to only alleviate earthly suffering. We must think in terms of the gospel and how we can share it with those who don't yet know Jesus. When we lived in France, our eldest daughter, Sophie, befriended a girl who was an atheist. The girl worried about what would happen when she died—a fear she confided to Sophie. A year went by. Sophie prayed for her friend constantly, seeking open doors. Eventually, Sophie's friend came to the end of her atheism and followed Christ. Bringing her atheist friend to Jesus was Sophie's part (along with God's huge part) in restoring this world. John Piper said this at the third Lausanne Congress on World Evangelization: "For Christ's sake, we Christians care about all suffering, especially eternal suffering."

Spiritual warfare is about setting things in proper order in our hearts and minds through the power of the Holy Spirit. It's about recognizing God's supremacy, Satan's defeat, and our humility. It's about His renown, His ability to change things. It's about His kingdom and the role He allows us to play in it.

Still, we struggle. How do we know when something is spiritual warfare? Maybe it's the bad pizza we ate the night before, or maybe it's just the fallenness of this world, or maybe we're willfully walking in sin. How do we discern what is happening? How do we know when the enemy is attacking? Here are 11 questions to ask.

1. Has your peace suddenly eroded? At what point did it flee? What was happening at the time when peace left?

2. What are your thoughts/inner voice saying? Are they accusatory, laden with despair? Are you hearing things like, "Your sin is too big for God to forgive" or "You'll never overcome that issue in your life" or "You are worthless"? Conversely, do you struggle with thoughts of over-worth? "You're better than that person" or "That person is stupid compared to you" or "You should've been the one to be recognized."

3. Is shame involved? Remember, shame is an overwhelming feeling that you'll never overcome a situation in your life. Its boast is to keep you overwhelmed by your sin. Shame floods us in unspecific ways, producing a general feeling of spiritual malaise. True conviction from the Holy Spirit is always accompanied by hope, within the context of a positive relationship with God. We can confidently approach God's throne of grace. (See Hebrews 4:16.)

4. Has a strange, out-there thought bombarded you, followed by a condemning voice that says, "I can't believe you just thought that! What kind of a Christian are you?"

5. Is this current struggle based on what you feel? If so, are your

emotions accurate? What is the truth about the situation? If another person looked at your situation, would they see the same thing? How much of your own tendency toward drama is coloring your view of the situation?

6. Have you just experienced a significant spiritual victory in your life? Often spiritual attack comes right after a victory. (Read the story of Elijah after his victory over the Baal prophets in 1 Kings 19:1-14.)

7. Have you explored other options? Are you exercising and eating right? How are your hormone levels? Are you disciplined in reading the Bible, praying, and sharing Christ? Do you have a broken relationship that needs mending?

8. Is what you are experiencing God's discipline? Have you neglected to reconcile with the difficult friend and now you can't sleep at night? This could be God's conviction and discipline in your life, not spiritual attack.

9. Are you experiencing consequences for your own sin? If you suffer in a relationship for telling lies, the other person's lack of trust isn't spiritual warfare, it's the natural consequence of your behavior.

10. Have other discerning believers perceived this as spiritual warfare? Once I was walking through a long, long period of extended trials. I wondered if I was simply being attacked. A wise friend watched my life, then said, "Mary, I think you're walking through a wilderness right now. Keep walking. The Promised Land will come." Her insight helped me press on, and it shed light on whether I was experiencing attack or simply walking through the mess of life.

11. Has a sin you've conquered suddenly become alluring to you? What brought about the enticing? Did you open the door to the sin in the past few weeks?

The story of spiritual warfare, like the quotation says at the beginning of the chapter, is a dynamic, kingdom-clashing story. It's about God's power, your weakness, and Satan's defeat. While it's not always clear when we're facing it—Satan loves to masquerade and deceive, so this makes sense— we can always be prepared by living according to Ephesians 6:13-18:

> Therefore, put on every piece of God's armor so you will be able to resist the enemy in the time of evil. Then after the battle you will still be standing firm. Stand your ground, putting on the belt of truth and the body armor of God's righteousness. For shoes, put on the peace that comes from the Good News so that you will be fully prepared. In addition to all of these, hold up the shield of faith to stop the fiery arrows of the devil. Put on salvation as your helmet, and take the sword of the Spirit, which is the word of God. Pray in the Spirit at all times and on every occasion. Stay alert and be persistent in your prayers for all believers everywhere.

As woman warriors we can resist, believe truth, live in righteousness, walk in peace, wield our faith, believe and quote God's Word, pray for ourselves and others, and live a persistent, dedicated life. There's no magic formula, no shortcut—just simple, dedicated obedience in a victorious, enabling God. As we engage daily with this beautiful God, we'll be better able to discern what is spiritual warfare and what is not. It's not always easy to determine, but the determination evolves the longer we walk with Christ.

———

Mind if I pray for you?

Lord, sometimes we don't know what is warfare, so we come to You and ask for help. I pray for my sister today, that she would buckle truth around her heart and mind and really, really believe that You are for her, that You love her. May she live believing in Your goodness and power, less concerned about her own penchant for sin and weakness. Elevate her eyes above the fray of today so she can see the battle You are waging on her behalf. Help her to discern practical matters, Lord—whether she needs to live in discipline or eat better or exercise. Protect her from the lies of the Evil One. Help her take every single condemning, shameful voice captive, believing only what You believe about her. Today I pray for mind rest, Lord. Settle her mind. Bring simplicity to her thoughts. And bless her with bubbling joy. Amen.

Part Two

PROACTIVE:
How We Participate
in the Beautiful Battle

I ended the last chapter with a quotation from Ephesians 6, a proactive Scripture about our responsibility in spiritual warfare. To have victory as a warrior woman, we must be proactive now, before an attack happens. The following section reveals eight holy habits a warrior woman must embrace if she wishes to live with freedom, empowered to discern Satan's attacks.

The eight holy habits are:

1. Breathing prayer
2. Loving truth
3. Practicing risk
4. Slaying idols
5. Worshiping God
6. Living the Bible
7. Embracing rest
8. Chasing healing

Chapter 6

Breathing Prayer

*Someday we may understand more fully why the Lord
seemed so urgent about our prayers, as if heaven and earth
depended on them. Who knows? Maybe it is His way of
making us feel fully engaged in the process, body and soul.*[1]

ANDRÉE SEU

In this chapter I wanted to share a devastating story of loss completely
reworked by the power of God. But I can't. Not yet. Even though I've
prayed. I've wept alongside. I've held the hand of a friend whose life has
fallen apart in every possible way. I've hollered, beseeched, begged. But
the painful situation persists.

What difference does the holy habit of prayer make? If you've walked
with the Lord long enough, you've had to deal with a prayer seemingly
hanging in the air between heaven and earth. Sometimes the answer is *no*
or *not yet* or *wait*. I've been praying fervently for a family member over 30
years, and she just seems to grow harder and harder. Sometimes the answer
is *yes*. I've seen profound healing in my heart over the past several years, all
God's doing as a direct yes-answer to my prayers.

Whether the answer is *no* or *yes*, when I pray the most extraordinary things
happen in me. I experience God. I sense His nearness. I come closer to His
heart. Perhaps that's the crux of prayer: relationship. If I view prayer that way,
I'll grow in my relationship with Him. I'll become not merely as an infant
demanding to have all my needs met, not merely a child asking for things-
things-things, not an adolescent longing for self-actualization, but an adult
seeking to know Him, understand His heart, and experience His friendship.

Freedom comes in moving from a request-based prayer life to a relationally-based one. Perhaps prayer becomes something dynamic—like breathing. It's a life-sustaining interaction between the Creator and the created. Prayer allows us to be alert and expectant in the moment, trusting God to speak, to encourage, to guide, to whisper, to help, to love, to correct. John Dawson, a well-known speaker about prayer and reconciliation, said this: "Everyone prays. Even non-Christians pray. The difference when Christians do it is that they are climbing into the lap of their heavenly father."[2]

> Prayer is a life-sustaining interaction between
> the Creator and the created.

Even though I know prayer is relationship, I'm still one of those people haunted by 1 Thessalonians 5:17. Paul urged the believers in Thessalonica to "never stop praying." This means we are to constantly be in breathed communication with Jesus—in the midst of casserole preparation, while chatting on the phone with a friend, or taking a bath—any time. Henri Nouwen helped me understand this verse a little better, though. "Praying always" is the Greek word *hesychia*, which literally means "come to rest." Nouwen explains, "*Hesychia*, the rest which flows from unceasing prayer, needs to be sought at all costs, even when the flesh is itchy, the world alluring, and the demons noisy."[3]

I want to foster a pray-without-ceasing habit, particularly in the restful way Nouwen explains it. I envision myself looking like a cross between a quiet girl-monk and Fraulein Maria of *The Sound of Music* fame—a contemplative sort who still knows how to engage life. Funny things happen when you try to live 1 Thessalonians 5:17. People appear out of the paneling needing prayer. It delights His heart when, instead of just saying you'll pray, you actually do pray, right then and there.

Along this journey of spontaneous and continuous prayer, I've been forced to change my paradigms. Prayer couldn't just be a thing I performed at designated prayer meetings; it became the air I breathed. Finding opportunities to pray transformed into a great adventure. Here are four ways God taught me how to pray for others as I attempted to "pray without ceasing," engaging in spiritual warfare on behalf of others.

Touch

I once consulted with a friend of mine who is writing a Bible resource for teen girls. When we finished our writer-talk, we prayed. I reached over and held her hand as we prayed for her new literary adventure. After we finished, she thanked me for touching her. "I get so tired of prayer times where people sit aloof and don't touch. Thank you for touching me," she said.

Strangers

One story stands out to me as I think about praying for strangers. I'd almost finished my first novel. Worn out by an endless day of frenetic typing, I couldn't stop to make dinner. I called out for pizza, much to the delight of my cheese-loving children. When the pizza man arrived, he looked tired, his eyes registering sadness. I tried to make light of his situation. "Too many pizzas to deliver today?" I asked.

He shook his head. As he held our two pizzas (with extra cheese), he told me he'd had a bad day peppered with family problems.

The Lord told me to pray for him. We had a little conversation, mostly me telling Him why this was not a good idea. Finally, though, I asked the man, "Would you mind if I prayed for you?"

He said no, he didn't mind, so I prayed.

When I finished, he was crying. He thanked me, handed me the pizzas, and left. A few hours later, I typed the last word of my novel and jumped up and down. (I do have some Fraulein Maria in me, after all.) In the quiet of my bed that night, the Lord whispered, "The most eternal thing you did today wasn't finishing the novel. It was praying for the pizza man."

Cyberprayer

Once I received a very sad e-mail from a friend. Her husband told her he did not love her and, in fact, had never loved her. I prayed for her as I responded to her. As I prayed, I decided to type the prayer I was praying on the spot. I've done this a lot over the past year. It's been heartwarming to see people being changed by simple e-mail prayers.

Gather Around

At a women's Bible study I taught about God's healing touch—how when He intersects our lives, He bandages our wounds because He loves us. As I planned the evening, I felt I should ask each woman to share a wounding from her week. The rest of us would gather around her and pray for her need. All through the study I struggled. *Will they think this is weird? Will they feel uncomfortable praying for each other?* I worried right until the moment I brought up the prayer idea. Turns out, it was the best study we ever had. We connected. We cried. We prayed. And the women left feeling God's love in a new way.

—

I wish I could decree, queen-like, that henceforth I shall pray nonstop. Instead, my frailty and my desire to be a prayer-woman intermingle daily. But I am thankful that when I do utter prayers to Jesus, He answers by helping me touch those in need, giving me boldness to pray for strangers, innovating my typed prayers for friends, and enabling me to take prayer risks.

Like writing this chapter. I realize entire books tackle prayer. Volumes have been written about it. Those facts fuel my insecurities, threatening to strangle my words. But as I've walked through spiritual warfare, I know the holy habit of prayer is central, and I've found ten types of prayers that will benefit a warrior woman.

1. Open-Eyed Prayers

While it's certainly the norm that we close our eyes when we pray, have you considered how your prayer life would change if you opened your eyes? Juan Carlos Ortiz, in his enigmatic book *Disciple*, writes about a prayer meeting he had with his staff in a park. At first they closed their eyes, but eventually they opened them and started seeing things to praise God for. Eyes-open prayers breed a natural thankfulness, to see what God has done and then thank Him for it.

Ortiz concludes, "Here is a very 'childish' revelation which came to me one day: Maybe the reason we don't have praises to give God is that we try to praise Him with our eyes closed. What can we think of when everything is dark?...But when we open our eyes and look around, we find all things to thank the Lord for."[4] My best prayers come on my morning run, where I hear the birds, smell the air, and watch God's sunrise erupt. I praise Him for everything on those runs. His creation, even in my little corner of the world, connects me with others, so that once I start praising God about trees and leaves and bunnies crossing my path, I end my run praying for people because of God's reminders. I become active in their spiritual warfare.

2. Community Prayers

Which segues nicely into praying with and for others. In the circle of community, something dynamic happens in our prayer lives. Personally, I experienced huge amounts of healing during college when folks dared to pray for me often. I shared my failures and sins with that group and watched God cleanse me. My deep insecurities from growing up in a painful home began to slough off under the prayers of my friends. I saw this verse unfold and play itself out in my life: "Confess your sins to each other and pray for each other so that you may be healed. The earnest prayer of a righteous person has great power and produces wonderful results" (James 5:16).

As people pray, we hear, feel, touch,
and experience Jesus through them.

Prayer in community is part of spiritual warfare because it shows the enemy that we can be unified in Christ. It gives us the opportunity to come clean about the sin and secrets we've let Satan torment us with. It reveals to us the beauty of the hands and feet of the body of Christ. As people pray, we hear, feel, touch, and experience Jesus through them. And comfort comes in the aftermath of our collective struggle.

3. Battle Prayers

Prayer empowers us in our war against Satan, his angels, and their schemes. However, it's important for us to think biblically about the way we pray. Many of us (me included) have used the words "binding" and "loosing" as we pray, rebuking Satan.

We find the binding and loosing passages in Matthew 16 and 18. The first time it's mentioned, Jesus has declared the beginning of the church, starting with Peter. It will be inaugurated on the rock of Peter's declaration that Jesus is the Christ. Just after this, Jesus says, "I will give you the keys of the kingdom of heaven; whatever you bind on earth will be bound in heaven, and whatever you loose on earth will be loosed in heaven" (Matthew 16:19 NIV). Jesus is not referring to Satan here, saying that we are to bind him. Instead, He's referring to the day-to-day operations of the burgeoning church. The ESV commentary for this passage states, "Peter also has authority to exercise discipline concerning right and wrong conduct for those in the kingdom, an authority that is not exclusive to Peter but is extended to the church as a whole."[5] Later, in chapter 18, Jesus gives believers instructions about church discipline, how we are to confront sinful believers one-on-one, then with a friend, and finally in front of the church. Only after that does He say, "Truly I tell you, whatever you bind on earth will be bound in heaven, and whatever you loose on earth will be loosed in heaven" (Matthew 18:18 NIV). Again, this refers to community living, telling us how to live in community when one of our members is blatantly sinning.

As believers, we are not to go around rebuking Satan. Only the Lord does that. In Zechariah 3:1-2, we see a picture of warfare as the Lord is cleansing the high priest. God gave Zechariah a vision: "Then the angel showed me Jeshua the high priest standing before the angel of the LORD. The Accuser, Satan, was there at the angel's right hand, making accusations against Jeshua. And the LORD said to Satan, 'I, the LORD, reject your accusations, Satan. Yes, the LORD, who has chosen Jerusalem, rebukes you. This man is like a burning stick that has been snatched from the fire.'" Note that it is God who rebukes Satan.

Let's become so passionately consumed with Jesus—His life, death, and resurrection—that Satan is but a fleeting thought.

In Jude 1:9, we see that even the angelic majesties don't rebuke Satan. "But even Michael, one of the mightiest of the angels, did not dare accuse the devil of blasphemy, but simply said, 'The Lord rebuke you!' (This took place when Michael was arguing with the devil about Moses' body.)" There is no biblical precedent for dismissively rebuking Satan. God has taken care of that for us. He is the One who rebukes.

How do we pray, then?

The simplest warfare prayer model is actually the Lord's Prayer because it focuses on God, His kingdom, and His plan—not on the evil one's schemes. Read through the prayer again, this time in the New Living Translation. Note how much God is mentioned, and how Satan is an afterthought:

> When you pray, don't babble on and on as people of other religions do. They think their prayers are answered merely by repeating their words again and again. Don't be like them, for

your Father knows exactly what you need even before you ask him! Pray like this:

> Our Father in heaven,
> may your name be kept holy.
> May your Kingdom come soon.
> May your will be done on earth,
> as it is in heaven.
> Give us today the food we need,
> and forgive us our sins,
> as we have forgiven those who sin against us.
> And don't let us yield to temptation,
> but rescue us from the evil one
> (Matthew 6:7-13).

The prayer is a good model for our lives as well. We should spend the bulk of our mind-time thinking about God, His beauty and strength, concerning ourselves with His kingdom being established in our lives. After that, we concern ourselves with asking God for our daily needs. Then we seek Him to be Lord of our relationships, determining to so experience God's radical forgiveness that we can't help but forgive others. We ask for protection against temptation. The footnote to the prayer, and our lives, is asking God to rescue us from the Evil One. My hunch is that if we spend most of our time in God's grandeur, the Evil One will be but a footnote in our lives as well.

Let's not become so captivated by Satan's activities that we're pulled into dark pursuits. Let's become so passionately consumed with Jesus—His life, death, and resurrection—that Satan is but a fleeting thought.

4. Journaled Prayers

I'm a forgetful girl. I pray throughout the day in bits and spurts, but then when God answers I forget to thank Him or even remember I prayed for that thing in the first place. To remedy this, I've journaled my prayers. This has taken several different forms, depending on my mood and time restrictions. When my children were younger, we had a large chalkboard in a prominent place in our home. There we listed a date on the far left-hand side, a prayer request in the middle, and a place for God's answer on the far right. It was a tangible way to write our requests and then see God's specific answer. I've also used this same abbreviated format in the back of my journals. It's incredible to see how beautifully God answered my prayers.

I've had times in my life, though, when listing my regrets didn't adequately address what was in my heart. In those moments, I took my pen and a notebook and poured my heart to God on the page. Page upon page of worry, entreaties, petitions. In that exercise I not only felt heard by God, but purged of my stress. If you're going through a dry spell in your prayer life, or there's a particular battle you can't seem to get beyond, give yourself permission to write it all—stark as you can—on the page. This emptying on the page becomes a tangible remembrance of God's faithfulness on which you can stand when you're attacked.

5. Gifting Prayers

Similarly, one of the most profound spiritual blessings I've experienced came from the heart and hand of a friend. We weren't close friends at the time, which made the gift even more extravagant. Patrick and I were stateside, battling through some difficult re-entry issues in our marriage—a dark, painful time. I often felt alone and bewildered as I tried to discern how to encourage Patrick in our new environment. I failed a lot. And I wondered if God saw me.

One particular month strained me to brokenness. At the end of that month, I felt a new sense of relief. A few days later, I received a stack of papers in the mail. God had directed my friend Tina to pray for me every day for a month—that particularly painful month. Instead of praying out loud, she journaled her prayers longhand. I marveled as I looked back on what she prayed and threaded her words together with what had been happening. Her written prayers were warfare on my behalf. They spoke truth. She prayed Scripture. God gave her insight only He could give.

I still have that outrageous gift. I count it as one of the most touching, profound gifts I've ever received.

Perhaps God is calling you to do the same for someone else. To stand in the gap for a period of time. To send on your prayers. I adore this creative form of prayer warfare as it fosters community, displays God's love, and gives room for God's curious answers to prayer.

6. Healing Prayers

When we lived in France, I had the privilege of welcoming a team of prayer warriors from Healing Rooms,[6] a ministry developed to help people walk through emotional, spiritual, and physical healing. At first, as is my nature, I was skeptical. How could this kind of prayer help me? Was it real? True? A bunch of bunk? How could God possibly give folks insights into the depths of my heart? Hadn't I already been profoundly healed?

So when the group gathered to pray for me, one man asked if I saw a picture as they prayed. I did, but I didn't answer. I saw myself in a crib at four years old. The man persisted. So I gave him another memory, one of the wild memories—where I was molested at the age of five. He persisted, "Is that really the picture that comes to mind?"

I didn't want to answer. After all, the memory was so pedestrian. It didn't mean a thing. Truly. So I shared another memory, this one of my parents' drug use. Still, the man persisted.

Finally I said, "I'm standing in a crib and I'm four years old." In the declaration, I suddenly understood how strange the memory was. Why was a four-year-old in a crib? At that time, I'd been living with my grandparents. My grandmother insisted I take a nap every day. I remember not being tired, so I sang. But I wasn't allowed to get out of the crib. Next to it was an intercom where, when my grandmother heard me singing, she would say, "Mary, lie down and go back to sleep." She wasn't malicious in her tone, just firm.

As the people kept praying, I felt a weight settle onto my chest—almost heart attack worthy. I couldn't roll off the weight. I realized in that moment that I'd placed a lot of emphasis on my grandparents. I'd rationalized that during my year-long stay in their home I was wanted and loved. That their love and protection for me during that time enabled me to survive my kindergarten year, neglected at home and molested by neighborhood boys. I always pointed back to that time in their house as a capstone, proving I had worth, that someone in my family wanted me. Problem was, as the people prayed for me in France, more memories came back—where I'd been an inconvenience to my grandparents, how I had to sit in a bedroom alone and play quietly while my grandmother played bridge. Cemented through the memories was this truth: my presence was an inconvenience.

Which weighted my chest even further.

It was only when God allowed one more picture that the steel ball of grief rolled off. I said, "If I say my grandparents didn't really want me, then no one did." At that point, I saw Jesus in that basement room where my crib sat. He lifted me from the crib and held me—all four-years-old of me—and loved me. That picture has proven to be one of the most profound moments of healing for me. I learned that even if folks on earth didn't want me, Jesus always did.

The experience, as I write about it, does seem esoteric in nature. But as I meditated on it later, I realized the picture God gave me was a true one. He is omnipresent. He is everywhere. Of course He was in that room—I just didn't know it then. Experiencing this kind of prayer opened my eyes to God's bigness, and for that I'm thankful.

7. Scripture Prayers

My friend Brandilyn Collins writes suspense novels. But she's more than an author; she prays—a lot. Her many prayers sustained me in France. One of the things I love about her is her desire to pray Scripture over people. If you get to a place where you're weary and don't exactly know what to pray or even how to battle the enemy in your life, Scripture is the best place to start, particularly the Psalms.

Brandilyn writes: "I'm continually praying for many Christian friends who are very sick. As many of you know, I use the psalms to pray for people. Nothing is more powerful in prayer than God's own Word. Psalm 31 is a particularly good one to use to pray against illness. Here's the BPV (Brandilyn's Prayer Version) for Psalm 31 (based on the New American Standard Bible.) Just fill in the names of your own friends and family members—or maybe pray it for yourself.

> In You, O Lord, ____ has taken refuge;
> May she (or he) not be ashamed.
> In Your righteousness deliver her.
> Incline your ear to me, rescue her quickly.
> Be to her a rock of strength, a stronghold to save,
> For You are her rock and her fortress.
> For Your name's sake, lead and guide her.
> Pull her out of the net this illness has laid for her,
> For You are her strength
> Into Your hand I commit her, Lord.
> Ransom her, O God of truth.
>
> I hate the regarding of vain idols,
> But I trust in You, Lord.

I will rejoice and be glad in Your lovingkindness,
Because You have seen ____'s affliction.
You know the troubles of her soul.
Don't give her over to the hand of this enemy.
Set her feet in a large place.

Be gracious to ____, Lord, for she is in distress.
Her eye is wasted away from grief, her soul and body also.
Her life is now spent with sorrow and sighing.
Strength fails her, and her body is wasting away.
Because of her illness she may feel
like she's a reproach to her neighbors,
An object of dread to her acquaintances.
Some may not want to see her.
She may feel forgotten, out of mind, like a broken vessel.
She may have heard the words
of many that terror is on every side.
Illness takes counsel against her, scheming for her life.

But she trusts in you, Lord, and I trust in You.
For You are our God.
Her times are in Your hand.
Deliver her from the hand of this illness
and from its persecution.
Make Your face shine upon her.
Save her in Your lovingkindness.
Let her not be put to shame, O Lord,
For she calls upon You.
Let this illness be put to shame, let it be silent.
Let lying lips be dumb that speak arrogantly against ___
With pride and contempt.

How great is Your goodness,
Which You have stored up for ____.
Which You have wrought for ____,
Because she takes refuge in You before the sons of men.
Hide ___ in the secret place of
Your presence from this illness.
Keep her secretly in Your shelter from
the strife of this disease.

Blessed be Your name, Lord,
For You have made marvelous
Your lovingkindness to ____
During this besieged time.
If she says in alarm, "I am cut off from God's eyes!"—
Even then You hear her prayers and supplications when she
cries to You.

I love You, Lord, I and all Your godly ones.
I know You preserve the faithful and fully
recompense the proud doer.
Help ____ be strong. Help her heart take courage
For she hopes in You, Lord.
Amen.[7]

8. Expectant Prayers

My husband relayed a story from his seminary days. He'd been in a class where the professor started with a question. "Does anyone have a prayer request?" A man raised his hand and shared a health need for a family member. The prayers in response went something like, "Lord, guide the doctors;" "Give him strength;" "Let the medicine accomplish its desired effect." The man who asked for prayer stopped the class and said something like, "Remind me not to ask for prayer again. None of you prayed as if you believed God could heal my family member."

While it is very true that God uses modern medicine to heal many, He is also the Creator of everything, including our bodies and minds. He is fully capable of the miraculous. It's not that we shouldn't pray for God to use medical professionals, it's that we should also pray with a holy expectation that God can heal. My friends in Ghana taught me this. They didn't have the luxury of running to the doctor when someone fell ill. Other than home remedies, all they had was the Great Physician to entreat. And entreat they did. They believed God could heal.

Of course, as in nature, balance is essential. While God can heal anything He wants (He is not limited as we are), He may, in His sovereign plan, choose not to. So we learn to pray with expectation over God's ability to heal balanced with a healthy belief in His sovereignty.

How do we pray that way? Part of learning to pray expectant prayers full of belief and trust is simply praying. C.H. Spurgeon wrote, "Prayer itself is an art only the Holy Spirit can teach us. He is the giver of all prayer. Pray for prayer. Pray until you can really pray."[8] As the 24/7 prayer movement took off, authors Peter Greig and Dave Roberts realized the apprenticing power of prayer—that people learned to pray simply by praying. They write, "In the prayer room, people were really learning to pray simply by praying. By locking ourselves alone in a room with God, we were encountering His presence night after night and learning to listen to the still, small voice of His Spirit."[9] We learn by practicing prayer. We grow in faith by believing God is bigger than our struggles or our friend's infirmity. And we grow in prayer by doing it.

9. Listening Prayers

Prayer is not merely listing a litany of requests. As I mentioned at the beginning of this chapter, it's about relationship. It's about sharing, yes, but it's also important that we cultivate the ability to wait on God, to listen to His voice. Jesus tells us that as sheep we hear and know the shepherd's voice (John 10:27). It's part of prayer to stop, to listen, to hear. Read through Psalm 29. Note how the psalm begins, with a nod to heavenly beings needing to honor God. Following that, we see the power and majesty of God's voice:

> Honor the LORD, you heavenly beings;
> honor the LORD for his glory and strength.
> Honor the LORD for the glory of his name.
> Worship the LORD in the splendor of his holiness.
> The voice of the LORD echoes above the sea.
> The God of glory thunders.
> The LORD thunders over the mighty sea.
> The voice of the LORD is powerful;
> the voice of the LORD is majestic.
> The voice of the LORD splits the mighty cedars;
> the LORD shatters the cedars of Lebanon.
> He makes Lebanon's mountains skip like a calf;
> he makes Mount Hermon leap like a young wild ox.
> The voice of the LORD strikes
> with bolts of lightning.
> The voice of the LORD makes the barren wilderness quake;
> the LORD shakes the wilderness of Kadesh.

> The voice of the LORD twists mighty oaks
> and strips the forests bare.
> In his Temple everyone shouts, "Glory!"
> The LORD rules over the floodwaters.
> The LORD reigns as king forever.
> The LORD gives his people strength.
> The LORD blesses them with peace.

There exists a strong juxtaposition between God's power and majesty with His voice. Yet we speak in prayer as if He doesn't have one. Still, we can obsess about hearing God's voice, worrying whether we're really "hearing" it. I love how Jack Deere clarifies this issue with our need for humility. He writes, "Humble people put their confidence in the Holy Spirit's ability to speak, not in their ability to hear, and in Christ's ability to lead, not in their ability to follow."[10] Trust that God has the ability to tell you what He wants you to hear. Trust that He will speak. And, as in any relationship, seek to hear Him. The more you listen, the more you'll recognize His voice, and the more you'll discern how to proceed in spiritual warfare. We'll explore the voice of God further in chapter 19.

10. Daring Prayers

The most dangerous spiritual warfare prayer is a daring prayer—an over-the-top request only God can answer. During one crazy week, I felt deeply frustrated with one of my relationships and I reeled from some difficult novel edits, making me question my abilities as a writer. In the midst of that, God saw fit to speak specifically to me at church one Sunday after I asked for some clarity in or relief from both situations.

God speaks to me in different ways, but mostly, as in this instance, He spoke words into my thoughts. They came out of the blue, were very specific to some recent fears and old wounds, and salved my heart like only He could. I'd been wrestling with a friend's misunderstanding and judgment of my heart. No matter what I'd done to clear the air or prove my innocence, I couldn't make my friend see my heart or understand my motives correctly. God said, "Mary, I know your heart. I know the situation. I see it all. But your friend is too wounded to see that. Rest in Me and give grace to your friend who doesn't understand yet."

He said this while I worshiped Him in song. I raised my hands a little higher, tears of thankfulness in my eyes. God sees me, I thought. He sees. And He understands. As if I needed a little more confirmation, I dared to pray, "Please show me specifically that You see me."

He answered in two ways:

One. The edits I received earlier in the week were making me feel terribly small as a writer. As in all my editor letters, though I agreed with what my editor asked for, I felt inadequate after reading all that feedback. I labored over that book, only to find flaws that needed to be worked out. I'd hoped for a "Brilliant!" Imagine my surprise when a woman came up to me after church—we attend a gigantic church—and told me she was reading my first novel, *Watching the Tree Limbs*. "I can't put it down," she said. "The way you write is beautiful. Thank you." Her words were exactly the encouragement I needed to hear. Proof one that God sees me and Jesus is real.

Two. I waited in our usual waiting place for our son to find us. While there, another lady approached me. "You don't know me, and I don't know you," she said. "But God wouldn't let me walk by you without telling you how much you are loved by Him. He has placed you on my heart to pray for you, and I don't even know your name. Be assured that He is mindful of you." I thanked her, marveling at God's swift double-punched answer to my small prayer.[11]

I left church knowing again that Jesus is so very real. And that He loves me enough to whisper encouragement in my ear during worship and lead two strangers to stop and give me the words I needed to hear. That's the power of daring prayer.

This week, I'd like you to pray the same way. Pour your heart out to Jesus, then ask Him this—perhaps the most daring prayer there is—"Jesus, will You show me specifically that You see me and love me this week? In a me-shaped way, speak to me."

Finishing this chapter, I feel the weight of my lingering inadequacy. There is so much to prayer, so many nuances, so many forms. I pray that as you explore the richness of prayer that you'll become so enamored with Jesus that your relationship with Him will shine all the more. In that, I pray your wrestling against Satan and his schemes would pale in comparison. And that you'd know today, right now, that you are wildly loved by the God who created you.

Mind if I pray for you?

Lord, help us to breathe prayer throughout the day, to see it as a continual relationship between You and us. Meet us there in our minutes of prayer. Hold us when we're perplexed about the cares of this world. Keep us alert to how You're guiding us to pray. Make the woman reading this book a woman of communion with You, a warrior after Your heart. Heal her in prayer, both alone and with a group of praying women. And use her prayers to be the conduit of Your healing in other hurting women. Give her Scripture to pray for her family and friends, and confirm to her today that You hear her and will answer her in Your perfect, sovereign timing. Amen.

Chapter 7

Loving Truth

*The perpetual delusion of humanity is thinking we're
better off hiding than confessing, avoiding rather than
facing, clinging to our sickness instead of taking the
remedy that's freely given and readily available.*[1]

MARK BUCHANAN

When we lived in France, our eldest daughter had a friend who was
experiencing some painful, scary issues. The girl's father tried to fix
those issues with mediums and spiritists. At first Sophie didn't let her
friend's frightening episodes affect her. But eventually, whenever Sophie
spent time with that girl she would come back to us altered. One such
time she'd become a different girl—kicking, growling, fearing. After one
episode, I followed her into her room, then started praying for her. Arms
across her chest, her eyes spewed an otherworldly defiance. Nothing got
through to her. I prayed. I fretted. Finally, I shared my heart with her. I
told her about a painful story from my life, how it affected me in France.
In that circle of truth and authenticity, Sophie snapped out of her funk.
That's the compelling power of truth.

Since Satan's native language is lying, he hates truth. He loves hiding,
aversion, and deception. One of his greatest weapons is whispering lies to
us so we will believe them, act in accordance with those lies, and seek to
cover up the hidden parts of us. When we keep secrets about ourselves or
our pasts, the power of that secret becomes an unruly monster, enslaving
us. It's only when we bring our fears, sins, and stories into the light that
we are set free in the light. Ephesians 5:13-14 shows us the importance of
bringing ourselves into the light. "But their evil intentions will be exposed

when the light shines on them, for the light makes everything visible. This is why it is said, 'Awake, O sleeper, rise up from the dead, and Christ will give you light.'"

Authenticity is the holy habit we give ourselves and, ultimately, the world. It is our declaration that we will live in the light, that the darkness has no power over us, that we can live as free women even if we have a painful past. One of the most powerful ministry moments I've ever experienced came on the heels of a Christian leader sharing a story of a man who years ago had been unfaithful to his wife. He spun the story so well, entangling us into the pain, the deception. At the end of the message, he confessed, "I was that man." The raw vulnerability of that moment spurred on weeping, confession, and renewed marriages within the group. His authenticity paved the way for others to be open about their sin, and it also caused a holy reverence for telling the truth.

Authenticity is our declaration that we will live in the light.

How, exactly, is authenticity part of spiritual warfare? Four ways.

Hiding faults and sins strengthens their hold. Revealing them breaks the power of sin in our lives.

Being truthful helps us expose our hearts before a holy God and His people, and that vulnerability frees us from the lies women warriors listen to. First John 1:6-10 illuminates this perfectly. "If we claim to have fellowship with him and yet walk in the darkness, we lie and do not live out the truth. But if we walk in the light, as he is in the light, we have fellowship with one another, and the blood of Jesus, his Son, purifies us from all sin. If we claim to be without sin, we deceive ourselves and the truth is not in us. If we confess our sins, he is faithful and just and will forgive us our sins and purify us from all unrighteousness. If we claim we have not sinned, we make him out to be a liar and his word is not in us" (NIV).

These are communal, not personal, verses. Used to be, I read the famous portion of the verse this way: If *I* confess *my* sins, He is faithful and just and will forgive *me my* sins. And yet, John uses *we* and *us*. Why? Because true, redeeming power arises in confessing to community. There have been times I've been tormented about a particular sin in my life, pouring it out to God and God alone. And yet, I still struggled. Only when I let my struggle out to a trusted group of friends did the power of that struggle dissipate. It simply can't thrive in the light. Besides, it's easier to heal from your own sin or someone else's when you share it in community. When a friend comes alongside you, embraces you, and says "I understand, and I will pray for you," the burden suddenly lightens.

Sin simply can't thrive in the light.

Our first community is the family, and we must confess our sins in that first community. Why? To be an example to our children. To help them see we all fail and we all need Jesus. That the Christian walk is not about keeping a Christian list, it's about going to Jesus for help.

After our families, we should seek to be real with our friends who love Jesus, who will be trustworthy with our hearts and shortcomings. Confessing our sins and fears and stories to the significant people in our lives invites them into our hearts. And it also breaks the hold that sin has on our lives.

A word of caution, though. Some people are unsafe. In their own hiding, they cannot bear authenticity. They may listen to your heart, but use it against you later. Be hopeful, yet cautious, as you initiate a new friendship, doling out small parts of your heart to test the trustworthiness of your friend.

Confessing opens the door for healed and restored relationships.

We will not be healed in our relationships if we are unwilling to confess our sins and ask for forgiveness. And our relationships will never deepen beyond our willingness to speak the truth—about ourselves, about our friends. Paul asserts, "Speaking the truth in love, we will grow to become in every respect the mature body of him who is the Head, that is, Christ" (Ephesians 4:15 NIV). If we want to be like Jesus, we will speak the truth, even if it's painful.

In terms of spiritual warfare, I believe Satan loves it when we run to people to fill us first rather than Jesus. He knows other Christians will let us down, causing disillusionment and possibly an angry abandonment of the faith.

Authenticity reveals our weaknesses, which then reveals Christ's strength.

Satan revels in our own personal power and strength. Why? Because he knows that the Christian life cannot be lived consistently in human strength—it is only won through dependency on the Holy Spirit. The more he can distract us into thinking we can do things on our own, pulling ourselves up by our spiritual bootstraps, the more victory he can claim. The truth is that Christ's strength can only be found in our weakness. And sharing those weaknesses is a key component of an authentic Christian walk.

Consider these verses: "For to be sure, he was crucified in weakness, yet he lives by God's power. Likewise, we are weak in him, yet by God's power we will live with him in our dealing with you" (2 Corinthians 13:4 NIV). "But we have this treasure in jars of clay to show that this all-surpassing power is from God and not from us" (2 Corinthians 4:7 NIV).

The Christian life isn't about putting on a show. It's about truth from the inside out. It's about our outsides matching our hearts. If we believe (erroneously) that we simply have to tidy up our exterior, we'll be what Jesus called "whitewashed tombs," full of deadness inside, but shiny on the outside. I knew a woman once who appeared to be a Christian. She said all the right words. She knew her Bible. She passed judgment on anyone who differed from her particular beliefs in the way people should live. But when she opened her mouth, all sorts of evil spewed forth. She made fun of people who didn't look beautiful. She disdained all the "other sinners" out there in the world and reveled that she, thankfully, wasn't like them. She was bigoted and deeply prejudiced. She may have appeared strong, but that strength crowded out Jesus's tenderness toward people. And in her pride, Jesus had no room.

> The Christian life isn't about putting on a show. It's about truth from the inside out.

Contrast her with my friend Holly, who shares her hurts with a trusted group of friends, who prays for many, who takes the lowest seat. Even though right now she walks through excruciating trials, she had the wherewithal to e-mail me and tell me she's praying for me. Her weakness has become the power of the Holy Spirit. She walks closely with Him, responding to His leading—all because of her weakness and dependency.

Welcoming truth sets us free—and Satan, the Enslaving One, hates freedom.

I love that Jesus said "I tell you the truth" 78 times in Scripture. Everywhere He went, He spoke truth, and as He did so, He set people free.

As I mentioned before, Satan is the antithesis of truth. He delights when we live a lie, speak a lie, or live in a family of lies. Lying is the native language of Satan's kingdom, so telling the truth is a subversive act. It deals a decisive blow to the enemy of our souls. Honesty is spiritual warfare. It advances the kingdom of God because it sets people free. "Then you will know the truth, and the truth will set you free...So if the Son sets you free, you will be free indeed" (John 8:32,36 NIV).

I've listened to lies. Have you? I've taken them into my soul, nursed them, cemented them into my heart until they became like truth to me. But those words were not true. Words like:

- God is constantly disappointed in me and therefore can't really love me.
- I am not worthy to take up space on this earth.
- I deserve abandonment and harsh treatment from myself and others.
- My protection and safety are solely up to me.

See how destructive these four sentences are? By believing them, I can conclude that God doesn't love me; I am worthless; I deserve what I get; I have to be vigilant to protect myself. Thankfully, I have a dear friend, D'Ann, who saw the power of these lies in my life. She took me out to lunch one week and told me her story of believing lies and how she learned to overcome those lies. "I did it through Scripture," she said. Then she handed me a bound notebook of 3x5 cards. "I want you to identify the lies in your life, then dig through Scripture to find the truth."

The journey toward truth has been life-changing for me. I've come to taste freedom for the first time in many years, all through the power of truth and Scripture.

To combat the lie that God can't really love me, I read, "Don't be afraid... for you are very precious to God. Peace! Be encouraged! Be strong!" (Daniel 10:19). I remember the words of Romans 8 where I realize nothing can separate me from His love. To counteract the unworthiness I feel, I run to Psalm 139 where I remember God created me, is thinking of me, and walks before and behind me. When I feel I deserve harsh treatment, I remember "You can be sure of this: The LORD set apart the godly for himself. The LORD will answer when I call to him" (Psalm 4:3) and "Even if my father and mother abandon me, the LORD will hold me close" (Psalm 27:10). When I believe I'm the only one who can protect me, I reread "But You, O LORD, are a shield about me, my glory, and the One who lifts my head. I was crying to the LORD with my voice, and He answered me from His holy mountain. I lay down and slept; I awoke, for the LORD sustains me. I will not be afraid of ten thousands of people who have set themselves against me round about" (Psalm 3:3-6 NASB). Or "The LORD directs the steps of the godly. He delights in every detail of their lives. Though they stumble, they will never fall, for the LORD holds them by the hand" (Psalm 37:23-24).

Combating lies with the truth of God's Word has changed me. It has empowered me to live a more victorious, confident life—something I'm sure makes the Enemy angry. I've learned the joy of sharing my heart with others, experiencing the beauty of God's grace through the comforting words of friends. In that, I've been on a journey of freedom toward a heart that no longer condemns.

But this is not merely my journey to cultivate the holy habit of authenticity. You can experience this joy too. You can be freed from whatever it is you're keeping secret. You can be freed from a heart that constantly condemns you. Consider this verse: "This then is how we know that we belong to the truth and how we set our hearts at rest in his presence: If our hearts condemn us, we know that God is greater than our hearts, and he knows everything. Dear friends, if our hearts do not condemn us, we have confidence before God" (1 John 3:19-21 NIV).

What would it look like if you had a confident heart like that? And how would that confidence help you in your daily battles against the Enemy and sin? It's something to consider, to weigh. The freedom that comes from an authentic faith will revolutionize a warrior woman's life.

———

Mind if I pray for you?

Lord, we need You. We want to be real, to tell the truth about our past, our present. Help my sister today to find a safe community where she can share her heart openly. Give her holy grit to do so. Protect her from the lies of the evil one who whispers worthlessness and destruction in her ears. Instead, let her know the truth, the power of Your truth in her life. Speak it over her. Whisper her beauty as she falls asleep tonight. Thank You that You are an authentic God who loves us well. Amen.

Chapter 8

Practicing Risk

*Security is mostly a superstition. It does not exist in
nature, nor do the children of men as a whole experience
it. Avoiding danger is no safer in the long run than outright
exposure. Life is either a daring adventure or nothing.*[1]

HELEN KELLER

What is the enemy of the believer? Satan, yes. But what's one of his most effective hidden tactics? Boredom. Or anything that lulls the believer away from adventurous, risky faith.

Consider David's sin with Bathsheba. When the kings ventured off to war, David stayed in Jerusalem, abandoning his work. One night he couldn't sleep, so he meandered onto his rooftop. There, he saw the bathing Bathsheba. In the midst of his idleness and boredom, sin presented itself in all its splendor. In *The Screwtape Letters*, C.S. Lewis writes, "My dear Wormwood...I have always found that the trough [boring] periods of the human undulation provide excellent opportunity for all sensual temptations."[2]

When we are bored or we give in to idleness, sin lurks nearby. In Latin the word *acedia* is one of the seven deadly sins—and it connotes passivity. The French use the word *ennui*, which can also mean weariness, discontentment, or tediousness. I'm afraid those words sometimes describe my life, and all too often they describe the modern life of women today. We're victims of an unholy discontent, yet we're glutted on material possessions, overactive activity, in-your-face entertainment and advertising, way too many commitments, and very little peace. All these choices can overwhelm us into passivity.

How do we prevent ourselves from giving in to boredom? What's the remedy? It's one little word: risk. It's daring to step beyond that which is comfortable, to live Helen Keller's words about living the daring adventure. This is a holy habit we must not neglect because our faith stagnates in doldrums and monotony. When circumstances are too easy, when I'm lulled to lethargy by routine, I don't grow. And I tend to wander, which is something I'm sure Satan and his horde of demons applaud. If they can lull us, distracting warrior women from the work of God, they've won an important battle.

It's when I dare to risk, to step out of comfort, that I once again become dangerous to the kingdom of darkness.

Let's look at two stories of risk with two different endings.

Story one: My friend JR Vassar, a pastor in New York City, shares a story about standing on a precipice. He was visiting Hawaii, preaching at a youth camp. One day, he and the worship band hiked up to a precarious outcropping of rock. A patch of blue water preened 35 feet below him, beckoning. The lead singer said, "Hey, I'm going to jump."

"You go right ahead, my friend," JR said. "I'm going to stay right here. I have a wife and children." To clear the outcropping the worship leader had to leap far out into the air, but not too far, otherwise he'd smash himself on the rocks that flanked the pool's other side. He leaped. He screamed. He survived. JR paced.

Another band member jumped. Same leaping. Same screaming. Same survival.

Still, JR shook his head, muttering "No way," until the only two people remaining were the drummer and himself. "Are you going to do it?" JR asked.

"No way," the drummer said. Even the youth camp taunting from below could not sway them.

At this point in the story, JR pauses, smiles, and then says, "We were happy up there, proud even. Until a girl leapt into the air and splashed below. At that point, I knew what I had to do. Jump."

So, he jumped. He screamed. He survived. Upon reflection, he told us, "Sometimes, you just gotta jump."

Story two: A few years ago, my husband described a powerful word picture. I'd been struggling to connect with him and our children, partially as a result of my upbringing. "Mary, I see you on a high dive, pacing back and forth," he told me.

I stood there, tentative, entirely afraid to dive. (Oddly, I remember this feeling. I have paced my share of high dives in my life, not always taking the leap.) Down below me splashed my family: husband Patrick, and children Sophie, Aidan, and Julia. In their playful cacophony, they beckoned me to jump. "The water's warm, Mommy," Aidan said. "Jump!" I walked all the way to the edge of the board as it bent beneath my weight. My toes peered over the edge. I could hear the horseplay and giggling below. I bent forward, straining to hear my family better, but I did not jump. Instead, I turned around and descended the ladder. I sat on the edge of the pool, watching the joy on the faces of my family, but I did not jump in. I settled for dipping my toes on the pool's edge.

The first story involves a physical leap, the second an emotional one. Yet both are excruciating. Both involve hemming and hawing—choosing that which is safe and easy over that which is unknown. Neither is simple or easy. Yet when Jesus calls us, He calls us to leap off precipices of complacency. He calls us to a life of almost daily risk. His call to this holy habit is radical and excruciating. Consider His calling to Peter from the waves that licked at His holy feet. Defying gravity, Jesus tells His ghost-white disciples, "Take courage, it is I; do not be afraid" (Matthew 14:27 NASB).

> When Jesus calls us, He calls us to leap
> off precipices of complacency.

Only one disciple dared to say, "Lord, if it is You, command me to come to You on the water" (Matthew 14:28 NASB). Peter, a fisherman who knew well the physics of Galilee's water, made a choice to do the impossible. It's not that he was foolhardy, in love with risk for risk's sake. He loved the One who called. John Ortberg writes in his book *If You Want to Walk on Water, You've Got to Get Out of the Boat*, "This is not just a story about risk-taking, it is primarily a story of *obedience*. That means I will have to discern between an authentic call from God and what might simply be a foolish impulse on my part."[3]

Peter's faith-leap depended solely upon his relationship with Jesus and who he knew Jesus to be. When Jesus said come, Peter went. For a moment, his fisherman's feet touched a paradox: water that supported his frame. In another moment, his eyes caught glimpses of the raging storm and the impossibility of the situation.

Panic sunk him.

I thank God that the story does not end there. What a horrible object lesson that would be! Trust God beyond your comfort zone. Take a leap. Get sucked into raging waters and drown the moment you have one glimmer of doubt. As Peter sinks, he yells, "Lord, save me!" Jesus takes hold of him, saves him. Immediately, the seas calm.

I would personally like the story to end there. I've preached mini-sermons to folks along these lines. On the eve of the first day of French schools, I hugged my children and told them this story. I spoke about how going to school was like getting out of the boat. I encouraged them to look into Jesus's eyes and walk toward Him even when French words swirled around them. "But remember," I told them, "even if you become overwhelmed at the life around you, even when you are teased, even when you take your eyes off Jesus, you can ask Him to help you. He will reach out, grab your hand, and pull you up. You won't drown." I held my children close when I told them about Peter's initial triumph, his frailty, and God's ultimate ability to save. When I prayed for them, they wept. On the first day of school, they huffed lips in and out while I silently prayed, "Lord, save them."

Jesus doesn't call us to a life of little faith, but of
adventurous day-by-day faith, full of courage.

The walking on water story continues, though. Jesus utters perplexing words to Peter: "You of little faith, why did you doubt?" (Matthew 14:31 NASB). The audacity! At least Peter had the wherewithal to step onto the swirling sea. Who *wouldn't* be traumatized by the mounting waves and the fierce winds? This is perhaps where books on risky faith fall short. We cheerlead each other to take phenomenal risks, much like the youth group below the outcropping or my splashing family beneath the high dive. Yet the obedience God calls us to is often a long one; taking the initial risk is just the beginning of the journey. We can sometimes be swayed by our cheerleaders (or not, as in my case), and take a leap of faith into the empty air. Yet Jesus doesn't call us to a life of little faith, but of adventurous day-by-day faith, full of courage. Not boredom. Not idleness. But the raw, unadulterated, holy habit of risk.

But how? I remember being supercharged reading missionary biographies as a teenager. I'd want that kind of life, a life characterized by follow-Jesus-or-die. I know now that most biographies are merely high-lights, a string of victories with a few failures thrown in for good measure. Life is not like that. Satan's attacks can be relentless, insidious. More often than not, our own biographies have lowlights like Peter's—pocked with doubt and fear and failure. If we are honest, we'd have to say we're more like the other eleven, clinging to the side of the thrashing boat, believing Jesus to be an apparition.

The story, though, still does not end there. It ends with these words, "And those who were in the boat worshiped Him, saying, 'You are certainly God's Son!'" (Matthew 14:33 NASB). The hope in our journey of risky faith is Jesus. Betraying boredom, we may get out of the boat. We may shiver in fear in the hull. We may leap off the outcropping. We may pace the high dive and retreat. Yet Jesus is still there. Still doing miraculous things in front of our very eyes. He lifts us when we risk and fail. He returns to us when we shudder. He stills the furious seas of our lives. He sees our utter frailty.

But He still gets back into the boat with us. He gives us a chance to wonder at Him, to marvel at His power, to worship Him. I once heard a pastor say, "Worship is our primary occupation in heaven. What are you doing today to prepare for your eternal job?" Perhaps the gist of this water-walking story is simply worship. I wonder what would've happened if David had taken his moment of idleness to sing praises to God. No matter where you find yourself in this faith walk, whether you're cowering under the attacks of the enemy or bored silly, Jesus is the constant One, the One who deserves extreme, constant worship. Whether we take the first step or the last step before we face Him in glory, His call to us is always the same.

Dare to believe Him.

Dare to believe there is more to life than an endless series of monot-onous tasks.

Dare to believe Him enough to take one step.

Dare to believe He will walk the faith journey with you, day by day.

Dare to believe He will be the cheerleader *and* the enabler.

Dare to believe that in our collapse, He offers His saving hand.

Dare to believe that in our fallibility, He still shares a boat with us.

Dare to believe it's all about Him, His renown.

Dare to believe His reality in such a way that worship exudes from us.

JR jumped. I paced. We are all reticent. But, like Helen Keller's quo-tation at the beginning of this chapter, I believe we all long for daring adventure. It's either risk or boredom. We've paced on risk's precipice too long. If we stay there, we'll build our lives there. We'll become so secure we'll never jump, never feel the empty air beneath our kicking feet. We'll miss the opportunity to feel the strength of Jesus's hand lifting us from the sea. We'll forget He's with us for the long, risky journey. We'll lose the opportunity to praise Him for His power because we have settled for safe rather than faith. Won't you join me on this adventure?

Spiritual warfare is risk. It's making decisions based on what God says versus what you may feel. Sometimes it's illogical. And always, a life of risky faith is opposed by your enemy who prowls and lurks and gives you all sorts of reasons why you should settle for mediocrity.

Mind if I pray for you?

Jesus, forgive us for living safe, easily-managed lives. We've failed to risk. There are times we've let boredom lull us into sin. But, Lord, I pray for my friend reading this book today, that You would pull back the curtain of her life right now and show her where she's holding back, where she's afraid to embrace the holy habit of risk. I pray You'd beckon her in a very specific way today. Give her unction and verve to take the leap, to live for Your kingdom and not the kingdom of her control. Make her life a daring adventure through the power of Your Holy Spirit. Amen.

Chapter 9

Slaying Idols

Little children, keep yourselves from idols.

1 John 5:21 KJV

In the spirit of boredom, I've been a bit of a sloth-girl this past week, forsaking exercise. But this morning the sun shone so brightly I couldn't resist its invitation. So I ran. Thank God, I ran. I circled a familiar path in the park and saw it: a dead autumn leaf clinging to an up-and-coming green tree. Though the brown leaf didn't know it, spring would come in a matter of days. And that's when the Lord spoke to me. "The brown leaf will fall. Life always pushes out death."

It reminds me of the cure for idolatry that Timothy Keller writes about in his book *Counterfeit Gods*. We can't simply forsake our idols (whether they be materialism, achievement, lust, the desire to please, food, porn, reputation, or anything else). Instead, we must worship that which is higher. Repentance must hold hands with rejoicing. That's how life pushes out the dead leaves in our lives. We rejoice. We embrace the Life Giver and praise His worth. And His life, because of its sheer power and beauty, pushes away death.

I want that kind of life with Jesus. I don't want to cling to the dead parts of me that I feel are important and valuable—often idols—forsaking the emerging green of spring. I want spring. I want life. I want to run in the freedom of His love. But idols seem to worm their deadly way into my heart. They're not easily slayed.

That's why I laughed when I heard a televangelist proclaim, "Well, we all know America doesn't worship idols, so we can skip that verse."

Really?

An idol is something with which you replace God. It can become a foothold Satan uses to climb his way into your affections. It's something you fill yourself up with, revere, pay homage to. Tim Keller wrote, "Idolatry is always the reason we ever do anything wrong."[1]

With that in mind, the televangelist was wrong: America is full of idols. Maybe we don't offer incense to a golden statue, but we do offer up our lives, our reputations, our money. In the Old Testament, idolatry is linked to spiritual adultery, and often what people worshiped had a sinister, satanic element. Idols are often interchangeable with demons. Love of idols made people do Satan's bidding—to steal, kill, destroy. Which is why slaying idols is such an important holy habit.

Consider this sobering passage: "They [the Israelites] worshiped their idols, which led to their downfall. They even sacrificed their sons and their daughters to the demons. They shed innocent blood, the blood of their sons and daughters. By sacrificing them to the idols of Canaan, they polluted the land with murder. They defiled themselves by their evil deeds, and their love of idols was adultery in the LORD's sight" (Psalm 106:36-39).

Again, God equates the Israelites' idols with demons: "They offered sacrifices to demons, which are not God, to gods they had not known before, to new gods only recently arrived, to gods their ancestors had never feared. You neglected the Rock who had fathered you; you forgot the God who had given you birth" (Deuteronomy 32:17-18).

In the New Testament, we see this same correlation made by Paul—idols and demons. "What am I trying to say? Am I saying that food offered to idols has some significance, or that idols are real gods? No, not at all. I am saying that these sacrifices are offered to demons, not to God. And I don't want you to participate with demons. You cannot drink from the cup of the Lord and from the cup of demons, too. You cannot eat at the Lord's Table and at the table of demons, too. What? Do we dare to rouse the Lord's jealousy? Do you think we are stronger than he is?" (1 Corinthians 10:19-22).

It's easy for us to look into the biblical narrative and be like the TV host who proudly proclaimed we are idol-less. As warrior women, though, we must take seriously the idols in our lives.

What is an idol?

There's more to idolatry than a stone statue. An idol is anything you run to that replaces your need for God. Idolatry is forbidden in the Ten Commandments: "You shall not make for yourself an image in the form of anything in heaven above or on the earth beneath or in the waters below" (Exodus 20:4 NIV). In the New Testament, Paul clearly describes idolatry in Romans 1:25: "They traded the truth about God for a lie. So they worshiped and served the things God created instead of the Creator himself—who is worthy of eternal praise!" An idol is anything you fashion, whether physically or in your imagination, that becomes an object of worship.

Here are some other ways to look at idols. You might have an idol if:

- You set your heart on something other than God.
- You need something other than God to be happy.
- You allow something to capture your imagination more than God.
- You seek something outside of God that only God can give.
- You say, "If I have _____, then my life will have meaning; I will have value; I'll be significant and secure."
- You believe there is something you can't live without or imagine your life without.

To pinpoint your idols, ask yourself:

- What is operating in the place of Jesus as my salvation or savior?
- What am I most afraid of?
- What do I run to first when something in my life falls apart?
- What is the worst thing that could ever happen to me?
- Where does my mind wander when I'm not thinking of other things? What do I daydream about?
- What worries keep me up at night?
- Where do I spend most of my resources (money, time, etc.)?
- What sparks my most uncontrollable emotions?
- What must I have at any cost?
- Fill in the blank: I would be horrified and humiliated if _____.

Take some time to reread and think through those questions. Ask God to sift your heart, to show you what exactly it is you may be worshiping in place of Him. Journal your thoughts.

A List of Possible Idols

If you're struggling to pinpoint your idols, here's a list of common idols women worship.

- Love, romance
- Sex
- Pets
- An unhealthy tie to someone who doesn't share your faith (someone to whom you are unequally yoked)
- An obsessive relationship
- Chaos (Some of us prefer chaos over order because it's what's familiar to us.)
- Morality, perfectionism, virtue, personal piety
- Invincibility, risk-taking, thrill-seeking
- Something tangible that shows worth: a building, a ministry, a house, a car, a promotion, a successful hobby, an empire, a business, a perfect family
- Allowing yourself to be exploited (having a victim mentality)
- Appearing or being better than someone else, having an insatiable need to be right
- Peer approval, people-pleasing, reputation, critical acclaim, achievement
- Money, prosperity (conversely: austerity, poverty)
- Work, workaholism
- Looks, body image, beauty, getting or being in shape, being thin
- Avoidance (of enemies, criticism, uncomfortable situations)
- Control (your children, your world, your life, your job, your relationships)
- Stability, safety, security, lack of change, lack of suffering
- Peace, lack of conflict

- Harmony in relationships at any cost
- Children (having your identity fully wrapped up in them)
- Favorable political climate (your party in power, the laws you like passed)
- Success (in work, ministry, parenting, relationships, sports, etc.)
- Knowledge, education, competence, skill
- Discontentment and a constant comparison to others, what they have
- Addictions (porn, shopping, alcohol, food, drugs, video games, approval)
- Art, creative expression, music
- Entertainment, recreation, vacation
- Sloth, lethargy

What Now?

It's not enough to identify our idols. It's not simply repenting. It's repenting connected to rejoicing, as Timothy Keller expounds in *Counterfeit Gods*. You must worship the One who is greater. You must place God at the center of your life. Anything short of that is idolatry.

I write this with trepidation, with fear. Because I know myself. I know how much I "need" approval from others. How I long to feel pretty to experience deep satisfaction. How I equate my output with my worth. I have worshiped idols. Given my life for them on many levels. And I've experienced the emptiness that comes from such worship.

I've been reading through Jeremiah and Isaiah as I've researched idolatry. God's wrath seems to be especially reserved for those who worship idols. That had always been an abstract concept to me until I visited Malaysia one summer and saw actual idols housed in little shadow boxes outside of people's homes. Incense and fresh fruit graced the idol boxes, even while the occupants inside the home went without food.

So that made sense. God hates idols.

Idols = Control

In working through that list of idols, I've tried to discern what's beneath our worship of them. In doing so, I revisit those idols in Malaysia, what they represented. Worshiping little gods meant having some sort of control. *If I pay homage to the god of rain, maybe, just maybe, it will finally rain.* It's their way of feeling like they possess some sort of control over the chaotic world.

That hits too close to home. The underlying need for control is alive and well in my life. Is that true for you?

Has God become convenient for us, like a Starbucks on every corner? Have we minimized Him to the god of what we want, when we want it, and how we should receive it?

We may not offer fruit or incense to stave off its hunger, but we do jump through all sorts of hoops to get what we want. And sometimes we mistake the God of the Bible with the god of control. We tell God we want a, b, and c, and when we get what we want, we tout it as an answer to our prayers. If you're like me, you're weary of hearing stories about how God made someone's circumstances perfect or easy. Just as many folks could come back and say God didn't choose to make their circumstances perfect or easy. And how is that any less of His plan than lining our lives up perfectly, just the way we want them? How much holiness do we achieve in our hearts if we are spoiled brats, getting every single thing we want at the very moment we want it? What parent who deeply loves his child would do such a thing? Would allow such a counterfeit?

The question becomes: Why do we serve God?

To get what we want?

To have control over our environment?

Has God become convenient for us, like a Starbucks on every corner? Have we minimized Him to the god of what we want, when we want it, and how we should receive it? I'm shouting these things to myself. I wonder how much I've trivialized God. I wonder how much I've served a god of control, preferring a life that fits my own expectations to a scary, faith-filled life that ruins my preconceived paradigms.

Richard J. Foster illuminates an interesting irony about control and giving it up. "In prison, Alexander Solzhenitsyn discovered that whenever he tried to maintain a measure of power over his own life by acquiring food or clothing, he was at the mercy of his captors. But when he accepted and even embraced his own vulnerability, his jailers had no power over him.

In a sense, he had become the powerful, they the powerless."[2] When we allow our need for control to reign over our need for Jesus, we give Satan a foothold in our lives. We place ourselves on the throne of our lives, desperately trying to fill our needs and wants. Eventually we become enslaved to lesser things.

I wonder how much we worship idols, putting our pennies and treasures into a holy bank in hopes that God would work everything out right, to our specifications—only to find out that kind of lifestyle shirks God's renown in our lives. I wonder if our perspective would change if we truly equated idols with demons. Would that shock us from our idolatry? How has worshiping idols, including our need for control, hindered our walk as warrior women?

I'm ending this chapter with those questions—to stir you, to welcome you to reread the lists and prayerfully consider where you may have worshiped something other than God. Ask God to search your heart, to highlight your idols. And as He illuminates them, may you lay them at His feet as an offering of worship.

Mind if I pray for you?

God, help us. Help us to see it's all about You. It's not about us. Nor is it about Satan's enticements to worship that which is lesser than You. Help us embrace You whether You send convenience or inconvenience. Help us to trust You in the storms that test and try our faith. Help us to forsake the god of what we want for the God of the universe, who is not so easily understood or captured. Amen and amen.

Chapter 10

Worshiping God

Always be joyful. Never stop praying.
Be thankful in all circumstances, for this is God's
will for you who belong to Christ Jesus.

1 THESSALONIANS 5:16-18

Worship is an everyday habit. Whether we worship ourselves, our agendas, another person, an idol, or God Almighty, we assign worth and value to people, things, or God.

But God created us to worship Him.

Unfortunately, we're far too fascinated by the latest gadget or self-help trick or pathway to success to realize we're worshiping something that doesn't fill. Sam Storms, in his fascinating book *Pleasures Evermore*, illuminates the truth that we're misguided when we place our affections in the wrong place. "God built us to be fascinated, to be intrigued, to be exhilarated, to be stunned. Our desire for these experiences will never let up. There are no breaks, no rest, no sabbatical. There is no surface, fleeting diversion, but a basic, foundational, instinctive orientation of the human soul. Fighting it is like trying to hold your breath."[1]

With this fascination comes the inevitable problem of filling. Like the woman at the well, we long to be filled up with something minute by minute so we don't have to keep carting water from a well to our homes. We'd prefer to forsake the holy habit of constant worship. Isn't it fascinating and ironic that Jesus speaks about worship in the context of their conversation about living water versus plain old well water? He says, "Believe me, dear woman, the time is coming when it will no longer matter whether you worship the Father on this mountain or in Jerusalem. You Samaritans know very little about the one you worship, while we Jews know all about him, for salvation comes through the Jews. But the time is coming—indeed it's here now—when true worshipers will worship the Father in spirit and in truth. The Father is looking for those who will worship him that way. For God is Spirit, so those who worship him must worship in spirit and in truth" (John 4:21-24).

This passage illuminates some important points about worship:

- You can worship God anywhere.
- Worshiping the One who provides salvation is what God desires.
- We must worship with our spirit. This is a supernatural act.
- We must be authentic and true in our worship. We must come before God as we are.
- God is seeking worshipers! He seeks after those who love Him and revere Him. This is reminiscent of 2 Chronicles 16:9: "The eyes of the LORD search the whole earth in order to strengthen those whose hearts are fully committed to him." He seeks people who bow before Him in order to strengthen us.

These are important lessons to remember—that we can worship Jesus truthfully anywhere, any way. But what about the *why*? Why should we worship? And what bearing does the holy habit of worshiping God have on spiritual warfare?

Because God deserves it.

The simple reason we worship is because God, in His infinite other-than-us otherness, is worth it. He is beautiful above all beauty. True above all truth. Strong above all human strength. He made everything you see right now. He created you. As the instigator of the universe, He is above all things. John, in the book of Revelation, puts it well: "You are worthy, O Lord our God, to receive glory and honor and power. For you created all things, and they exist because you created what you pleased" (Revelation 4:11). Simply put: we worship because He is everything.

Because He is ultimately victorious.

We worship God because He will gain the victory at the end of time when Satan and his demons are thrown once and for all in the lake of fire, when God establishes the new heavens and new earth. Yet even now, we serve a victorious Savior. We worship when we see His strength in our lives, enabling us to continue on. We worship Him when we watch Him deliver a friend. The psalmist writes, "Sing a new song to the LORD, for he has done wonderful deeds. His right hand has won a mighty victory; his holy arm has shown his saving power!" (Psalm 98:1).

Because He helps us.

We praise God because He comes to our aid, particularly in the dark places. He shelters us, protects us, and holds us. Nothing that happens to us hasn't first filtered through His sovereign hand. Like a wonderful father, He disciplines us for our own good. "But as for me, I will sing about your power. Each morning I will sing with joy about your unfailing love. For you have been my refuge, a place of safety when I am in distress" (Psalm 59:16).

Nothing that happens to us hasn't first
filtered through His sovereign hand.

Because He does great things.

Not only does He help us, He does mighty, amazing, soul-stirring, mountain-crumbling acts. Our worship is one way we declare His ability to a disbelieving world. In that act of worship, we are also sharing the power of Christ to transform lives. The habit of worshiping God becomes a form of holy evangelism. "Give thanks to the LORD and proclaim his greatness. Let the whole world know what he has done. Sing to him; yes, sing his praises. Tell everyone about his wonderful deeds. Exult in his holy name; rejoice, you who worship the LORD. Search for the LORD and for his strength; continually seek him. Remember the wonders he has performed, his miracles, and the rulings he has given" (Psalm 105:1-5).

Because it makes Satan angry.

In Satan's fall from heaven, we see a creature longing to be worshiped. When he tempted Jesus, he longed for Jesus to fall down and worship him. So when we actively seek to worship God, no matter what form that worship takes, we anger Satan and his demons. We remind him of his proper place and our allegiance to the only One worthy of our worship. "Say to

God, 'How awesome are your deeds! Your enemies cringe before your mighty power'" (Psalm 66:3).

Because it's our offering.

Our worship is our offering to God, what we bring Him of ourselves, our work, our creativity, our relationships. It's our privilege to shout praises to a holy God, to declare His sufficiency, to lay down our idols and reorient ourselves to His plan, His majesty. Mark Buchanan puts it beautifully: "The opposite of a slave is not a free man. It's a worshiper. The one who is most free is the one who turns the work of his hands into sacrament, into offering."[2]

A Picture of Worship as Warfare

In 2 Chronicles 20, we see worship as a strategic, albeit counterintuitive, aspect of warfare. The Israelites under the rule of King Jehoshaphat shook in fear as the armies of Moabites, Ammonites, and Meunites threatened to invade. Jehoshaphat made a choice to seek God by praying and fasting. As a result, a prophet told the king these hope-filled words: "Listen, all you people of Judah and Jerusalem! Listen, King Jehoshaphat! This is what the LORD says: Do not be afraid! Don't be discouraged by this mighty army, for the battle is not yours, but God's" (verse 15).

In response, the king bowed prostrate on the ground. His people followed. Other clans stood and shouted praises to God. The next day, the king organized the people for war, but not in the way you would expect. "After consulting the people, the king appointed singers to walk ahead of the army, singing to the LORD and praising him for his holy splendor. This is what they sang: 'Give thanks to the LORD; his faithful love endures forever!'" (verse 21).

The moment the Israelites praised, the invading armies turned on each other. When the Israelites arrived in the arena of combat, they saw corpses of former warriors. Not one enemy soldier survived. It took them three days to gather the plunder. On the fourth day, they convened in what they now named the Valley of Blessing. After that, the people returned to Jerusalem, rejoicing. "They marched into Jerusalem to the music of harps, lyres, and trumpets, and they proceeded to the Temple of the LORD" (verse 28).

God's principles are similar today. We face an overpowering, cunning enemy. He prowls like a lion, seeking to devour us, to overthrow our lives.

He is intimidating and forceful. Our strange defense doesn't rest in ramparts of our own strength, but in voices lifted in victory. Our praise shudders Satan. It infuriates him, hog-ties his will, and reminds him of his place on this planet. God uses praise, thanksgiving, and worship to overcome Satan's plans, not by our own strength, but by His.

I asked some of my readers to share stories of how warfare helped them overcome the enemy. Their stories illustrate the power and importance of worship.

Julie writes, "I was 17 and in the last month of my senior year of high school. As the youngest of our family, my graduation present was going to be my parents' divorce. My mother and I were living with my grandmother in her big, rambling house in Portland, Oregon. The family's emotions were raw and dark and I felt them engulfing me. I had recently learned to play the guitar, so I took [my guitar], a pencil, and an old hymnal down into my grandma's echoing basement, where I scribbled penciled guitar chords into the hymnal. As I sang hymn after hymn after hymn, I could feel the Holy Spirit calming me and blanketing me in peace. That's how I got through that period, me and Jesus in the basement, finding guitar chords and singing hymns."

Danica writes, "When I was visiting a missionary to a small community in South Dakota, the first thing another friend and I noticed was how dark and oppressive it felt in that corner of the United States. Our first night we felt such an oppressive presence that it woke us up. I stayed in bed, but I kept singing a worship song over and over (quietly, so I wouldn't wake anyone) and after a while, that feeling left. In the morning I woke, and my friend had a CD playing the exact same song. She told me that she'd woken up in the night with a similar feeling, and the only thing that calmed her spirit was that CD. She, too, had put it on really low so it wouldn't wake anyone, so neither of us had heard the other or knew what was going on, but for both of us, that feeling of oppressiveness was overcome by worship."

Ellen tells the story of a distraught friend and how worship over the phone had a deep impact: "A good friend of mine went through postpartum psychosis after the birth of her first child. She was 3,000 miles away so I couldn't see her, but would call almost daily. Her mother and husband said she would hold the phone to her ear and listen, but there were many phone calls when she wouldn't respond to anything I said. I was afraid for her, for her baby. During long phone calls when she hadn't spoken at all, I'd wonder if I'd lost her or if I was still reaching her on any level. When I ran out of prayers and things to talk about, I'd sing praise songs. She wasn't a believer, but one day when I sang 'You Are My Hiding Place' she sang part of it with me. After that, whenever I felt I wasn't reaching her, I'd sing that song, and she would sing with me and I knew she was still there. Eventually she got better. She came out of the postpartum experience believing in God and our friendship has been a continued blessing. Her daughter has thrived and has a sweet and amazing faith."

Warrior women are women who worship, who take their eyes off the circumstances swirling around them and look into the eyes of Jesus. When we practice the holy habit of worship, we hasten God's smile, reinforce Satan's demise, and find joy in the moment.

Mind if I pray for you?

Jesus, You are worthy of our worship. Lift our gaze from today's worries and help us see You. Forgive us for worrying about everything else, for forgetting that life is all about Your renown and fame. Lord, I give You my sister reading this prayer in this moment. Teach her new ways to worship You as she shops, pays bills, and loves her family. Help her make worship a holy habit she delights in. Enable her to see the power of praise over the shrill voice of the evil one. Settle her calmly in Your embrace today. Amen.

Chapter 11

Living the Bible

*What if the condition of one's heart is more important for
understanding the Bible than the ability of one's mind?*[1]

JACK DEERE

In Ephesians 6:13-17, we find one of the most famous passages on spiritual warfare. Notice how it ends in verse 17: "Put on salvation as your helmet, and take the sword of the Spirit, which is the word of God."

A sword is an offensive weapon, intended to fend off, maim, or kill. Such is our greatest weapon in spiritual warfare. When Satan tempted Jesus in the wilderness, Jesus retorted with Scripture. What's fascinating about their interchange is that Satan, too, used God's Word in his attack. This shows how vitally important it is for the believer to not merely know God's Word, but understand it in the context of a reverential relationship with Him. Satan used an exact quotation—right from the belly of the Bible—about God commanding His angels, but he twisted the context to undermine God's authority, supremacy, and power. He said the right words, but his intent remained diabolical in nature.

The Pharisees, who played a crucial role in crucifying Jesus, also knew the Scriptures well, but this knowledge did them no good in terms of living for the kingdom of God. Jesus told them these sobering words: "And the Father who sent me has testified about me himself. You have never heard his voice or seen him face to face, and you do not have his message in your hearts, because you do not believe me—the one he sent to you. You search the Scriptures because you think they give you eternal life. But the Scriptures point to me! Yet you refuse to come to me to receive this life" (John 5:37-40). Jesus illustrates the importance of relationship here.

The Pharisees search the Scriptures, yes, but they can't see that the Word Incarnate is standing right in front of them. Their effective Scripture wrangling did nothing to change their hearts because they trusted more in tradition than they did in God.

Jesus continues, "Your approval means nothing to me, because I know you don't have God's love within you. For I have come to you in my Father's name, and you have rejected me. Yet if others come in their own name, you gladly welcome them. No wonder you can't believe! For you gladly honor each other, but you don't care about the honor that comes from the one who alone is God" (verses 41-44). Here we see the Pharisees' lack of reverence for God and their inability to understand and practice God's love. Without that understanding, accompanied by deep humility, they cannot know Jesus. They honor only themselves and their fellow Pharisees and their superior knowledge.

Jesus further says, "Yet it isn't I who will accuse you before the Father. Moses will accuse you! Yes, Moses, in whom you put your hopes. If you really believed Moses, you would believe me, because he wrote about me. But since you don't believe what he wrote, how will you believe what I say?" (verses 45-47). Here, Jesus equates belief with the Scriptures. It's not enough to know the words of Moses, but to live in such a way that proves your belief. More than knowing, we must obey. We grow through obedience to the hard truths of Scripture. James 1:22-25 is clear on this point. "But don't just listen to God's word. You must do what it says. Otherwise, you are only fooling yourselves. For if you listen to the word and don't obey, it is like glancing at your face in a mirror. You see yourself, walk away, and forget what you look like. But if you look carefully into the perfect law that sets you free, and if you do what it says and don't forget what you heard, then God will bless you for doing it."

The Word of God is a weapon, yes. But it must be wielded from a yielded heart, a heart bent on obeying it first, keeping it in high view.

The Unsafe Bible

Yet we struggle with the Bible. Obeying it is hard. Sometimes understanding it eludes us. And some of us, in our desire for antiseptic lives, read only the happy parts of Scripture, forsaking a realistic view of this sometimes raw book. Recently, I read an Amazon review of the ESV Study Bible. The reviewer had given it only one star. Since I'm a masochist and read my own one-star reviews, I clicked over to see how in the world someone could give the Bible such a low rating. The reviewer wrote: "Some paces [*sic*] were violent and even sexual in nature, I was led to believe this version was going to make the bible more kid friendly, I was wrong."[2]

Since when has any version of the Bible, right down to the original Hebrew, Greek, and Aramaic, ever been safe? Noah's flood isn't exactly a heartening tale, yet we (oddly) decorate our church nurseries with the big boat and happy animals (never showing the waves and drowning people gasping for breath). The Bible is a dynamic, scary, amazing, freaky story about a holy God and a sinful society, and with that sin comes all sorts of vice: sex outside of marriage in various forms, murders, thefts, swindlers, betrayal, scheming, violence, and the very present activity of Satan and evil in the world. Why? Because it represents reality.

No, the Bible isn't safe. But it's real.

The Bible will never be safe. But it is precisely its authenticity that helps us see how powerful God's redemptive plan was and is, how stunning God's victory over sin and Satan became. Imagine being God, then slipping into the clothes of humanity, experiencing tragedy, gossip, plotting, hatred, and misunderstanding, yet still loving the very people who mud-slung pain your way. Imagine going one step further by choosing to die for all that filthy sin by taking it on your perfect, unmarred self, dying an excruciating death. Imagine then rising to life again, conquering the biggest fear of man: death. That birth-death-resurrection story is the centrality of the Word of God, which is why Satan cowers when we read it, study it, memorize it, declare it, and live it.

No, the Bible isn't safe. But it's real. Yet sometimes it feels stale. Sometimes it feels mundane and pedestrian. How do we cultivate a love for God's Word, particularly if we've walked with God a long time and begin to feel staleness as we study? What if we lose our awe of the Book?

Time with the Bible

True confession: I shudder at the words *Quiet Time.* Those two words have unwittingly heaped loads of guilt upon my desire to connect with God. Because of those words, I've believed that to know God deeply I had to adhere to a series of spiritual lists. Read the Bible like an instruction manual. Dissect the Bible. Pray, but not too much about myself. Maybe sing. Write in a journal. Spend at least an hour, and of course it must be at 6:00 a.m. or it's not sanctified. And if I don't do it, I have to deal with the accompanying shame and guilt.

But everything changed when I considered that we served a creative God who designed us to be creative. The God we serve fashioned the beauty of this earth with a word. Songwriter and recording artist Michael Card illuminates the amazing truth that we are God's creation, designed to be creative: "The Bible tells us that we are God's masterpieces (*poiema* in Greek); not only creatures, but His creations, His poems. We are living epistles. And so, our lives are meant to be listened to, because it is God who is speaking into and out of and through the symphony of the years, and the masterpiece of a lifetime."[3]

If He is the Master, and we the masterpiece, why do we settle for rote methods to reach for Him? Why do we believe monotony is the way to His heart? Author Ken Gire wrote, "We reach for God in many ways, through our sculptures and Scriptures. Through our pictures and our prayers. Through our writing and our worship. And through them, he reaches for us."[4]

Here are some creative ways to sharpen your sword—to fall in love with the living, breathing, dynamic Word of God, and to better battle the enemy.

Memorize

At our last Sunday school class, a friend stood up front. He said, "I could never remember a Scripture, let alone its address. Then I spent time with a friend who memorized the book of James. That challenged me to memorize the first chapter of John, then the second." As our class prepared for Advent, thinking about the coming of Jesus as a baby, he recited from memory the first chapter of John. I teared up through his retelling. There's something dynamic and powerful about committing Scripture to heart. And we rattle hell when we do so.

In college I wrote down every Scripture that had special meaning to me, particularly in my healing journey. I bound the 3x5 cards with a D-ring clip and memorized them as I stood in line for meals or during lulls in the day. Those Scriptures still come back to "haunt" me today. Recently when I had to write a Bible study curriculum (an entire book) in three weeks, those Scriptures came back to me. You will never regret committing God's

Word to memory, particularly when you encounter temptation. Those Scriptures, sharper than any double-edged sword, will help you resist. They will remind you of the truth of who you are in Christ. They will reorient you. And they might just save your life.

The Manuscript Method

Similar to the inductive Bible study method, the manuscript method breaks things up in your study of God's Word. First, go to an online Bible site like BibleGateway.com and copy a chapter or an entire book of the Bible. Paste the text into a document oriented as a landscape (11 inches long, 8½ inches high). Instead of one large column, divide the document into two columns per page. (This will look like an actual Bible page). Add pages as needed, then print the entire document.

Since the passage is on regular paper and not bound within a Bible, you'll feel more freedom to make marks and observations directly onto the text. Go crazy! Find similar words. Circle verbs. Draw pictures. Make comments. Journal alongside the passage. Simply removing a portion of Scripture from the Bible will give you more freedom in study.[5]

Scripture Journals

My friend Erin started a revolution in my heart when she sent me one of her amazing art journals (a book full of small-scale art projects) as a gift. She'd been going through a move, so she decided to create artistic responses on the pages of a journal as a reaction to all the changes she'd encountered. She cried out to God. She pasted house listings inside and wrote Scripture over them. She painted some of the pages and highlighted key verses God breathed to her during the tumult.

For the first time in a long time, I longed to connect to God, but this time through art. So I bought myself a cheap journal. When a verse touched me, I wrote it down, adding magazine pictures to illustrate it. I created several pages where I wrote simple words of prayer, words I could go back to and recognize God's answer. When I worried about how many hats I wore, I placed different hat stickers all over one page and defined my many roles. Seeing them all there helped me to realize I needed to trim down my world.

Connecting to God through art journals has revolutionized my time with Jesus. I look forward to it. I revel in discovering new Scriptures to illustrate in simple, stick-figured ways. When I've taught this to others, I've emphasized that one doesn't have to be an artist to create a highly personal, deeply spiritual art journal.

A Word for the Year

Over the past few years during the month of January, I've asked God to give me a word for the year. This word or verse shapes the way I walk through the year. It's a small way to build deep anticipation into my heart as I wait on Him and then implement the word. Last year the words were, "Joy in rest. Truth in love." As things got difficult, I remembered to choose to rest and let God restore the joy in my heart. When painful relational difficulties threatened, I remembered the importance of being both truthful and loving.

This year the words He spoke to me were, "Be comfortable in your own skin" and "Abundance." I'm learning the joy of being happy with how God made me. And I'm learning to go to Jesus for abundance, where He fills me up with rivers of living water. Those words to me help me shape my year. They help focus me as I search the Scriptures. I love how Scriptures I hadn't noticed before jump off the page as they relate to the word I'm given.

It's possible to experience newness and surprises in your time in the Word. We can respond to His words for us with creativity as we embrace the fact that He is our creator. We can wait in expectation for His ways to surprise us. And we'll be forever changed in the process.

That's my prayer and desire for you. Not only that you'd give yourself permission to interact creatively with God's Word, but that you'd simply and powerfully obey it. As you do so, the Word of God will jump from the page because the more you obey, the more you understand.

As warrior women, the holy habit of living and studying the Bible will equip us to overcome Satan's attacks. Committing God's Word to our minds and hearts will empower us to be confident against his schemes. May it be that we become women of the Word who fall in love with the thoughts of God.

———

Mind if I pray for you?

Lord Jesus, You are the Word incarnate. Every thought of God is found in You. Help us to see the words between the pages of the Bible as life—not a stale manual or a book of condemnation. I pray for my friend reading this chapter, that she would be freed today to study your Word creatively, in a her-shaped way. Give her permission to doodle, sing, obey, create as she reads Your words. And Lord, please help her understand afresh that her heart and mind will grasp the Bible better when she lives it. Amen.

Chapter 12

Embracing Rest

*That's the irony: those who sanctify time and who
give time away—who treat time as a gift and not
a possession—have time in abundance.*[1]

MARK BUCHANAN

When we were missionaries in France, I occasionally had to fly back to the States for publishing business. Extreme trials and overt spiritual warfare marked our time there, so much so that we were diagnosed with Post-Traumatic Stress Disorder after our first year on the field. I understood the diagnosis because when I flew back to the States, I'd ask people to pray. Once someone started, I would break down and weep. All I could say was, "I feel like I've been in a constant war."

Combat weary, I leaned on others, sought the Lord, and tried to discern how to get through our fiery trials. I realized some important things—things you might not expect. I learned that the holy habit of rest is part of God's strategy for women warriors. Consider Moses and his inability to keep his hands skyward when the battle waged below him. "So Joshua did what Moses had commanded and fought the army of Amalek. Meanwhile, Moses, Aaron, and Hur climbed to the top of a nearby hill. As long as Moses held up the staff in his hand, the Israelites had the advantage. But whenever he dropped his hand, the Amalekites gained the advantage. Moses's arms soon became so tired he could no longer hold them up. So Aaron and Hur found a stone for him to sit on. Then they stood on each side of Moses, holding up his hands. So his hands held steady until sunset. As a result, Joshua overwhelmed the army of Amalek in battle" (Exodus 17:10-13).

Even Moses needed rest in the midst of the conflict. Who are we to think we don't?

God understands rest. He instigated it on the seventh day, making it a holy time of recreation, reflection, and trust. He gave the Israelites rest after war. In the aftermath of a large battle, the Scripture says, "the land had rest for forty years" (Judges 5:31 ESV.) He blesses us with restorative sleep, yet we often press our lives to exhaustion. "It is useless for you to work so hard from early morning until late at night, anxiously working for food to eat; for God gives rest to his loved ones" (Psalm 127:2). Even Jesus didn't violate His need for rest. Often He went off by Himself to pray, to restore. Before He faced Satan in the wilderness, He fasted and prayed 40 days, spending time in solitude as He awaited the confrontation.

Yet we as women warriors have falsely believed that we must go-go-go. Whether we do this because we won't feel adequate if we don't, or we fear God won't like us unless we're productive, or we base our self-worth on what we produce, the truth is we live as if the world depends on us, as if we are God. Rest and Sabbath, therefore, are a counterintuitive warfare strategy. Learning to pull back when we're exhausted and overwhelmed is actually beneficial. We may say that, but we don't live as if we do.

Dr. Richard Swenson wrote a groundbreaking book about time and rest entitled *Margin*. He asserts that believers, to be effective in this world, must build in periods of rest into their lives. This space is margin, though the metaphor of margin can also extend to relationships, health, and money. He writes, "Margin is the amount allowed beyond that which is needed. It is something held in reserve for contingencies or unanticipated situations. Margin is the gap between rest and exhaustion, the space between breathing freely and suffocating. It is the leeway we once had between ourselves and our limits. Margin is the opposite of overload."[2]

I wrestled with this when we lived in France where the warfare swirled thick and my nerves wore thin. I knew God called me to find pockets of rest, but it seemed counterintuitive to add one more thing to my life. As full-time writer, church planter, and the mother of three children, I lived life to the edge of my margins. Exhausted and weary, I turned to a life coach for help. She asked me pointed questions, like, "How do you *want* to feel at the end of a day? A week? A month?" I answered using words like rested, peaceful, unharried. I told her I was tired of real life passing me by while I dutifully and doggedly tackled an endless to-do list. Eventually, I decided I needed rest. But how did rest fit into my daily life or my weekly rhythm? How could I learn to value rest as a spiritual warfare strategy? And what did Sabbath have to do with it all?

The Change

It wasn't until I read a fascinating book entitled *The Power of Full Engagement* by Jim Loehr and Tony Schwartz that I began to understand my deep need for rest. In the book, the authors write about the productivity of people who powered through their lives without rest versus those who took strategic breaks during the day and week. To my surprise, the people who rested were happier, produced more, and felt better about their lives. Coupling this with the Bible's admonition to take a day out of the week for rest and worship, I felt God's conviction to move toward Sabbath-izing my life.

As a result of all this internal wrestling, we began to observe a weekly day of rest as a family. And since we are learning to be freedom-loving folks, we tried to observe the day without a lot of rules. We chose to set aside one day a week to do life-giving things—activities that enhanced our love for each other and for Jesus.

Our family's Sabbath

What does the holy habit of rest look like for our family? I create brunch the night before and assemble an easy dinner that can be placed in a slow-cooker the next morning. I make sure we have a ready supply of paper plates and cups so we don't have many dishes to wash. We pick up the house the night before so we can feel restful the next day (and I won't be tempted to clean). On our day of rest we create cards for friends and family, read good books, write letters, make movies, put photos in albums, play games, hike in the hills around our house, take drives, look through old photo albums and reminisce, ride bikes, read Bible stories and respond to them through art projects, and garden—among many other things. Anything life-recharging we considered a Sabbath activity.

The result? Changed lives. A less-hurried family. A more connected family. At first, I longed to work—to get to "just a few" e-mails, but eventually I settled into the new rhythm as an offering to Jesus. Through this grand experiment, I realized that God is God and I am not. That He didn't need my frenetic activity to carry out His amazing plans. This holy habit of rest was a form of surrender and worship I'd seldom experienced before. And as I faced a new week, I was less overwhelmed when spiritual attack came. My head and spirit cleared. I found margin.

What else I discovered

I also learned that the quality of my life on this earth is directly linked to my ability to rest. In my forties, I saw how I could no longer keep the pace I'd kept for years. Eventually the stress and worry of living within my type-A lifestyle would take its toll on my health, my soul, my heart. I saw firsthand how beautiful God's command to rest was and is. That it's for our preservation and His glory.

Gandhi said, "There is more to life than increasing its speed." As I've learned to rest not only once a week, but in between my spurts of work, I've experienced more of life's beauty than when I ran-ran-ran through life. Life is relationships. Life is worship. Life is slowing down long enough to hear the still, small voice of God. Life is being in awe of God's creation. And rest is God's avenue for us to experience what is truly life. In that sacred space of rest, I am less apt to listen to the lies of the Evil One, more apt to respond to the still, small voice of my Creator.

What about you?

Maybe you're tired of the battle. Maybe you're reading this with a deep sense of longing for true life, for connection with your family, for sleep that restores, for a quiet mind that hears God's voice, a new ability to discern the battle. Have you considered that God may be calling you to rest? To slow down? To love Him enough to entrust your schedule, to-do list, and lack of time to Him? Perhaps it's time to rest, to set aside weekly time to recharge, to take strategic breaks throughout the day to sing a song, take a walk, bless a friend.

The rest of your life is ahead of you. And your ability to rest, to slow down long enough to worship God, will enhance the quality of the rest of your life. Like Mary who sat at the feet of Jesus, we won't miss the good parts of life. We'll become an interruptible people. Mark Buchanan writes, "The devil distracts. God interrupts. And for some reason, we fall prey to the one and grow oblivious to the other."[3] Rest is our way of letting go of the devil's distractions and re-attuning ourselves to the God who gives us the power to win the beautiful battle.

—

Mind if I pray for you?

God of the Sabbath, I pray for rest for my sister reading this prayer today. She is weary, overburdened, and dog-tired. Lift her head. Help her see where she's replaced You with hurry. Give her perspective on life. Help her see that life doesn't consist in what she does but what You do through her. Make her an interruptible woman today, Lord. Enable her to see her life from a distance so she can evaluate it, dissect it, and see how she can institute rest in her life. Warfare rages all around her, Lord, and her arms are tired of lifting to the sky. Hold her arms heavenward, Lord. Bring other women who will help lift her. And woo her today with the promise of Your Sabbath rest.

Chapter 13

Chasing Healing

As a pastor, I've spoken to hundreds of people held hostage by
these kinds of memories. Old wounds they keep reopening. Old
glories they keep reliving. Old grudges they keep nursing. Old
taunts they keep rehearsing. Old fears they keep reviving.
Their minds curve back to and curl around these with
virtually no provocation. These memories are a prison they've
lived in so long they don't know how to live outside it.[1]

MARK BUCHANAN

As I mentioned in the first chapter about the gaping hole, Satan exploits us where we're wounded. A significant part of spiritual warfare, then, has to do with the holy habit of chasing after our own healing. As a survivor of neglect, sexual abuse, my parents' substance abuse issues, my mother's three divorces, and the death of my father, I had plenty to heal from. Any one of those issues could've resulted in terrible choices. Any one of those wounds could have led to me giving Satan a foothold in my life. My insecurity alone was enough to allow him unfettered access to my heart, so willing was I to fill up my insecurity with anything and anyone.

I received Jocelyn's comment in one of my blog posts, dealing with this issue of healing. She wrote, "It's just beyond me how God has restored you and the life you live for Him. This is one of my greatest areas of weakness. I've always battled so much with God over children and women getting hurt. I've hated men for a good part of my life, though God has been so gracious to not let me encounter such pain myself. Mary, how did you move on? How did you keep going before you knew Him and how did you get healed to the point of being able to spit at the devil?"

My response to Jocelyn: Jesus. He utterly rescued and healed me. At five years old I was a made a victim of sexual abuse by older neighborhood boys. I carried that secret with me for many years. It wasn't until I met Jesus that I became brave enough to let the secret out. And that's when the healing began. It continues today. I can feel used very easily, and I have a deep insecurity about myself. Those feelings have gotten better with age, but it has been a very slow process. Sometimes it's hard for me to know—really *know*—that Jesus loves me.

The years of healing took a lot of vulnerability on my part—probably too much at times. I basically wept my way through college as many of my childhood issues came to the forefront. I had a great group of friends who laid hands on me in prayer and believed God was big enough to heal the wounded parts. He did a lot of healing during that time of my life.

I won't sugarcoat the healing process, though. It's one of the most excruciating things a warrior woman can walk through. It's like stepping into a dark tunnel. And when you step inside, two things happen:

1. The movie of your life plays out before you in the darkness.

2. Jesus holds your hand as you watch the movie together.

Yet healing isn't a one-time event. Even today, a memory returned and I had to reprocess some grief, give it back to Jesus, and ask Him to help me digest it. The cliché is true: healing is like peeling an onion. The more layers you dig into, the more tears will come. Still, I am living proof of two things:

1. That God can utterly transform a life.

2. That you have to *want* to be transformed.

Jesus asked the paralytic, "Do you want to get well?" Notice that the man, lame and crippled, didn't answer the question. And yet, even in his frail state, not knowing how to answer such a question, Jesus reached out His hand to the man and restored him. This man had been waiting for healing at the pool for years, not knowing he would meet the Living Water.

My question to you: How have you placed yourself near Jesus? How have you sought healing? I'm convinced that often the difference between those who are emotionally healed from the past and those who are enslaved by the past is this: tenacious pursuit of healing.

Your past will either haunt you or it will break you enough to reach for rescue. Which will you choose? Haunting? Repeating the same sins that were done unto you? Listening to Satan's lies about your worthlessness? Or will you be one who says, "Enough!" Will you chase instead after Jesus, the Author and source of all healing?

Eugene Peterson translates 2 Corinthians 7:10 this way: "Distress that drives us to God does that. It turns us around. It gets us back in the way of salvation. We never regret that kind of pain. But those who let distress drive them away from God are full of regrets, end up on a deathbed of regrets."

The truth? We all have distress from yesterday. The question becomes, then: Will you let it drive you *to* God or *from* God, making yourself vulnerable to Satan's lies and schemes? God is able to transform your heart. He is. I'm living proof. He can salve the bitterness, slake the fear, giving you a heart of compassion and forgiveness. But you have to choose—actively choose. Running from God will only lead to a lifetime of bad choices, deep regret, and an open door for Satan's activity.

I experienced significant, deep healing after reading Walter Wangerin's *The Book of the Dun Cow*. I realized, through an interesting interchange in the book, that I'd been masking God with my own pain, projecting my own warped perspective on Him. Many of us view God as if He wears a disguise—a costume that looks like all our pain and fear and worry woven together. When we see Him, we see our experience. Those who have happy lives tend to view God joyfully, as a Father who takes great care of His children. Those who live difficult lives tend to view God skeptically, intellectually knowing He is good, but not truly embracing His goodness.

Pertelote, a young hen in Wangerin's book, had the latter experience. Bent under the tyranny of Cockatrice (who acts quite a bit like Satan), a rooster who ruled with an iron beak, Pertelote recoiled in his presence. Half gray-scaled snake, half rooster, Cockatrice was the poultry world's Hitler. One day, Pertelote escaped Cockatrice's domain, but her pain and fear still resided within her. She made her way downriver, tattered and worn out. There, across from her, stood another rooster, Chauntecleer.

Chauntecleer, a kind rooster, had been wading through mud, graying his lower feathers. He did not know it, but the dried mud made him resemble the evil-scaled Cockatrice.

When Pertelote spied him, she screamed. She thought he was Cockatrice, coming back to torture her.

Later, when Pertelote felt safe within Chauntecleer's kingdom, she agreed to marry him. But before they were married, Chauntecleer was troubled afresh by her first reaction to him at the river.

"My beautiful Pertelote," he said. "Are you afraid of me?"

She said no.

He puzzled over her response. "But there was a time…when you were afraid of me, isn't that so?"

Again she said no.

He asked again.

Again she said no.

By now, he felt really confused. "But you screamed at me!"

"Yes, I screamed at you," she said.

Eventually, Pertelote shared that she thought he had been the evil Cockatrice. "Chauntecleer, what I thought I saw in you was not there. What I saw I should not have seen. My seeing was not true: The thing was not there, nor could it ever be there in you. I know that. My imagination made me afraid."[2]

We are a lot like Pertelote.

When we see God, His goodness is masked by the pain of our past. We assign His muddiness to scales. We scream in fear because we cannot conceive of God as being *for* us. Many of us fail to risk because we cling to an inaccurate view of God. He's wearing the distressing disguise of our pain. We project on Him our humanness. We misunderstand Him. And sometimes we mistake Him for Satan.

We forget that God is utterly different, that His ways are unfathomable. "'For My thoughts are not your thoughts, nor are your ways My ways,' declares the LORD. 'For as the heavens are higher than the earth, so are My ways higher than your ways and My thoughts than your thoughts'" (Isaiah 55:8-9 NASB).

Understanding the perplexity of God's ways gives us a higher view of God's sovereignty in our lives. Like Joseph, we can look back on our lives, see the people who harmed us, and be able to declare, "You intended to harm me, but God intended it for good to accomplish what is now being done, the saving of many lives" (Genesis 50:20 NIV). We can learn to see the past, even if it's checkered with pain, regret, and neglect, as a gift—a strategic part of God's redemptive plan for the world. Healing allows warrior women, through God's grace, to walk alongside others who face pain, bewilderment, and fear. Our healing becomes the venue God uses to crush Satan's activity in others' lives.

Healing isn't easy.

Healing involves dogged, tiring pursuit. L.B. Cowman expands on this idea: "The reason so many fail in this experience of divine healing is because they expect to have it all without a struggle, and when the conflict comes and the battle wages long, they become discouraged and surrender. God has nothing worth having that is easy. There are no cheap goods in the heavenly market. Our redemption cost all that God had to give, and everything worth having is expensive. Hard places are the very school of faith and character, and if we are to rise over mere human strength and prove the power of life divine in these mortal bodies, it must be through a process of conflict that may well be called the birth travail of a new life."[3]

The difference between someone who's dared to walk through healing and one who shrinks back afraid is this: one had grit; the other gave up. You have to want to be well. You have to want to push through. You have to be so sick of your own bad behavior that resulted from your past pain that you run to Jesus seeking help. It's not enough to casually want to get well. You have to yearn. You have to hate Satan's whisperings, his deceit, his enticements toward addictions and poor relational choices.

It's not enough to casually want to get well. You have to yearn.

It's not only for your sake.

Not only must you be tired of living life in response to the past, you have to make a choice to open your eyes as to how your behavior affects your loved ones. You have to love God enough to be healed, hate Satan's ploys enough to turn away, and love those close to you enough to seek healing. If you find it selfish to concentrate on your healing, do it because God is wooing you to, do it to thwart the enemy's plans to steal, kill, and destroy you, and do it for the sake of your loved ones.

The best gift you can give others is your healing. Your walled-off heart is no good to your children, your spouse, your friends. Your bitterness hurts every current relationship you have, and it gives Satan a foothold in your life. "Look after each other so that none of you fails to receive the grace of

God. Watch out that no poisonous root of bitterness grows up to trouble you, corrupting many" (Hebrews 12:15).

Remember forgiveness.

Consider too, the importance of forgiveness in the healing journey. Part of Satan's scheme is to wrack you so deeply in unforgiveness that you remove your heart from people. In the field of unforgiveness, hatred grows. And where hatred grows, Satan's direct influence in your life flourishes. "Anyone you forgive, I also forgive. And what I have forgiven—if there was anything to forgive—I have forgiven in the sight of Christ for your sake, in order that Satan might not outwit us. For we are not unaware of his schemes" (2 Corinthians 2:10-11 NIV).

Chasing healing involves the daring act of forgiveness. But that doesn't mean you're excusing bad behavior, or letting anyone off the hook. On the contrary, forgiveness is a revolutionary act because it involves remembering the pain and sin and forgiving it anyway. It's a holy letting-go, allowing God's justice to pervade the situation. And it releases you from bitterness and feeling like you have to punish. Lewis Smedes writes, "When we forgive evil we do not excuse it, we do not tolerate it, we do not smother it. We look the evil full in the face, call it what it is, let its horror shock and stun and enrage us, and only then do we forgive it."[4]

One pivotal Scripture came to me on the heels of listening to a speaker from Rwanda. He talked about the genocide and the country's need to integrate the perpetrators back into society. He spoke of Jesus being both the sin bearer and the pain bearer. Not only does Jesus bear the weight of the sins of the ones who perpetrate (including us), He also bears the weight of the pain the sin caused. That coexistent truth comes to glorious light in 1 Peter 2:24. "He himself bore our sins in his body on the cross, so that we might die to sins and live for righteousness; by his wounds you have been healed" (NIV). Jesus, the broken One, is broken for our sin, and He comes alongside us in healing and fellowship when we are broken.

How can we chase healing?

How do we let go of the past so Satan can't get a foothold in our lives? Twelve ways.

1. Acknowledge what happened. Hidden secrets never heal. You

can't heal in unreality. Our pastor likened our wounds to a beach ball in the ocean. When we try to push it down, it will eventually pop back up. You may be adept at pushing your pain down, but it's exhausting work and it will eventually resurface, usually in your behavior.

2. Share your story with a trusted friend. Be sure the friend has a heart to pray for you and will listen instead of just dictating answers.

3. Grieve. It's okay to say that what happened back there hurt terribly. If you don't grieve now, you'll have to revisit the grief again.

4. Ask others to pray for you if you get stuck. This is how I healed. For four years, people prayed for me consistently.

5. Consider counseling. It's not a dirty word. Sometimes we need a trained professional to help us sort out the past and figure out why we're making destructive choices today.

6. Journal your journey. Giving words to your pain helps lay it all bare and it frees your mind to let it go.

7. Seek a mentor in someone who's experienced the same kind of pain you've been through.

8. Let go of your status as a victim. Staying in that place will forever tether you to the past. You are no longer a victim. You are wildly loved by God. You are an overcomer.

9. Find Scripture that relates to your struggle. Write it down. Put it on your mirror, in your car, any place you frequent. Memorize it.

10. On really bad days, crank up the worship music and sing praises to the One who took on all sorts of abuse.

11. Move beyond your pain for the sake of helping someone else.

12. Realize that the hallmark of growth in the Christian life is self-awareness. The more you are aware of who you are, what motivates you, how you respond to wounding, what scares you, who pushes your buttons, why you're afraid, and where you're tempted, the more you're able to discern the healing path. If you

have a hard time knowing yourself, dare to ask a trusted friend for feedback. Be willing to be open. Share your struggles. Hear feedback without retaliation.

God's desire is that warrior women be whole. He goads us toward the holy habit of healing, not to mess with us or remind us of the pain, but to set us free—to love our families well, to be better used by God, to experience joy in the here and now.

—

Mind if I pray for you?

Jesus, we need to heal. We need Your help. We can't heal on our own. The pain is too much sometimes. But we want to heal for the sake of our own health and the people in our lives. Take us down the path of healing—gently, though. Do something new in my sister today. Create joy where pain lived. Inaugurate hope where despair camped. Rejuvenate resilience where lethargy reigned. Heal, Jesus. Please heal. Amen.

Part Three

REACTIVE:
What We Do in the Midst
of the Beautiful Battle

While it's imperative we become proactive warrior women, sometimes life's circumstances, our flesh, and the devil come at inopportune times. In those moments, we react. How can we face those interruptions with grace and confidence? In this section I've identified seven common warfare areas warrior women face in their daily lives, and I offer biblical support to help you overcome in the moment.

1. When fear rushes in

2. When Christians hurt you

3. When your mind attacks

4. When your family faces a battle

5. When sin and addictions threaten

6. When the mouth becomes a weapon

7. When overt attack assails you

Chapter 14

When Fear Rushes In

We are women warriors, not women worriers.

Mary DeMuth

I'm a fearful girl. Sometimes I crane my neck so far into fear's woods that the devil grows more fear in the fertile soil of my imagination. When I allow him that kind of frenzied, worried access, my fears deepen, like trees rooted to the dirt while trying to touch the sky. If I keep my heart in fear's forest, I'll never fly.

Here's a peek into my heart—a listing of my fears. Perhaps mine are yours. Perhaps yours are mine. Or maybe we all have a laundry list of unique fears.

I'm afraid to be alone.

Not alone in merely the empty-house-dark-night type of alone, but in the loneliness sense. I fear my husband will die. I fear my kids will die. I actually think about this a lot, which distresses me. Like I'm preparing for the worst. I suppose a lot of that comes from having a parent die when I was only ten. Death shakes the world of one so young. But maybe it's because when those neighborhood boys took me at five years old, they took me alone—and raped me as I lay helpless. And alone, I had to figure a way to save myself. Such a huge responsibility, that, for a kindergartener. So I don't like thinking about life without relationships, without the safety of those who love me gathered around.

I'm afraid of sickness.

Maybe I'm this way because the perpetrators who stole me away did so without my consent, without my knowing that what would happen would be so soul-killing. To me, sickness looms that way. It surprises. It steals. It shocks. It's often outside your sphere of control.

I'm afraid of rejection.

This may be more related to other issues in growing up, as those boys didn't reject me. They embraced me—in the worst possible way. But they cemented a belief in my mind that I was completely unworthy of normal affection, of tender care, of kindness. So I nurse those same feelings when others reject me. I fall into the pit where I believe those strange lies as truth. Rejection has come to indicate my worthlessness.

I'm afraid of creepy men.

I guess this goes without saying, right? But the creep-o-meter ding-ding-dings in me when I meet one. And I run away as best I can. I block some on Facebook. I am cautious about being alone when I travel. I worry about being raped again, and whether I'll be able to handle it, survive it.

Even so, God has truly, truly walked me farther along the fearless journey. These fears all used to scream at me; now they whisper. I also think if I let my mind linger too long on a particular fear, I'll give the enemy of my soul a welcome mat to my heart. He wreaks havoc in there, through the threshold of my fears. So I pray. And pray. And ask others to pray. And I rest in eternity, knowing someday all my issues will be wiped away, all my fears relieved. I may be walking fearful at times on this earth, but these are numbered days. Eternity will be fearless for me. In that, I rejoice.

I think of missionaries in India, women, who ventured into villages to tell people about Jesus. They prayed for people who were sick. God healed many. They prayed for people to meet Jesus. People met Jesus. They risked their lives. They did not fear. And God changed the spiritual landscape of the villages they visited. Vina, one of the missionaries, said these words that rocked my own spiritual landscape: "I am feeling very proud of my Jesus."

How often do we exclaim that? How often do we live in such a way that *only* Jesus could do the miracles before us? Have we micromanaged our lives to be fear-avoidant so that Jesus can't work? And do we live with holy anticipation at the greatness of Jesus? Are we willing, after a spiritual victory, to redirect our praise not to ourselves but to the greatness of Jesus?

Oh, how I want to be uttering those words every day.

I am feeling very proud of my Jesus.

I am feeling very proud of my Jesus.

I am feeling very proud of my Jesus.

Let those words roll off your tongue. Let them be reflective of surrendered, Holy Spirit-infused lives. Let them be the nursery rhyme we can't get out of our heads, sung ad infinitum. Lord, have mercy. We've forgotten the joy of living minute-by-minute in anticipation of God's greatness. We've cowered in fear. We've forgotten how to risk. We've forsaken the deeper waters, preferring the shelter of our own comfort zone.

A widow of a martyred man killed in Afghanistan a few months prior stood at the podium, poised, soft-spoken, and resolute. She spoke to over 4,000 Christian leaders, sharing fondly of her husband, of the team trekking through a treacherous mountain pass to provide medical care to the forgotten there. She shared the last conversation she had with her husband before his death.

"We'll call you from the other side," he said. "I love you."

She spoke of a particular kind of goat cheese in the Nuristan area, where they had been working. "Nuristani cheese," she said "is an acquired taste." It's pungent, sour, and hard to get used to, but once you do, you're hooked. She equated it to God's grace. "In these difficult places God's grace is not something to debate. It has to be seen, experienced." She paused. "The vulnerability of God is too foreign, too distasteful. It needs to come in small doses over a long stretch of time. We have to acquire a taste for grace."

She read a poem found in John Piper's book *The Misery of Job and the Mercy of God*:

> Behold the mercy of our King,
> Who takes from death its bitter sting,
> And by His blood, and often ours,
> Brings triumph out of hostile pow'rs,
> And paints, with crimson, earth and soul
> Until the bloody work is whole.
> What we have lost God will restore
> That, and Himself, forevermore.[1]

When she finished reading those words that echoed her husband's fearless sacrifice, the crowd was brought to its feet. Tears spilled down my face. It was one of those kingdom moments for which I lack words. The people around me joined hands and cried. We all prayed simultaneously in our own languages, weeping, some sobbing. The beauty of the widow's message, as she spoke it without guile, washed through me. Her husband had died because of his love for people. Because of the gospel. Because of Jesus. He most likely spoke to the team about Nuristani cheese and God's grace—something his widow learned when the FBI gave her a piece of paper with his sermon notes on it, including the story of the cheese and several kingdom-minded Scriptures. His last words on earth were of grace—not fear.

I put my head on the table. I couldn't get low enough. I wept and wept and wept, remembering our time in France, remembering the sacrifice, the pain, the injury, the unrelenting fear. It was as if it all flew into me in the moment. I remembered the suffering. I remembered our friend Dr. Scott Horrell's words to us afterward: "Nothing significant happens in the kingdom unless death occurs." Then, in between catching my breath and the tears wetting the papers beneath my face, the Lord asked, "Are you willing to suffer again?"

I didn't want to say yes. I remembered the fear, as if I could taste it. But I said it. "Yes, Lord," I said. "Yes."

He then reminded me of Acts 14:22 (esv), in which Paul says, "Through many tribulations we must enter the kingdom of God."

As I shared this with my tablemates for the conference, my new friend Malcolm reminded me of God's path. "That time in France," he said, "was a stepping-stone. You will have your joy reinstated, and you will battle the enemy more easily." I so appreciated his words.

Then Ebenezer, a pastor from Nigeria, said, "The three things I see in missionaries are these: fear, discouragement, and doubt." Oh, how I felt those things on the mission field and in everyday life. And yet Jesus is bigger still. He is worth it all. Worth the suffering. Worth the joy. Worth the sacrifice. Worth moving beyond the fear.

God caused that holy moment to welcome me to mourn, to die, to remember. But He did this to prepare me to live, to experience joy, and to find the wherewithal to joyfully suffer again for His sake. He did this to remind me that a life lived in fear of pain is no life at all. He showed me that He alone can help me forsake fear.

But how? How do we move beyond our fears? Fears lurk like monsters in our souls—fear of failure, disaster, death, prodigal children, disease, strife, depression, bankruptcy, addiction, abandonment, adultery, loneliness. We fear because of what happened to us in the past. We fear because something terrible might befall us today or tomorrow. We fear because we're ensnared by our own idols. We fear simply because it seems to be our nature to do so. We give in to our fears because Satan tends to megaphone them when we've lost our trust in God.

I wish I could tell you I'm fear-free. I'm not. But I've learned a few biblical principles that help me combat fear in my day-to-day life.

God made, redeemed, and called you.

Because God made you, you can rest in His ability to help you. Not only that, but He sent His Son to bear the penalty for your sin. In short, He took every fear, including the power of hell, upon Himself in order to redeem you. Beyond that, He also called you. Notice how Isaiah highlights all three of these amazing things God does: "But now thus says the LORD, he who created you, O Jacob, he who formed you, O Israel: 'Fear not, for I have redeemed you; I have called you by name, you are mine. When you pass through the waters, I will be with you; and through the rivers, they shall not overwhelm you; when you walk through fire you shall not be burned, and the flame shall not consume you'" (Isaiah 43:1-2 ESV).

God is for you.

When you face your fears, it's best to remind yourself that God is not acting against you, but *for* you. He cheerleads. He fights on your behalf. Although this passage from Romans is familiar, I want you to read it in *The Message* to recapture this truth afresh.

> So, what do you think? With God on our side like this, how can we lose? If God didn't hesitate to put everything on the line for us, embracing our condition and exposing himself to the worst by sending his own Son, is there anything else he wouldn't gladly and freely do for us? And who would dare tangle with God by messing with one of God's chosen? Who would dare even to point a finger? The One who died for us— who was raised to life for us!—is in the presence of God at this

very moment sticking up for us. Do you think anyone is going to be able to drive a wedge between us and Christ's love for us? There is no way! Not trouble, not hard times, not hatred, not hunger, not homelessness, not bullying threats, not backstabbing, not even the worst sins listed in Scripture: "They kill us in cold blood because they hate you. We're sitting ducks; they pick us off one by one." None of this fazes us because Jesus loves us. I'm absolutely convinced that nothing—nothing living or dead, angelic or demonic, today or tomorrow, high or low, thinkable or unthinkable—absolutely nothing can get between us and God's love because of the way that Jesus our Master has embraced us (Romans 8:31-39 MSG).

What would your life look like if you truly believed the words of Romans? To live as if nothing fazed you in the light of Christ's amazing love? Not even the demonic can separate you from God's love. Rest in that. Believe that. Live that.

God is your confidence.

We don't have to muster up confidence in the face of fear. We don't have to feel invincible to engage in spiritual warfare. We need not allow ourselves to be captured by fear. We simply need to rest in God's ability. Consider this proverb: "You need not be afraid of sudden disaster or the destruction that comes upon the wicked, for the LORD is your security. He will keep your foot from being caught in a trap" (Proverbs 3:25-26). Some of us worry of sudden terror. In a world bent on terrorism and unmitigated acts of violence, this is normal. And yet we can live without dread. How? By resting in God, by being confident in Him. "But all who listen to me will live in peace, untroubled by fear of harm" (Proverbs 1:33). Note that the writer of Proverbs doesn't say we'll be free of disaster—just the *fear* of it befalling us.

God holds our hand.

As children, our natural bent is to grab for a grown-up's hand when we're afraid. As parents, we don't begrudge our children that right. We gladly hold their hands to reassure them of our presence and protection. God does the same for us. He tells us, "Don't be afraid, for I am with you. Don't be discouraged, for I am your God. I will strengthen you and help you. I will hold you up with my victorious right hand…For I hold you by your right hand—I, the LORD your God. And I say to you, 'Don't be afraid. I am here to help you'" (Isaiah 41:10,13).

God owns it all and knows it all.

Knowing that God owns everything should give us peace. Even when financial ruin threatens, we can be confident of His ownership of everything. As my friend Jill Savage says, "It's no problem for God to sell some cows." She's referring to this verse: "For all the animals of the forest are mine, and I own the cattle on a thousand hills" (Psalm 50:10). Jesus reminds us, too, of how much He knows His creation. He numbers our hairs. He sees us when we sleep, wake, walk, fear, rejoice, eat. Understanding our intrinsic value combats Satan's slick lies about our worthlessness and helplessness. "Are not two sparrows sold for a penny? And not one of them will fall to the ground apart from your Father. But even the hairs of your head are all numbered. Fear not, therefore; you are of more value than many sparrows" (Matthew 10:29-31 ESV). Beyond even that powerful truth, Jesus promises much more to us than merely what we see. When we look at the things, traits, relationships we don't have, we must remind ourselves that we are created for a different kingdom. Jesus said, "Fear not, little flock, for it is your Father's good pleasure to give you the kingdom" (Luke 12:32 ESV).

God has adopted us into his family as a good father.

When we were helpless against the schemes of the devil, God rescued us. But more than that, He adopted us into His family. We need not fear His wrath, thanks to Jesus's death on the cross. "For all who are led by the Spirit of God are children of God. So you have not received a spirit that makes you fearful slaves. Instead, you received God's Spirit when he adopted you as his own children. Now we call him, 'Abba, Father'" (Romans 8:14-15). With this knowledge, we learn to let go of fear. Why? Because the God of the universe loves us, adopts us, leads us, blesses us.

God is our refuge.

Storms come. Even what we fear will sometimes come upon us. And yet we have a God who loves to shelter us. "God is our refuge and strength, a very present help in trouble. Therefore we will not fear though the earth gives way, though the mountains be moved into the heart of the sea" (Psalm

46:1-2 ESV). This is one of those verses warrior women should memorize, particularly when fear lurks everywhere.

God gives us power.

If we fear, not only are we imperfect in our understanding of God's love, we are not grabbing onto something God has given us. He doesn't give fear. His Holy Spirit, dynamically residing within us, breeds courage. "For God has not given us a spirit of fear and timidity, but of power, love, and self-discipline" (2 Timothy 1:7). How encouraging that we don't have to muster up power—all power comes from a powerful, enabling God.

God won't leave or turn His back.

One of the verses I memorized early on in college has stuck to my ribs when my stomach knotted in fear. "It is the LORD who goes before you. He will be with you; he will not leave you or forsake you. Do not fear or be dismayed" (Deuteronomy 31:8 ESV). Even when our emotions dictate otherwise, God will never leave us. He will not turn away from us. If we are His children, He remains with us every moment of our lives.

God is bigger than man.

Sometimes it's not that we fear things. We fear people. We worry what they think of us. We fret about what they will say or what they've said against us. We've elevated people so high that God is dwarfed in our fear. I can imagine Satan enjoys it when we devalue God and worry over people. Even so, it's important to remember that God is big and people are small. "So we can say with confidence, 'The LORD is my helper; so I will have no fear. What can mere people do to me?'" (Hebrews 13:6).

We may be a fearful lot, but we need not stay in that constant state of fear. God is big. His ability to rescue us from our fears, though they be aplenty, is supernaturally strong. The Bible is replete with encouragement to *fear not*. It's a choice. A daily, hourly, minute-by-minute choice to believe in the bigness of God over the smallness of our fears.

Mind if I pray for you?

God of all power and might, please release us from the restriction that fear brings to our lives. I pray for my friend today reading these words, that You would show her where she's feared people instead of fearing You. Help her to lay that relationship at Your feet, entrusting her friends and enemies alike to You. Release her from debilitating fear, particularly fear of the future. Thank You that You are enough today. Help her to rejoice in what she has in this moment, that right now she is beautifully provided for. Invade her fears, Lord, and give them wings. May my sister no longer be tormented by fear, but settled by Your sovereignty. Amen.

Chapter 15

When Christians Hurt You

But Jesus on his part did not entrust himself to them, because
he knew all people and needed no one to bear witness
about man, for he himself knew what was in man.

JOHN 2:24-25 ESV

The most defeated times in my life resulted from other Christians disappointing me. Or downright hurting me. Or acting so unlike Jesus I couldn't be sure of their intentions. Reeling in the aftermath of Christians living unchristianly, I've been tempted to give up.

What does this type of Christian-initiated discouragement have to do with spiritual warfare? Everything. Because Satan wants nothing more than to point to the fallibility—and sometimes the evil intentions—of other Christians as evidence of God not being good. It's a powerful ploy. How many times have you heard that those who don't believe in God came to that conclusion because someone in the church hurt them?

How do we deal with people who disappoint us, particularly Christians? First, we must recognize them. For the sake of clarity, I've categorized them into three camps: wolves, weeds, and weasels.

Wolves

I told my friend Susan a perilous ministry story about meeting and dealing with wolves in sheep's clothing. I told her how I'd read all those false-prophet Scriptures and the wolves passages, never realizing that I'd interact with one directly in ministry one day. I guess I thought those warnings were for "back then" when the church was new. We walked a long stretch of the Pacific Ocean, she listening, me spilling the story.

When I first met the wolves, they appeared so sheeply I felt sheepish in their presence. I didn't measure up, certainly not to their standards. And I felt the weight of their judgment. Everything they said sounded like a sermon—a good one. Slick, polished, beautifully presented. But then fissures formed. Their actions didn't match up with their words. At first it was subtle, but after a few months everything came out. Lies. Deception. The real truth about the state of their hearts.

These were leaders. Wolves in shepherd's clothing. They'd been ministry leaders for years and years. Surely I must've read things wrong. But as their story played out, I understood their wolf-like ways, using people for gain. It broke my heart. Jaded me. Made me cynical. All their words sounded Jesus-y in the beginning, and I had believed them, taken them at their word, pointed to them as examples of Christendom. And yet they were far from Jesus.

In the end, they exemplified Matthew 7:15-23: "Beware of false prophets who come disguised as harmless sheep but are really vicious wolves. You can identify them by their fruit, that is, by the way they act. Can you pick grapes from thornbushes, or figs from thistles? A good tree produces good fruit, and a bad tree produces bad fruit. A good tree can't produce bad fruit, and a bad tree can't produce good fruit. So every tree that does not produce good fruit is chopped down and thrown into the fire. Yes, just as you can identify a tree by its fruit, so you can identify people by their actions. Not everyone who calls out to me, 'Lord! Lord!' will enter the Kingdom of Heaven. Only those who actually do the will of my Father in heaven will enter. On judgment day many will say to me, 'Lord! Lord! We prophesied in your name and cast out demons in your name and performed many miracles in your name.' But I will reply, 'I never knew you. Get away from me, you who break God's laws.'"

The end of our time enmeshed with the wolves turned messy. Terrible. Confusing. Painful. Lots of wreckage and heartache. I tried not to cry when I told Susan the story. But tears leaked out, as they are wont to do. Walking back to the car, I looked down in the sand. There, a small white figurine peered up at me. It looked like our cat, Madeline. I thought of my youngest, how she loved little things like this, and bent down. The "cat" was a wolf. A white wolf. A plastic white wolf that looked like a white sheep.

So Susan and I walked back to the shoreline. I wondered at the irony God placed in my path, how that white wolf peeked out from the sand at such a moment. With all the strength my wimpy arms could muster, I threw the wolf into the Pacific—an ocean whose name means peace. I watched its whiteness sink beneath the waves. And a little part of me felt free.

How about you? Have you met a wolf in shepherd's clothing? Has a ministry leader wreaked evil in your life? Have you considered that he or she might actually have been a ploy used by Satan to dismember the body of Christ? While it's never easy to discern a wolf versus a deeply wounded lamb, understanding the nature of wolves can help you heal from the bite.

Weeds

What if some people in your life are weeds—folks who take over your life, not just physically or with time, but emotionally too, where they crowd the space in your mind? I know some weedy people. Thankfully, they're not deeply imbedded in my day-to-day activities because God has uprooted them. But if I let these weedy folks who have spoken destructive, painful words over my life take up residence in my mind, I will constantly mull over their mean-spirited words, ruminating on what I possibly could have done to change their minds about me.

In that conundrum, there are three primary ways of weed removal:

1. We can simply pretend the weeds are pretty, tolerate them, even water them. Often, I've done this. I've tried to hope for the best with some painful relationships, doing my best to jump through hoops so all will be well. The result? Those weeds take over my heart, choking me.

2. We can spray toxic chemicals on them. This happens during direct confrontations with said weeds. If we allow someone to hurt us so much that we retaliate with words, then we've given in to sin. Better to take the pain to Jesus and ask Him to be our defender.

3. We can ask the Master Gardener to fully uproot the weeds, not only from our day-to-day lives, but from our hearts and minds. When He does this, healing begins. We simply can't be beautiful, lush gardens with weeds invading. The hard part? Sometimes weeds pose as flowers. And sometimes flowers look like weeds. Only the Master Gardener knows the difference and can order our lives and relationships accordingly. The key to weed removal is close proximity to the Master Gardener.

I invite you to evaluate your life right now. In what ways are you throwing your relational pearls before swine? Who are the weeds in your life? Who are you afraid to let go of? Who has acted like an enemy, speaking words of discouragement over you? Perhaps it's time to press into the Master Gardener, to trust Him to pull the weeds that need to be pulled, and plant the flowers that need to be planted.

It may be that God is calling you to confront in the manner of Matthew 18:15-17. "If another believer sins against you, go privately and point out the offense. If the other person listens and confesses it, you have won that person back. But if you are unsuccessful, take one or two others with you and go back again, so that everything you say may be confirmed by two or three witnesses. If the person still refuses to listen, take your case to the church. Then if he or she won't accept the church's decision, treat that person as a pagan or a corrupt tax collector." Conversely, God may be using a person who looks like a weed to you to be the confronter in Matthew 18. Don't easily dismiss a friend's words if they have the ring of truth. Be willing to hear hard things about yourself.

If the person isn't bringing truth, but their words are primarily meant to overwhelm and discourage you (without a constructive element), you may need to limit contact.

It may mean leaving behind a friend completely so you have enough space to heal and forgive.

Or it could mean that God is asking you to engage so much, you'll have to turn the other cheek. Regardless, it's His leading that matters.

Weasels

Weasels are tricky animals. They kill more than they eat. They can change their coat to suit their environment. They put on a good show to mask their cowardliness. They're sneaky. While some people may be wolves masquerading as sheep and some may crop up like weeds in our souls, weasels find specific ways to undermine our confidence, to rattle us.

On the phone, a tax official spent several minutes insinuating something untrue about me. Her tone and words niggled me. Later I realized this woman and her words rattled something deeper than a simple bureaucratic manner should have. They shook my heart. Why?

Because I value integrity. I value doing the right thing, even when no one's watching. I have a healthy fear of wrongdoing, and I'm passionate about being a good citizen, law abider, friend, and worker.

Her insinuations weaseled their way into me, corrupting my day.

Another weasel-like person completely misread my heart. The repercussions of her words still hurt. Deep. There are nights I have dreams about her and wake up afraid. In the melee, I realized quickly that nothing I could say would convince her of my heart or show her my innocence. So I stopped trying to convince her of my innocence. I cried instead. I gave my reputation to Jesus to manage, since I'm not so great at that task.

How do we get freedom from weasels? One way is to remember this: God sees.

He sees your heart. He sees your motives. He sees the bureaucrat's heart. He discerns my friend's heart. He knows our desires. It's completely freeing to know that even if someone else doesn't believe me, I don't need to "protest too much." I can rest. God sees. He knows. He rewards those who are faithful in little.

The weasels in my life remind me not to be so quick to pass judgment on someone's motives or heart, not to accuse blindly, not to jump to conclusions without patiently listening and asking questions, not to jump to bitterness before I have a chance to exercise forgiveness. Bitterness, if I let it take root, does one awful thing. It makes me blind to the heart of another. It assigns negative intent to that person. It only sees the bad, oblivious to the good. There have been far too many times in my life when I've listened to gossip about someone else. If that's the first thing I hear about him or her, it forever colors my view. The older and wiser I get, the less weight I give to the first thing I hear. I try to meet people fresh, try to draw them out and discover their heart. Not always, but I try.

Because I know how painful it is to be misunderstood by weasels, and I don't want to become one.

I thank Jesus, though, that He truly understands what it's like to be misunderstood, to be insinuated against, to be judged wrongly. Consider this from John 2:24-25: "But Jesus on his part did not entrust himself to them, because he knew all people and needed no one to bear witness about man, for he himself knew what was in man" (esv). He let the Father hold His reputation. He understood the fickleness of the crowds. He felt the weight of their judgments, which ultimately led to His death.

If you're in that place where weasels insinuate evil in you, press into Jesus. Give Him your worries and fears. He can shoulder such things. He already has.

Move Beyond Wolves, Weeds, and Weasels

It's not easy to live well in the aftermath of pain, particularly when other Christians cause that pain. Our tendency is to let the circumstances of betrayal overwhelm and embitter us. But there are ways you can move beyond the pain—healthy ways to cling to God and resist Satan. Here are six ways.

Be thick-skinned, yet tenderhearted.

Vulnerability is both overrated and underrated. It's underrated because so few do it well. It's overrated because when some folks do it well, it leaves them open for vicious attack. Have you been in a relationship where you've given every shred of you to someone, only to have him or her cut through you? A hairbreadth line exists between being thick-skinned, yet tenderhearted. God wants us to be tender, forgiving, loving. Yet He also wants us to be tough. That's where the wise as serpents, innocent as doves Scripture comes in. But it's hard to negotiate, isn't it?

Life seldom ties up neatly. We are vulnerable. People may take advantage of that vulnerability, using it as a road into our hearts. They stab at us with words. We recoil, cry, lament, and pray. We walk through recovery and healing, holding Jesus's hand, empowered. Warrior women choose not to let the devil have a bitterness foothold in our lives. And then, by God's grace, we dare to be vulnerable again, albeit more cautiously.

Embrace the vulnerability of Jesus.

I've had times when I swore I wouldn't let anyone else in. I deadened myself to life. I recoiled from sharing my real self. But I'm always miserable there. There's something about the human heart that needs to be known *and* loved. We can't be fully loved unless we are fully known. If someone knows very little of you, how can she love you? And would that love really satisfy? You might think, *if she knew the real me, she wouldn't love me.*

So it's a risky dance, this vulnerability, sometimes involving more heroics than many of us are willing to muster. Sure, it's brave to climb a daunting mountain or complete a marathon. But relational risk with vulnerability is probably the hardest task we will ever perform as warrior women. Relationships involve sacrifice, forgiveness, grace, courage, and a view to eternity. Pursuing the hearts of others takes grit. Guts. Wherewithal. Self-awareness.

The only way we can be vulnerable is to consider Jesus Christ's vulnerability. He dared to sacrifice the comfort of heaven to be with *us*. We crucified Him and He knew we would. But He still came. The *only* way I can go forward in vulnerability is by sticking very closely to Him. Because He's been there.

Heal in community.

The painful but true reality is this: we are wounded in community, yet the way through healing is also through community. It seems paradoxical, doesn't it? If we're deceived by a wolf, overtaken by a weed, or insinuated against by a weasel, the last thing we want to do is hang out in an overgrown garden populated by howls and weaseling. Yet God chooses to heal us through the organic beauty of His church. If Satan can get you to isolate yourself from others as you lick your wounds, he will win. Because isolation breeds all sorts of sin.

Of course if you've been hurt, it's not wise to trust again immediately. Trust is earned, not granted, after all. Be cautious as you approach new friends. Ask questions. Observe. Don't throw yourself into a relationship. Hesitate at first as you take tentative steps toward trustworthy believers. Then tell your story, ask for prayer, and enjoy the fellowship of those who don't howl, overtake, or insinuate.

Trust first in God.

Jesus didn't entrust Himself to the heart of man. Neither should we—fully. Our full trust and allegiance must first be to God. Paul recounts a time when he faced extreme stress in Asia. He describes the situation in dire terms. "We think you ought to know, dear brothers and sisters, about the trouble we went through in the province of Asia. We were crushed and overwhelmed beyond our ability to endure, and we thought we would never live through it. In fact, we expected to die. But as a result, we stopped relying on ourselves and learned to rely only on God, who raises the dead. And he did rescue us from mortal danger, and he will rescue us again. We have placed our confidence in him, and he will continue to rescue us" (2 Corinthians 1:8-10). Paul learned to place his trust in God, the One able to raise the dead. He learned the power of God in his weakness. In our relational pain, we do well to remember this. God is strong. He is trustworthy. And He will rescue.

Use what you've learned to strengthen your discernment muscle.

In the aftermath of dealing with the wolves in our lives, I've become far more discerning. The trick is to not let skepticism override everything. A healthy skepticism helps us step back and assess a situation and the people within it. Jesus elaborates, "Look, I am sending you out as sheep among wolves. So be as shrewd as snakes and harmless as doves" (Matthew 10:16). We need to be wise and discerning, understanding the schemes of the enemy and how he works in the hearts of people.

Remember, the battle isn't against people.

Our battle isn't ultimately against people. It's against principalities and strongholds. It's against the ruler of this world. If we believe our fight is against people, we'll be more apt to give up, to let people's betrayal undermine our faith and embitter us against those folks. Remember, God loves all people, even those you perceive as enemies. In His sovereign plan, He allowed for those wolves, weeds, and weasels to crowd into your life. And He loves them passionately. The real enemy is Satan. Direct your rage there.

When Christians hurt us we can turn our backs on God or throw ourselves into His embrace. Jesus empathizes like no other. Hebrews 4:15-16 confirms that "this High Priest of ours understands our weaknesses, for he faced all of the same testings we do, yet he did not sin. So let us come boldly to the throne of our gracious God. There we will receive his mercy, and we will find grace to help us when we need it most." He brings grace to the darkest relational situations. He is able to help us overcome that type of pain. When Christians hurt you, run to the Person who understands misunderstanding, who took on the sins of all of us—including the wolves, weeds, and weasels.

Mind if I pray for you?

Lord, more than anything we need discernment. Help us to understand the people in our lives and the roles they play. I pray for my friend today, that You would show her where she's interacted with wolves. Give her insight into the weeds in her life. And if there be weasels, I pray You'd help her to turn her ear away from weasel words. Beyond all this, protect her heart from bitterness. May she not view You as she does Christians who disappoint. You are the God who is perfect love. Help her rest her assurance and confidence there alone. Please, please heal the wounds she's received from other believers. May those wounds bring discernment instead of bitterness. Amen.

Chapter 16

When Your Mind Attacks

When words from the pit assail us, we are not to entertain
them, try to figure them out, languish by them, feed on them,
ruminate on them, but instead to silence them. Immediately.

MARY DEMUTH

ost of our battle on this earth takes place inside ourselves—the way
we think, process, and believe. As warrior women, we not only have
to work through how we think, but also walk through the minefield of hormones and the resulting emotions they bring. Right after we were married,
I spent our first months crying all the time, thinking about death, and worrying incessantly. My poor husband wondered what had happened to the
girl he'd slipped a ring on. The culprit? I took "the pill" and it messed me
up.* Thankfully, I went off it and became my happy self once more, no
longer crying through church services or dwelling on my unworthiness. In
varying degrees, I've seen how hormones can deeply influence how I process my world, how quickly they can become a doorway for dark thoughts.

But if I believe in the power of the Holy Spirit to help me think rightly
about myself, this world, and God, I have to believe He is strong enough
to help me de-mine my hormonal land mines. I have to believe God is
bigger than estrogen.

That being said, of course not every negative thought can be blamed on
hormones, nor can wild hormones become a scapegoat for our bad behavior. The key to winning the battle of the mind is truth. Huge heaps of truth.

To bring this to a practical level, I'm going to share three common lies

---

* This is not meant to be a condemnation against the pill. It simply made me crazy.

we women believe and work through what God's Word has to say about them. Read through these sections prayerfully, seeking to see where God would have you re-evaluate how you think. Also, note the connection between how Satan tempted Adam and Eve and then Jesus with the three lies—pleasure, stuff, achievement.

Lie #1: Pleasure. Your looks are the gateway to pleasure and contentment.

Psalm 139:14 says, "I will give thanks to You, for I am fearfully and wonderfully made; wonderful are Your works, and my soul knows it very well" (NASB). I resonate with *fearfully* when I think of my aging body, but I can't seem to shake hands with *wonderfully*.

Every time I see a celebrity on a magazine, preening in airbrushed beauty, or I look at pictures of myself years ago, how young I was, I shake my head. I'm having a hard time grappling with my aging body. How can it be wonderful? As I age, does it mean my capacity for joy decreases?

My teenage daughter has said, "Mom, you're pretty," several times in the past few months. Right around this time, the Lord saw fit to send me to a mother-daughter conference where author Vicki Courtney was the keynote speaker. She spoke about five things our daughters needed from us. Number three? *Make friends with your own reflection.*

I realized why my daughter built me up—because I wasn't happy with my own reflection. And my daughter caught how I viewed myself. She will be insecure if I am insecure. She will reflect my own paranoia. She will get her attitude about how she looks by how I feel about how I look. If I'm stressing about extra pounds, chances are, she'll follow. So, in a roundabout way, her compliments served as a reminder to make peace with myself, choosing not to listen to Satan's lies that my worth rested in my looks.

Matthew 5:25 says "When you are on the way to court with your adversary, settle your differences quickly. Otherwise, your accuser may hand you over to the judge, who will hand you over to an officer, and you will be thrown into prison."

Many of us are guilty of disobeying that verse, only the opponent isn't someone else. It's ourselves. We need to learn to make friends with our reflections, denying the nagging voice in our heads that says we're not Angelina Jolie, comparing ourselves mercilessly to the latest beauty queen.

We are not doing any favors by constantly worrying about our physique. And this worry can open the doors to destructive behavior.

Even if we don't have daughters watching us, there are women everywhere who need to see women warriors befriending their reflections. We could start a positive revolution by simply embracing contentment, spending our energy on loving others, and rejoicing that our bodies enable us to give hugs, listen to hurts, bear burdens. We're all aging. We all face these issues. How, though, can we make friends with our reflection?

Here's a surprising truth: those who love Jesus are actually God's sacred dwelling place. "Don't you realize that all of you together are the temple of God and that the Spirit of God lives in you?" (1 Corinthians 3:16). Why would we spend so much time discrediting God's temple? Why would we deny it nourishment (or offer it more than it needs by overeating), level scorn its way, or let it atrophy through lethargy? If God created our bodies to house His spirit, then we can rest in knowing we are wonderfully made while we embrace the responsibility of keeping healthy.

We must choose to push against our culture's superficial tyranny of beauty. We can defy the culture that glorifies youth and puts asunder anything less than perfection. Is that what Jesus would do? Would He flock only to the beautiful people? Since He created us all, we're all beautiful people. To place on each other this yoke of hierarchy is to discredit Jesus. Mother Teresa speaks of us finding Jesus in "distressing disguise." How sad that we miss Him when we value external beauty over genuine beauty. I wonder how many times Jesus has appeared to us from the unlovely, and we've looked away. But when we embrace those whose hearts outshine their beauty, we become countercultural in the best possible way.

Whenever I worry about my looks, I think of heaven, how this body will not remain, that a new body will replace it. Paul writes we should anticipate heaven "while we look not at the things which are seen, but at the things which are not seen; for the things which are seen are temporal, but the things which are not seen are eternal" (2 Corinthians 4:18 NASB).

Everything I see in the mirror is temporary. It won't last. But what I choose to do in this body God's given me is what will last. I fear that all my worrying is adding to the wood, hay, and straw Paul addresses in 1 Corinthians 3:12-13: "Now if any man builds on the foundation with gold, silver, precious stones, wood, hay, straw, each man's work will become evident; for the day will show it because it is to be revealed with fire, and the fire itself will test the quality of each man's work" (NASB). Let's be less consumed with a body that is fading and more consumed with the fire of God's testing. Let's strive to live a life worthy of Jesus's words, "Well done, good and faithful servant!" As woman warriors, we should value faithfulness over youthfulness, our service over our appearance.

When I find myself slipping into sadness over my appearance, one of the best ways I pull out is to look at others in a different light. I compliment a friend of mine who's recently lost weight. I tell older women they're beautiful. I strive to point out beauty when I see it. If we take our focus off ourselves and think about the rest of the women suffering from body image issues and seek to encourage them, we'll embody the words of Paul. He wrote, "Don't be selfish; don't try to impress others. Be humble, thinking of others as better than yourselves. Don't look out only for your own interests, but take an interest in others, too" (Philippians 2:3-4).

We need to remind ourselves that God looks at the heart, and that our goal in life should be pursuing the kind of beauty He rewards, developing a heart that runs quickly to Him, a heart full of mercy and patience and kindness. Project yourself in the far future, when you've had a passel of grandkids and maybe even a few great-grandkids. You will be old, then. Will you have smile lines? Will children want to scamper on your lap because you exude the irresistible Jesus? Will your heart be beautiful?

Lie #2: Stuff. You are what you have (so if you don't have, you're nothing).

Although I don't think of myself as a materialist, I probably am. I could say I believed that God would provide, but my praxis, the way I live my life, indicates otherwise. Never did this become so evident than when we were the victims of a conman. Before leaving for France to become missionaries, we allowed our panic over selling our house to influence our decision-making, which involved selling our home to a man we met at church. We did check him out, but we should've investigated further. Two weeks before Christmas, after only four months on the mission field, we got a call from our bank asking us why we weren't paying our mortgage. We explained that we'd sold our home months ago.

But it turned out that while the conman owned the title of our home, we still owned the mortgage. The situation forced us to go into foreclosure. As Christmas neared, I struggled with the betrayal, our loss of credit, and our financial situation. Quietly, God reminded me again that He owned the cattle on a thousand hills. Then He whispered, "Do you really believe this?"

Of course I believed God owned everything. Of course I knew our lives consisted of more than just our stuff. But as His question sunk into me, I knew the answer. I didn't believe. At least I didn't live as if I believed. It took quite some time for me to surrender my fear to God. To believe that He owned it all anyway and that He was truly our provider.

Peel away stuff and money, and you get a word called *security*. Fundamentally, I wanted security—and many warrior women do as well. I believed Satan's stealthy lie that stuff and money would provide that. And yet Jesus said our lives don't equal things. In our love of security, we fall prey to a love for money, believing it to be the ticket to security. We stumble into all sorts of sin because of that love of money. Consider these truth-laced verses:

> For the love of money is the root of all kinds of evil. And some people, craving money, have wandered from the true faith and pierced themselves with many sorrows. (1 Timothy 6:10)

> Don't love money; be satisfied with what you have. For God has said, "I will never fail you. I will never abandon you." (Hebrews 13:5)

> The Pharisees, who dearly loved their money, heard all this and scoffed at [Jesus]. (Luke 16:14)

> Those who love money will never have enough. How meaningless to think that wealth brings true happiness! (Ecclesiastes 5:10)

> No one can serve two masters. For you will hate one and love the other; you will be devoted to one and despise the other. You cannot serve both God and money. (Luke 16:13)

> So my people come pretending to be sincere and sit before you. They listen to your words, but they have no intention of doing what you say. Their mouths are full of lustful words, and their hearts seek only after money. (Ezekiel 33:31)

The truth is that no matter what you have or what you don't have, God's grace is sufficient. He *does* own the cattle on a thousand hills. He is your provider. Panic is Satan's tool to get you to doubt God's provision and goodness. As warrior women choose not to panic, but to reinforce our belief in God's ownership, we will keep our hearts unhurried and unworried. The remedy for believing the lie that stuff and money are everything is deliberately deciding that God is your everything.

When I finally admitted I believed in God's ownership, something new settled into me. A deep peace. All those years previous I'd spent worrying suddenly halted. As I ventured forward as a missionary with a foreclosure on another continent, I stopped worrying. I'm sure Satan's plan to steal, kill, and destroy loomed, but by God's grace I learned the power of simple belief.

Lie #3: Achievement. You are what you do.

I'm a doer. Always have been. And since I grew up in a home where I felt I had to justify my space on this earth by doing things, I've slipped into that mode far more than I wish to admit. I've also fallen prey to Satan's lies that I consist solely in what I do. And if for some reason I don't do enough, I won't be enough. Not lovable to others. Certainly not lovable to God. The lie that doing reflects our worth harkens back to our need for control and our tendency toward legalism. The great truth of the Christian life is this, though: God is the One who does things, and it is what *He* does that makes us right with Him.

Oswald Chambers reminds me of the settled life God wants. He writes, "It is much easier to *do* something than to trust in God; we see the activity and mistake panic for inspiration."[1] I've been living in that place of panic for several months. I've taken panic into myself, digested it, then produced more work and more to-do lists than anyone could finish. Has that frenetic activity helped me rise above my stress? No. Instead, trapped in myself and my worry, I've settled into Satan's lies, let stress have its way.

Again Chambers slays me: "We would much rather work for God than believe in Him."[2] I prefer activity over trust. Do you? And yet belief and trust in Jesus should be the hallmark of my life. Why do I think I can solve all my problems merely by hard work, relegating God to the background? He is that splendid power within, but I forget so easily. I prefer cultivating my own splendid power. Chambers continues: "The degree of panic activity in my life is equal to the degree of my lack of personal spiritual experience."[3] In reading that, I'm convicted. How long have I panicked instead of prayed?

And yet there is hope for me, for you. God is the One who causes growth despite our frenetic work. Panic won't grow us; He does. Our plans will burn into ash, but His will flourish. Because He is God. And we are not. We are more than workers; we are children, wildly loved by God simply because we are His offspring.

Nothing you *can do* will separate you from His love.

Nothing you *don't do* will separate you from His love.

Nothing *done to you* will separate you from His love.

It is a truth worth noting: God loves us. Deeply. Widely. Extravagantly. Whether we feel we deserve it or not.

Which brings us to something that makes Satan shudder: a woman fully enmeshed in God's love for her, who believes firmly in who she is in Christ. She is settled. She is rested. She is loved. She is hopeful. She is trusting. She is peace-filled. Her steady belief in God's ability to trump her own abilities shatters the kingdom of darkness.

God loves us. Deeply. Widely. Extravagantly.
Whether we feel we deserve it or not.

How do we counteract lies? I've only listed three, yet there are hundreds we believe (and maybe don't even know we believe). Read through this list and see which ones resonate with you. Underline or highlight them, then write them down on a piece of paper or in a journal and ask God to reveal the truth to you through the Scriptures.

Lies

- You will never amount to much.
- If you only had $_____, you would be happy.
- You must take care of everyone or no one will be taken care of.
- Because you continue to struggle in that area, God has not chosen you to be His child.
- If you're to be protected, it's entirely up to you.

- You are not worthy to be loved.
- Bitterness is a benefit because it keeps your heart safe.
- Church is full of hypocrites. You don't need it.
- God helps those who help themselves.
- You are not spiritual enough to tell others about Jesus.
- God cannot be trusted. He's fickle and capricious.
- God adopts people into His family, but He will not adopt you. You're unadoptable.
- When God created you, He made a mistake.
- You must be perfect for others and God to love you.
- To prove your worth, you must do a lot of tasks—and do them well.
- You don't really need the Bible.
- Beautiful, smart, and talented people are more blessed.
- If Jesus walked the earth today, He wouldn't want to be your friend.
- This terrible day proves God doesn't love you.
- Prayer is just a waste of time.
- Life is fair.
- It's entirely all your fault.
- Because you failed in the past, you will fail in the future.
- Your depression defines you and proves you are unworthy of love.
- Everyone's happiness depends on you.
- You will never experience true freedom.
- God does not see you.
- You deserve ridicule.
- If something is to be accomplished, it's entirely up to you.
- Your pet (or hobby or passion or entertainment) is a perfect substitute for human relationships.
- To be worthy, you must be in perfect physical shape.

- Spiritual disciplines are for legalists.
- This little indulgence won't hurt you.
- Your sickness is proof that God doesn't care.
- God owes you a pain-free life.
- You deserve abuse.
- Even if you don't sin, your motives will be impure. (Some of us are cursed with an overactive conscience that turns anything we do into sin in our minds.)
- You are ugly.
- God is a policeman in the sky who holds everything against you.
- You must caretake your life because God is not dependable.
- You can't know truth.
- It doesn't matter that your business partner (or boyfriend) isn't a Christ-follower.
- You can't trust God to act justly, so take your vengeance now.
- Being feminine is the same thing as being weak.
- You don't need other Christians.
- God chose not to heal you, so numbing yourself through medication, food, illegal drugs, or alcohol is acceptable.
- Pleasure is far better than obedience.
- God is holding out on you.
- You have nothing for which to be thankful.
- God will never answer your prayer.
- It's just a minor flirtation. It will never amount to anything.
- The home isn't that important.
- Your calling and ministry is less important than a man's calling and ministry.
- You will never suffer as a Christian.
- God is too lofty to be knowable. Why even try?
- God cannot use you.

- Satan doesn't exist.
- Your gifts are unnecessary in the kingdom of God.
- It's your prerogative to keep some sins private. Your sin is your business.
- Your words are unimportant.
- You can't help but duplicate the mistakes and sins of your parents.
- Satan already has a hold on you and cannot be defeated.
- Your sin is someone else's fault.
- God doesn't exist.
- The world would be better without you.
- How you look = who you are.
- You will never move beyond _____, and you will never be happy because of it.
- If you're friendless, it's always your fault.
- You have to earn your way to heaven.
- You deserve pain, particularly the pain you inflict on yourself.
- Every thought you have originates from you, and the evil thoughts prove you're unworthy.
- You don't need to repent.
- You must have it all together for God to use you.
- You must have control to feel safe.
- You will only be whole if you have a husband or boyfriend.
- Something other than God (food, sex, money, possessions, relationships) brings happiness.
- Telling the truth about the sin in your life is unnecessary.
- Grief will always be your constant companion.
- You don't have to ask _____ for forgiveness.
- You can never forgive _____.
- The best part of your life was _____ years ago, and you'll never be happy today.

- Sin isn't that big of a deal—particularly the little sins.

- You deserve poor treatment.

- Your feelings are 100% trustworthy and reveal what is true.

- Reconciliation is unnecessary.

- Your friend's advice trumps God's direction.

- You will never overcome that repetitive sin.

- What your enemy says about you is always true.

- God's requirements are too burdensome.

How do we combat such lies? The obvious answers are: read the Bible, allow the Holy Spirit to counteract the lies, and fellowship with other believers who will help you discern the lies.

Beyond that, in observing how and why Jesus silenced the demons when He walked the earth, I've learned a valuable insight. I used to wonder why Jesus silenced the demons. They'd say things about Him being the Son of God. In an odd sense, they told the truth about Jesus, yet Jesus would have none of it.

When something vile says something true, it is an affront. Especially when it is said with dripping disdain. I can imagine the sarcasm and the humiliating tone the demons used when they revealed Christ's identity to the crowds. Why did He silence them?

It was not yet Jesus's time to be "outed." The demons tried to usher Jesus into the spotlight in their wicked timing, not God's. Jesus knew there would be a day when children and parents lined a palm-strewn street proclaiming Him, heralding Him. Being proclaimed by evil ones sullied that future proclamation, so He silenced their words.

Jesus was also jealous of the glory of God. So desirous of God's glory, He felt it disdainful to hear hellish voices proclaim Him. It would be like Hitler praising the very people he murdered. He was obviously not sincere; in fact if he had said glorious words about the people he killed, he would be considered a horrific liar—to praise, then kill. The glory of God is too precious to be spewed by evil ones.

Perhaps it was as simple as not wanting to hear the voices of rebellion. Jesus was utterly perfect, utterly obedient to God the Father. Perhaps it rankled Him, grated on His sensibilities to hear such rebellious, hateful words.

And maybe, Jesus was teaching you and me a lesson. That when words from the pit assail us, we are not to entertain them, try to figure them out, languish by them, feed on them, or ruminate on them, but instead to silence them. Immediately. Eve would've been better off if she had just said, "Silence!" Instead, she listened. And reasoned. And rebelled. The demons spoke truth, and yet Jesus kept them quiet. Sometimes the enemy's voice has a familiar ring of truth, but the underlying motivation is always theft, murder, and destruction. The only proper response is to say, "Silence!"

Mind if I pray for you?

Lord, forgive us for believing lies about our appearance. Help us develop contentment in what we have. Free us from believing our worth lies in what we do. I pray for the warrior woman reading these words right now, that You would clearly and distinctly show her the lies she believes. Remedy those lies with a supernatural blast of Your truth. Infuse Your truth deep into her marrow, reminding her of how widely and wildly she's loved by You. Amen.

Chapter 17

When Your Family Faces a Battle

Avoiding a fight is a mark of honor;
only fools insist on quarreling.

PROVERBS 20:3

Satan hates the family. Despises it. Fights against it.

Why? Because the family, whatever form it takes, is a metaphor for God's kingdom. A marriage represents Jesus's relationship to the church. Children represent how we must interact with each other as a body. Parents model God to their children. When the family structure breaks apart, we lose the metaphor. We begin to believe lies about God's lack of goodness. We project onto God what we experience in our families. And some of us turn away.

As warrior women engaged in a beautiful battle, we have a unique role to play in the family. We tend to be nurturers. We try to protect, help, rescue, build up. We want to save. But sometimes we can't. And in that, we may despair. What can we do as women warriors? How can we love-pray-encourage our families to walk with Jesus, to make great choices, to pursue relationship?

Bind kindness around your neck (and heart, and actions).

Romans 2:4 tells us how God woos us, His children, toward a repentant, right life: "Don't you see how wonderfully kind, tolerant, and patient God is with you? Does this mean nothing to you? Can't you see that his kindness is intended to turn you from your sin?" God's kindness beckons us, and yet we forget as we deal with stressful family members and situations that kindness is what wins hearts. We resort to bullying, manipulation, control, and hollering. Proverbs 3:3 encourages, "Do not let kindness and truth leave you; bind them around your neck, write them on the tablet of your heart" (NASB). Being kind, as we see in this verse, doesn't mean we divorce truth from our tenderhearted ways. We are to speak the truth with love.

The sad tragedy of our day is that we treat those people we love most with disdain or distance. We sometimes treat strangers better than we treat our family members. Kindness woos, entices, beckons. Unkindness derails, pushes away, undermines—and it allows for Satan to instigate grudges and strife.

Leave the drama.

Sin abounds when drama explodes. As one who tends to be reactionary, I've seen firsthand how I can let my emotion, fear, and imagination get the best of me. When I don't slow down enough to hear God's voice, I tend toward panic, and panic leads me to listen to the Enemy's voice to stir up strife, take things under control, or simply overreact. And yet we are called to live in peace. Peace is the opposite of drama. The author of Hebrews tells us peacemaking is work: "Work at living in peace with everyone, and work at living a holy life, for those who are not holy will not see the Lord" (Hebrews 12:14). This verse connotes that it may seem natural to become a drama-queen, but we must labor to live in peace.

In the book of James we see the importance of seeking God first, to look for His wisdom when family issues escalate: "But the wisdom from above is first of all pure. It is also peace loving, gentle at all times, and willing to yield to others. It is full of mercy and good deeds. It shows no favoritism and is always sincere. And those who are peacemakers will plant seeds of peace and reap a harvest of righteousness" (James 3:17-18). Instead of planting seeds of dramatic discord, we are called to plant peace, to be gentle, to have a yielded heart. Remember, "Avoiding a fight is a mark of honor; only fools insist on quarreling" (Proverbs 20:3).

Gather at the table.

The family dinner table is threatened with extinction. As women warriors, we need to value our children and families enough to reorient our lives toward the table. Marjorie Thompson elaborates on the importance of the family table in Jewish families: "The Jewish faith has been characterized as a 'table spirituality' in which the central feasts and holy days are celebrated around the altar of the family table."[1] Our table is an altar, the place where we share our victories and defeats. It's where we learn how to process life. And, in an indirect but compelling way, it's where we help our kids make life choices.

A 2010 survey also undergirds the importance of the family table. "The magic that happens at family dinners isn't the food on the table, but the conversations around it…The more often children have dinners with their parents, the less likely they are to smoke, drink, or use drugs."[2] In that sense, the act of coming together at the family table is spiritual warfare. It's the place we debunk Satan's lies, unpack our children's hearts, hear and help form their theology, and offer wise, biblical counsel. It's the forming center of relationship—a key preventative measure of spiritual warfare in our family's lives.

Pray like crazy.

Simple enough, right? But we forget, don't we? We rush to worry. When we hear bad news about a family member, we're more apt to pick up the phone than we are to drop to our knees. But prayer changes us. It changes others. It's our direct, relational connection to the One who bears every family burden. Consider this: God is the Father of all His children. He knows how to come alongside mothers, grandmothers, aunts, cousins, and nieces. He's in the business of building families. He watches all of us walk our own paths at one time or another. And He keeps pursuing. Always loving.

What do you do when you have wayward relatives? Pray sin will find them out. Pray God will bring circumstances to teach them. Pray God will place people in their lives who share Jesus in a dynamic way with them. Pray God's will be done, whether that means success or failure, whatever it takes to bring your relative to Himself. Pray that the influences of the world will feel empty. Pray the thrill of sin will wane. Pray God will grant your relative discernment between evil and good. Pray God will birth in them the desire to live a better story. Pray that Satan's ploys will derail, that his voice will be heard as evil, not enticement.

Express your love.

Showing our love is perhaps the most important thing we can do as we fight for our families. Love shines through words like, "I love you," or "You're valuable to me." Love is expressed with specifics like, "I love the way you work hard at a project," or "I noticed how you helped that elderly man yesterday." But it's also manifested in actions—how you treat your family members in day-to-day life, how you sacrifice yourself for their sake. How you lay aside your agenda. How you joyfully serve. These actions communicate love beyond mere words, as actions add cement to the words you say. Paul wrote, "Love does no wrong to others, so love fulfills the requirements of God's law" (Romans 13:10). If we love, we do no wrong.

Retaliate by de-escalation.

In the heat of argument, you have a choice to escalate or de-escalate. If you choose to escalate, sin will abound and arguments will grow. Scripture is clear: "As the beating of cream yields butter and striking the nose causes bleeding, so stirring up anger causes quarrels" (Proverbs 30:33). Escalating an argument delights Satan because it places people in a swirl of anger and terrible words. And it means that the person stirring up wrath has chosen to take God's place to take things under her control. But the Bible says, "Don't say, 'I will get even for this wrong.' Wait for the LORD to handle the matter" (Proverbs 20:22).

Instead of escalation, choose to let kindness reign. Refrain from payback. "See that no one pays back evil for evil, but always try to do good to each other and to all people" (1 Thessalonians 5:15).

Create boundaries.

When we love our families, we want what is best for them. We want to see them walking successfully with Jesus, making wise decisions, and exhibiting a humble heart. We certainly can't make that happen, particularly when our family members make destructive choices. It seems counterintuitive, but if a family member is not acting as her best self, we must create strong boundaries to protect ourselves and to delineate acceptable behavior. For instance, if a son is doing drugs, it's not loving for us to accept his addiction and allow him to do whatever he wants. It's loving to provide or allow consequences to teach him. We cannot change him, but we can love him enough to want his best. If he doesn't give it, we love through boundaries.

Assume positive intent.

Marital researchers at the University of Washington found that a hallmark of the best marriages had this one thing in common: the spouses assumed positive intent in each other. What does that mean? It means that when something came up where a spouse could jump to a negative conclusion, he or she chose instead to think positively. Assuming negative intentions kills relationship. And as Paul writes in the famous 1 Corinthians 13 passage, we are to "believe all things" and "keep no record of wrongs." Assuming positive intent means we do both.

Ask God to change you.

Although it's good and right to pray for your family members to change or be changed, the most effective prayer to pray is, "God, change me." That's the only place you have the ability to see positive change. When we're suffering through painful family discord, it's easy to point to all the problematic people and demand they change. Harder still is looking inside yourself, asking God to search your heart, and being willing to see how your reaction to someone else's sin might just be sin too.

As Judy Douglass watched her adopted son make terrible choices, her heart broke. Her prayers rested on changing his prodigal behavior. But something unexpected happened as she prayed. She changed. She grew. "But for me, as difficult as this journey has been, God has enabled me to see this wayward son as an incredible gift to me. God has used him to reveal weaknesses I didn't know I had—and strengths I didn't realize I possessed. And God has used him to show me so much more of Himself. I understand unconditional love at a much deeper level—and that unconditional love doesn't demand love in return. In urging me many times not to give up on my son, God has reminded me that He has never given up on me. And certainly I have made many stupid and sinful choices that merit grave consequences, but His mercy has prevailed. When my feelings turned to anger and vengeance, God reminded me that he has redeemed me with tender mercy and wooed me with lovingkindness."[3]

Sacrifice.

Sometimes God calls us to sacrifice for family. Patrick and I had the opportunity once to do this. We'd sold our car to a family member who made payments to us each month. But then he totaled the car, ending up in the hospital. We prayed about what to do. God clearly guided us to not only erase the debt, but to give him back the money he'd already paid—a sacrifice for our family. But we knew in this instance that sacrifice was merited, and we prayed that the Lord would use that sacrifice to remind our relative about His extravagant grace and generosity.

Listen.

In family situations, we tend to want our opinion heard. We don't always assess a situation as it really is, but instead bring in our own biases. But James tells us to be quick to listen: "Understand this, my dear brothers and sisters: You must all be quick to listen, slow to speak, and slow to get angry" (James 1:19). Instead of nursing an insatiable need to vent our views, we need to ask the Holy Spirit to give us a holy curiosity about others and their perceptions. "Fools have no interest in understanding; they only want to air their own opinions" (Proverbs 18:2). We need to refrain instead of spewing. "Spouting off before listening to the facts is both shameful and foolish" (Proverbs 18:13). And we need to be humble enough to hear advice from our family members. "If you listen to constructive criticism, you will be at home among the wise" (Proverbs 15:31).

Forgive.

In the classic allegory *Hinds' Feet on High Places* by Hannah Hurnard, we follow a young doe named Much Afraid as she ventures to the High Places in search of healing. Exhausted, she reaches a high peak where only rocks are her footing. She spies a lone flower pushing its way up through the crags. She asks the flower its name.

"My name is Bearing the Cost, but some call me Forgiveness."[4]

She asks the flower how it arrived there.

"I was separated from all my companions, exiled from home, carried here and imprisoned in this rock. It was not my choice, but the work of others who, when they had dropped me here, went away and left me to bear the results of what they had done."[5]

In families, we'll experience the most excruciating, debilitating pain. And like Bearing the Cost, we are left on a rocky surface with a choice to bloom there or wilt. Our decision to forgive gives us the ability to bloom. We cannot control what our family members say or do. Nor can we prevent ourselves from being dropped from the valley to the precipice of rocks. But we can choose to forgive. In that forgiveness, we deal another blow to the enemy who delights over our bitterness.

Bitterness separates us from the God who freely forgives. Forgiveness frees our hearts to love, just as Jesus did.

Be wary of oversensitivity.

I love how the Amplified Bible renders a portion of 1 Corinthians 13:5: "[Love] is not touchy or fretful or resentful." When a family member injures us, our tendency is to live in reaction to that hurt. If we don't step back to heal and regroup, if we nurse bitterness, if we think over all the wrongs the person has enacted against us, we'll become oversensitive.

Part of overcoming oversensitivity is realizing that people will never satisfy deeply. We have to first entrust ourselves to God, to give Him our fears, worries, relationships. He is the one who can fill. With Him as our reservoir, we will be less apt to be touchy.

Say the seven magic words.

They're quite simple, but they involve humility and authenticity: "I was wrong. Will you forgive me?" Nothing changes the dynamic of a heated argument or an estranged relationship quite like the seven words. We will not prosper in our family relationships until we dare to swallow our pride and admit our wrongdoing. "People who conceal their sins will not prosper, but if they confess and turn from them, they will receive mercy" (Proverbs 28:13).

Trust in sovereignty.

Beyond all these things, we cannot control our families, how they behave or misbehave, or how they treat each other. But we can rest in God's loving control of the universe. That's what sovereignty means. It means God is the father of all things, the patriarch of the universe who breathed it and us into existence. He has a master plan that we cannot understand with finite minds. All we can do is trust in His plan, particularly when things swirling around our family seem dark. A resolved trust in God's sovereignty rattles the kingdom of darkness and it settles our souls, even when our families are restless.

Mind if I pray for you?

Instead of me praying for you, I'd like to offer you a gift—a portion of a prayer you can pray for a wayward family member, adapted by Judy Douglass.

> Heavenly Father, I bring before You and the Lord Jesus Christ one who is very dear to You and to me: _____. I have come to see that Satan is blinding and binding her in awful bondage. She is in such a condition that she cannot or will not come to You for help on her own. I stand in for her in intercessory prayer before Your throne. I draw upon the Person of the Holy Spirit that He may guide me to pray in wisdom, power, and understanding.
>
> I bring in prayer the focus of the person and work of the Lord Jesus Christ directly upon _____ in His strengthening and help. I bring the mighty power of my Lord's incarnation, crucifixion, resurrection, ascension, and glorification directly against all forces of darkness seeking to destroy _____.
>
> I pray, heavenly Father, that You may open _____'s eyes of understanding. Remove all blindness and spiritual deafness from her heart. As a priest of God in _____'s life, I plead Your mercy over her sins of failure and rebellion. I claim all of her life united together in obedient love and service to the Lord Jesus Christ. May the Spirit of the Living God focus His mighty work upon _____ to grant her repentance and to set her completely free from all that binds her.
>
> In the name of the Lord Jesus Christ, I thank You for Your answer. Grant me the grace to be persistent and faithful in my intercessions for _____ that You may be glorified through this deliverance.[6]
>
> Amen. Thank You, sweet Jesus!

Chapter 18

When Sin and Addictions Threaten

Although Satan is behind every temptation, blaming him does
not absolve us of any responsibility for sin and doing that which is
contrary to God's will. In Christ we have been given power over sin,
and Satan cannot make us do anything we do not choose to do![1]

JERRY RANKIN

The devil entices you to choose the wicked road, but he doesn't have the power to make you walk it—or run it, or revel in it. Though we are tempted, we have the ability to say no, not by sheer grit and determination, but through the power of the Holy Spirit who lives within us. He is the warrior woman's power source to withstand temptation. He gives us the ability to do what is right. He calls us to righteous action, holy inaction (in the things of sin), and correct reaction.

But all those words sound preachy as I write them. I remember battling a deep-seated repetitive sin in high school and college that debilitated me. Every time I engaged in it, I'd heap shame upon myself in shovelfuls. I'd read verses like this: "If we deliberately keep on sinning after we have received the knowledge of the truth, no sacrifice for sins is left, but only a fearful expectation of judgment and of raging fire that will consume the enemies of God" (Hebrews 10:26-27 NIV). I wondered if I still loved Jesus, or if He still claimed me as His child. I couldn't break free. Years of sin, years of making the same choice, debilitated me.

God eventually delivered me. (Note that I could not deliver myself.) How? Through an incredibly gradual process of teaching me how much He loved me, which reveals the surprising mysteries of His ways. We are a formulaic people, wanting five steps to overcome this, eleven keys to a better you, eight ways to lose weight now. The sanctification journey takes more than instantaneous now. It takes time. It twists and moves and steps forward and backward, in circles and oblongs. And yet, if we are God's children, His hand continues to guide us, and His heart continues to be for us. A beautiful mystery, indeed. To overcome our sinful behavior or our addictions, we must first find our place in that mystery.

Settle who you are.

We're a forgetful people. We forget who we are. We forget we are wildly loved by our Creator—chosen, set apart, redeemed. Throughout the Bible, we're told to remember, to look back, to recall what God has done for us. Not only has He rescued us from our former life, but He has already disarmed Satan's influence on our behavior. Consider: "You were dead because of your sins and because your sinful nature was not yet cut away. Then God made you alive with Christ, for he forgave all our sins. He canceled the record of the charges against us and took it away by nailing it to the cross. In this way, he disarmed the spiritual rulers and authorities. He shamed them publicly by his victory over them on the cross" (Colossians 2:13-15).

We are alive in Christ, forgiven, set free from the record of our past. If you're constantly being nagged by a little voice in your head about past sins, it's time to remember that God has wiped all those sins out. That voice is not God's. His delight is in you. He sent His Son to die for your sins, my sins, our sins. Therefore, it's important to resolve the issue first that we are made new by Jesus and that His blood is sufficient to forgive every sin.

When we settle who we are, we are less enticed to follow after things that don't fill us. When we understand what price it took for Jesus to save us, our gratitude overflows into obedience. It reminds me of my time in high school when I had several Christian friends who chose to have sex outside of marriage and fill their weekends with drugs and parties. My hunch is that they didn't yet know who they were. They didn't understand what God had already accomplished on their behalf to set them free.

During that time I was new to the whole Jesus-thing. I spent my days thinking about how greatly God had rescued me. I was so grateful, so astounded, so relieved, that the appeal of sin waned. Not to say I never sinned. I did. I struggled. But as I came to know myself and who I was in light of what God had done, sin lost bits and pieces of its hold.

Settle Whose you are.

Beyond who we are—wildly loved and rescued by God—we must settle Whose we are. We are no longer enslaved in the realm of Satan's domain. We are not his servants, or even servants of our own sin. We are God's children. "And because we are his children, God has sent the Spirit of his Son into our hearts, prompting us to call out, 'Abba, Father'" (Galatians 4:6). We have an intimate relationship with the God who wants us to call Him Daddy. We are directly born into God's family when we give our lives to Him. "Yet to all who did receive him, to those who believed in his name, he gave the right to become children of God—children born not of natural descent, nor of human decision or a husband's will, but born of God" (John 1:12-13 NIV).

In light of that truth, we need not fear. We don't need to walk around with our heads hung low, fretting about our sins, giving in to temptation day upon day. We can live in light of God's astounding adoption of us. "For all who are led by the Spirit of God are children of God. So you have not received a spirit that makes you fearful slaves. Instead, you received God's Spirit when he adopted you as his own children. Now we call him, 'Abba, Father'" (Romans 8:14-15).

Settle the questions.

One of the most helpful ways to move beyond a repetitive sin or addiction is to ask yourself questions like:

- Why does this sin appeal to me?
- What do I gain by participating in this sin?
- What need am I trying to fill in myself by doing this sin?
- Who do I become (that I like) when I do this sin?
- Who do I become (that I don't like) when I do this sin?
- What would freedom from this sin look like?
- Do I really want to be free from this sin?
- How does my sin affect those I love?
- What does God feel about this sin?
- Why does God call this particular sin a sin?

- What harm does this sin bring to me?
- What are the long-term consequences of my sin?
- How does living in this sin affect my ministry to others?
- How does living in this sin affect my family life?
- What shame lies beneath this sin?
- Why can't I stop choosing this sin?
- Did someone model this sinful behavior to me?
- How have I asked the Holy Spirit to overcome this sin?
- Have I invited others into my struggle, or have I kept it secret, trying to conquer it alone?
- Have I acknowledged my helplessness to conquer this sin in my own strength?
- How has this sin prevented me from truly living my life for Jesus?
- What do I feel God has not given me that makes this sin so appealing?
- Where have I lacked faith in regard to this sin?
- Who are the people in my life influencing me to sin?
- When have I listened to the lies of the enemy that say I'll finally be happy, satisfied, fulfilled, and complete if I sin?
- Have I so totally given in to my sin that I no longer feel lovable to others? God?
- What lies have I believed about my standing with God because of this sin?

Self-examination is part of the journey toward conquering repetitive sin. Spend some time with a pen and paper and answer these questions honestly. Ask Jesus to meet you where you are, in your pain and frustration. Ask Him for His perspective on your walk with Him. Ask that He will give you a deeper understanding of His holiness and a true desire for repentance. Pray for a desire to live right, not just to check things off on your Christian to-do list, but because you deeply love Him. The more you look at Him instead of harboring your sin, the more you'll grow in your desire to have a close, intimate walk with Him and the less Satan's hold on your life will be.

Settle your helplessness.

But as you walk through this time of self-examination, trying to figure out why this set of sins has a hold on you, you must settle your helplessness. Roy Hession contrasts the hold of sin versus our need for brokenness: "For sin is like an octopus. Its tentacles are everywhere. It has a thousand lives and a thousand shapes, and by perpetually changing its shape it eludes capture. If we are to see sin in all its subtle shapes and forms, and prove the power of Jesus to save us from it, we need to pray daily: Keep me broken, keep me watching at the cross where Thou hast died." [2]

We are weak. He is strong.

We can't do it. He can.

We are helpless. He is the Helper.

If we think we'll be able to pull ourselves up by our spiritual bootstraps and conquer sin, we're sorely mistaken.

Paul talks often about our weakness being a place for God to display His strength. Problem is, we spend a lot of our lives trying to make ourselves strong. Yet God seeks our dependence, not our independence. Independence is self-centeredness simplified. Jerry Rankin states, "We need to realize that blatant, immoral evil is no worse than a self-centered life. All rebellion against God and living for self deprives God of His glory and is contrary to His will." [3]

Settle the bigger story.

It's not just that we need to settle our helplessness. After that comes the important step of surrender, giving up, letting go. The Christian life does not consist of us micromanaging our reputations; it's about us surrendering to God's ways. To finally place ourselves before the Lord, begging Him for help. To recognize that He is big and we are small. To surrender to His kingship as we crawl off the throne of our own mess-making.

But surrender has another component. After surrender comes a going-after. Once we realize we've gone astray, not living according to who we are or Whose we are, we must replace our pursuit of sin with our pursuit of the things of God—first His heart, and then His plans. We must pursue a different, dynamic story. As I think on a friend of mine who is currently living in hellacious sin, devastating to his family, I can't help but think he's living a lesser story. He's given up and started pursuing pleasure in all the wrong places. As I pray for him, I ask God to woo him to that better story. A pursuing of the things of God, the adventure of risky faith.

It's not enough to merely turn our back on sin, but we must turn toward the God who ultimately fulfills us, then surrender ourselves to His outrageous story. And that story involves the re-creation of our hearts. Jesus spoke about the importance of heart, how we must be filled first with Him, how He came to change our hearts from the inside out. Consider this story from Mark 7:17-23:

> Then Jesus went into a house to get away from the crowd, and his disciples asked him what he meant by the parable he had just used. "Don't you understand either?" he asked. "Can't you see that the food you put into your body cannot defile you? Food doesn't go into your heart, but only passes through the stomach and then goes into the sewer." (By saying this, he declared that every kind of food is acceptable in God's eyes.) And then he added, "It is what comes from inside that defiles you. For from within, out of a person's heart, come evil thoughts, sexual immorality, theft, murder, adultery, greed, wickedness, deceit, lustful desires, envy, slander, pride, and foolishness. All these vile things come from within; they are what defile you."

To pursue a new story means seeking God for that new heart. He granted that when we came to first know Him, but He grants it afresh when we humbly ask again. He can cleanse. He can heal. He can renew. He can give us a new today, so that our lives are spent not in chasing the trinkets of sin, but in yielding fruit from a healed, settled heart. John 15:16 reminds us that, "You did not choose me, but I chose you and appointed you so that you might go and bear fruit—fruit that will last—and so that whatever you ask in my name the Father will give you" (NIV). From His divine initiation, He chose us. Not to give in to a reckless sin over and over again, but to something higher, a greater pursuit, the best story. He gives us the power and the privilege to bear fruit.

Note that I haven't spent a lot of time in this chapter talking about

Satan's story or his tactics. He can cleverly entice and hook us into sinning, but he is helpless against us living a better story. The more we concentrate on our sin or Satan's ability to mess with us, the better he likes it. When we lay down our pride, ask God for help, then live a better story, we diminish Satan's influence. He becomes a flitting pest, something we swat away in annoyance, and his power suddenly diminishes in the light of God's great power and the amazing life He beckons us to.

One last note: Remember community.

Concealed sin prospers and flourishes. Revealed sin weakens its resolve. To truly be set free from addictive behavior and repetitive sin, we must be willing to share our hearts in community. (Read more about that in chapter 23.) It takes humility to share our addictions or repetitive sins with close friends, but the reward is accountability, prayer on our behalf, and a secret let loose. Freedom comes from living in the light.

Mind if I pray for you?

God above all this crazy world, please bring order from our chaotic lives. Help us to see where we follow after sin instead of chasing You. I pray for my sister today, that You would use the questions in this chapter to help her identify the root of her bent toward sin and addiction. Reveal Your love for her as she explores the reasons why. I pray now that she would deliberately choose to turn away from that which ensnares her, to kick Satan from the foothold she's given him. Restore, restore, restore, Lord Jesus. Amen.

Chapter 19

When the Mouth Becomes a Weapon

The tongue has the power of life and death,
and those who love it will eat its fruit.

Proverbs 18:21 NIV

Words are powerful. They define who we are, who God is, how we relate to the world. And words have merit as women warriors engage in spiritual warfare. Often it's words that assail us. We use words when we face the Enemy. Words are the vehicle with which we entreat the Almighty God. It's important, then, that we first determine what words are not.

Words are not magical.

Some believe that wielding words in certain ways maneuvers God to do what we want, as if we can incant a special spell over the Almighty. Others mention words being the force of faith, that our words will determine what we believe and receive. While it's true that we must cultivate faith and speak words that coincide with that faith, it's *not* true that words alone determine what God gives or what He takes away. Our goal in this life is not to manipulate God to get things. It's to glorify Him and enjoy Him forever.

Words are not careless.

They mean something, whether we speak them over a child, sing them to Jesus, or whisper them to no one. Sticks and stones are better than ill-meaning words. Words have the power to slay a person, to ruin a day, to plunge a warrior woman toward depression. Therefore, we must be wise in the way we speak.

Words are not everything.

We can say all sorts of well-meaning words about our love for our family or our care for a friend, but if those words aren't backed by praxis (the practical working out of those words), our words lose all meaning.

Words are not defining.

How many of us have nurtured some untrue words close to our hearts, believing them, only to find out they weren't in the least bit true? I know a woman whose family convinced her she was shy and withdrawn. For years she believed those words, only to break out of her shell and become an extrovert. She defied the words spoken over her, but when she regrouped with her family of origin, they still held to those untrue words.

What are words, then? And how do they relate to our spiritual battle as women?

When we say a lot of words, sin lurks.

When we let go of self-control, one of the fruits of the Holy Spirit, we let loose our tongue. And when it flaps, we sin—something that makes Satan happy. The writer of Ecclesiastes warns us, "Do not be quick with your mouth, do not be hasty in your heart to utter anything before God. God is in heaven and you are on earth, so let your words be few" (Ecclesiastes 5:2 NIV). James equates the validity of our Christianity with our control of the tongue. "If you claim to be religious but don't control your tongue, you are fooling yourself, and your religion is worthless" (James 1:26).

Words have eternal significance.

The words we say count, not just in this moment, but for eternity. In the cosmic battle between God and Satan, culminating in the Day of Judgment, words last. Jesus warned, "You must give an account on judgment day for every idle word you speak. The words you say will either acquit you or condemn you" (Matthew 12:36-37).

Words can bring healing to a broken world.

One thing Satan hates is healing. Our words can bring healing to many, if we choose to take time to speak or write or encourage specifically. "Don't use foul or abusive language. Let everything you say be good and helpful, so that your words will be an encouragement to those who hear them" (Ephesians 4:29). Our words not only build up people fighting discouragement, but they advance God's kingdom. We can share Jesus with those who don't yet know Him. We can pray for someone who suffers. All those acts involve the risk of words.

Words reveal what's in our hearts.

Jesus said it's not the food we eat—what we take into our bodies—but the words we say that determine what is in our hearts. Therefore, it's important we examine those words as a barometer of where we are with Jesus. Having this type of self-examination grows us, pushes us to follow Jesus more closely.

Our ability to capture our thoughts and words is spiritual warfare.

Our thoughts are words strung together in our minds. And those thoughts may be wholesome or unwholesome. Part of a warrior woman's daily task is to capture the unwholesome thoughts, ask for forgiveness, and ask God to fill us with His thoughts. Paul writes, "We demolish arguments and every pretension that sets itself up against the knowledge of God, and we take captive every thought to make it obedient to Christ" (2 Corinthians 10:5 NIV).

Arguments and speculations are the devil's tools.

When we give in to argumentation and pick fights, we fight against what God wants to do in unbelievers' lives. If we want to dent the kingdom of darkness, we can positively influence people toward Christ, not through argument, but through kindness and humility. Consider Paul's sage advice: "Again I say, don't get involved in foolish, ignorant arguments that only start fights. A servant of the Lord must not quarrel but must be kind to everyone, be able to teach, and be patient with difficult people. Gently instruct those who oppose the truth. Perhaps God will change those people's hearts, and they will learn the truth. Then they will come to their senses and escape from the devil's trap. For they have been held captive by him to do whatever he wants" (2 Timothy 2:23-26).

One little word shall fell him.

Martin Luther's enigmatic hymn, "A Mighty Fortress Is Our God," contains the following stanza:

The prince of darkness grim—We tremble not for him;
His rage we can endure, for lo! his doom is sure,
One little word shall fell him.

People have speculated what that "one little word" could be. Luther is
reported to have said the word is "liar," though others believe the word to
be "Jesus." Regardless of its meaning, Satan can be felled with God's Word
by the person of Jesus. And it is true that Satan is a liar. We need not wran-
gle about with elaborate phraseology when we're engaged in spiritual warfare. Simply saying the name of Jesus or resting in His shed blood is enough.

How does a theology of words translate into the everyday life of the warrior woman? Here is one example, ripped from the pages of the DeMuth
family in France. Around the dinner table, for hours at a time, we argued
with our French friends. They argued with us and with each other. And
then we loved each other, kissed each cheek, and went along with our days.
At first the argumentation really bothered me. How dare my friends question my politics in such a vehement manner? How could they be so direct—
and yet, after the conversation, sidle up next to me, kiss both cheeks, and
joyfully continue being my friend?

The French tend to argue to understand, to share a part of themselves, to
put things out on the table, to stimulate a lively discussion. Sometimes they
play devil's advocate just to stir the pot. I'm not saying this is right or wrong,
just different. In America when folks argue, there has to be a "right" person.
In order for that person to be "right," he or she has to decimate the other
person's opinion. There's inherent fear behind everything. If I'm not "right,"
then something about me must be wrong. Therefore, I must find blame in
the other person's way of looking at things so I can feel secure. Right.

I've been deeply insecure about my opinions to the extent that I felt
I needed to undermine other people's opposite opinions just to feel okay.
Hopefully I'm growing. Hopefully I'm seeing that life is far too complex
and opinions too multilayered to have such a black-and-white perspective. And through all that, I think about Jesus.

We see Jesus sharing words with people who had vastly different life-
styles from what was considered holy in His day. Tax collectors and sinners
flocked to Him. He seemed to invite them near. Children ran to His irresistibility. He was not afraid of their opinions. He always spoke the truth,

but seasoned it with grace. He kept His harshest, most pointed words for those who appeared religious but were hypocritical, but He kept such an invitational stance to the masses that thousands of people followed Him.

My question: Do we represent the irresistibility of Jesus when we talk to people who differ from us? Would Jesus yell at someone who differed in her political opinion? Would He lash out? Would He scream? Does hollering and pouting and stirring up fear represent Jesus's manner of doing things? Warrior women are more winsome like Jesus when we listen, when we hold back our temper, when we choose not to stir up strife for the sake of proving our correctness. Our job is not to convince others of their wrongness and our rightness. It's not to change people's hearts— only God can do that. Our job is to represent Jesus, how He talked, how He acted, how He loved.

We should be so settled in His love for us that very little threatens us or shakes us up. We know how to entrust ourselves to God. We know how to wrestle. We know how to trust. And we know how to speak words of life, refrain from speaking for the sake of others, and use our words to praise God. Worship doesn't only happen when we're singing songs to Jesus. We worship God with our words in the day-to-day bustle of life. And we declare Whose we are to a world that desperately needs words of life.

Mind if I pray for you?

Lord, words are great and terrible and joyful and painful. Help my friend be a purveyor of strong, encouraging words. When she's attacked, I pray You would give her the divine gift of silence. When she wants to verbally assail someone, may Your Holy Spirit restrain her mouth from speaking. May her words today be seasoned with grace. And may she incline her ear today to hear Your amazing words, to truly and finally believe how much You love her. In that confidence, I pray You would enable her to use her words wisely. Amen.

Chapter 20

When Overt Attack Assails You

But you belong to God, my dear children. You have already
won a victory over those people, because the Spirit who lives
in you is greater than the spirit who lives in the world.

1 JOHN 4:4

When overt spiritual attack strikes, we tend to panic. I know I do. When I realized my youngest was hearing voices, I pressed the panic button far too many times. Why? Because the situation was scary. I didn't know how to navigate such an evil, all-out attack against my sweet, fun-loving girl. But in one way the attack made sense. Julia was not yet a Christ-follower.

Consider the surprise and shock we encounter when Satan attacks a believer. I knew a mom, Cathy, whose Christian daughter had a profound personality change after being exposed to a friend who dabbled in the occult. God had firmly shut a door on ministry in Cathy's life—a huge disappointment—and the family spent their last moments in ministry mourning. On the car ride home from the final event, her daughter Ellen started growling, then spewing belligerence from the backseat. It was such a profound change from her peace-loving, Jesus-following child, that Cathy turned around to see the eighth-grader's eyes and tell her to knock it off.

What Cathy saw was not her daughter. Ellen's normally happy self dissolved, her eyes defiant. No matter what Cathy said, Ellen barked back disobedient words. Then she kicked the back of Cathy's seat, although Cathy told her firmly to stop. Later, after the event in the car, Cathy found out that Ellen had also tried to open the back door. If she'd been successful, she'd most likely have caused her own death because the road they traveled had a severe ravine on the right side of the car.

When they arrived home, Ellen's exasperated father told her to go to her room. In that moment, Cathy felt the Lord tell her to follow Ellen and not to leave her side. So she did. She sat opposite Ellen on her bed, noting her blank, yet defiant, stare. Cathy prayed. Nothing. She shared her heart. Still no response. Where had Ellen gone? And why was she acting this way? Although she knew something sinister lurked beneath, she felt helpless to stop it. Eventually, she said the name of Jesus over and over again, knowing only Jesus could cut through whatever her daughter faced.

Suddenly Ellen pulled in a long breath. Her eyes morphed from distant to alive. She looked at Cathy, then said, "Mom, how did I get home?"

"We drove home in the car," Cathy said.

In that moment, Ellen cried. "I'm so sorry, Mom. It's like I knew what I was doing but I was helpless to stop it."

Cathy held her daughter, then prayed for her. Three days later they moved away. Ellen has never had an encounter like it since.

What confused Cathy is what would confuse us. We know Satan is powerful. We know he has demons at his beck and call. But can he possess a believer? Why did Ellen, who dearly loved Jesus, fall prey to such a severe attack?

Doctor Michael Pocock, a professor at Dallas Theological Seminary, believes that Christians can be influenced by demons. "I don't think that they're possessed, but the symptoms are very, very similar. They're not possessed because they're not owned. They are not a possession of Satan. They are a possession of Christ. So possession is not quite the issue, but control could be. And if they are controlled then they may manifest quite similarly to a person who is possessed."[1]

Another point to consider: if Satan can have no access to a believer, then why do we have Paul's admonition to put on the full armor of God? We wear armor because attack is imminent. Ellen must've laid down her armor, and she allowed her own anger about the dissolving ministry situation to become a doorway for demonic influence. We are no different. Our sinful responses to difficult situations can become open doors for Satanic attack.

So what do we do when Satan or his demons blatantly attack us? We find the answer in Scripture.

In 1 Samuel 7:1-12, we see the Israelites facing a formidable foe: the Philistines. And we see a wise prophet, Samuel, guide them through a scary confrontation. Read the Scripture, then glean understanding from the insights in italics.

"So the men of Kiriath-jearim came to get the Ark of the LORD. They took it to the hillside home of Abinadab and ordained Eleazar, his son, to be in charge of it. The Ark remained in Kiriath-jearim for a long time—20 years in all. During that time all Israel mourned because it seemed the LORD had abandoned them."

The Ark was the sign of God being with them, yet it no longer resided within the Israelite camp. This was cause for great mourning. However, the truth is that God does not abandon His people. They may have felt that way, but that feeling wasn't based on truth. Therefore, when we face spiritual battle, we need to remember God's constant availability and His ability to come alongside us, even when it doesn't appear He is there. That's the basis of faith, to believe even when we don't see.

Also note that God doesn't rebuke them for being in a state of lamentation. Perhaps He wants the Israelites' pain and bewilderment to lead them to Himself. Perhaps right now, God is allowing His seeming absence to produce a deep longing in you for Himself.

"Then Samuel said to all the people of Israel, 'If you are really serious about wanting to return to the LORD, get rid of your foreign gods and your images of Ashtoreth. Determine to obey only the LORD; then he will rescue you from the Philistines.' So the Israelites got rid of their images of Baal and Ashtoreth and worshiped only the LORD."

Samuel wanted to test the mettle of the Israelites' faith. He asked them to get rid of their foreign gods and idols. Before you go any further, take some time to identify and turn away from your idols (see chapter 9). Once you feel free from those idols, tell Jesus you're sorry for worshiping other things, and that you want to worship Him alone, particularly through this situation.

"Then Samuel told them, 'Gather all of Israel to Mizpah, and I will pray to the LORD for you.' So they gathered at Mizpah and, in a great ceremony, drew water from a well and poured it out before the LORD."

The Israelites allowed Samuel to pray for them. Sometimes we need to invite others into the battle on our behalf. And in the case of Samuel, there are times when the conflict is too overwhelming, so we need a leader to step beside us to intercede. And sometimes God asks us to pour something precious out before Him as a sacrifice. Maybe our addiction to food, believing it alone will satisfy, has become way too important to us. Perhaps giving up sugar or processed foods is part of our sacrifice.

"They also went without food all day and confessed that they had sinned against the LORD. (It was at Mizpah that Samuel became Israel's judge.)"

The Israelites fasted. They deprived themselves of food for the sake of having clear focus on what God required of them. This led to confession. In that place of worry and pain, they turned their eyes from the Philistines to their own internal enemy: their sin. As we engage in spiritual warfare, it's imperative we fast from something (food, TV, computer, music) in order to hear clearly from God about our sin. Then we can confess our sins to God and to each other.

"When the Philistine rulers heard that Israel had gathered at Mizpah, they mobilized their army and advanced. The Israelites were badly frightened when they learned that the Philistines were approaching. 'Don't stop pleading with the LORD our God to save us from the Philistines!' they begged Samuel. So Samuel took a young lamb and offered it to the LORD as a whole burnt offering. He pleaded with the LORD to help Israel, and the LORD answered him."

The Israelites show how common it is for us to become frightened. They asked Samuel to keep praying for them. One of the most beautiful parts of our New Covenant relationship with Christ is that we have an Advocate in the Holy Spirit. He enables us to pray when things are scary. He intercedes for us, much like Samuel interceded for the frightened nation of Israel. Samuel also offered something to God—a sacrifice. The completed picture of Jesus on the cross provides another staggering realization. God's Son became our sacrifice. So not only do we have the benefit of the Spirit interceding for us, but Jesus became our once-and-for-all perfect sacrifice.

"Just as Samuel was sacrificing the burnt offering, the Philistines arrived to attack Israel. But the LORD spoke with a mighty voice of thunder from heaven that day, and the Philistines were thrown into such confusion that the Israelites defeated them. The men of Israel chased them from Mizpah to a place below Beth-car, slaughtering them all along the way."

It's important to remember that the beautiful battle belongs to the Lord, not to us. He routed the Philistines. His voice conquered the mighty army. The Israelites played their part, but only after God had routed the enemy. The name and power of Jesus cannot be underestimated. As in Cathy's case, saying His name eventually led to her daughter snapping out of her funk.

"Samuel then took a large stone and placed it between the towns of Mizpah and Jeshanah. He named it Ebenezer (which means 'the stone of help'), for he said, 'Up to this point the LORD has helped us!'"

In the aftermath of victory, Samuel created a memorial so the Israelites would remember that God is mighty and able to fight their enemies. So many times we forget what God has done. When a fresh attack comes, we don't remember the great victories God has wrought in the past.

Building a remembrance (whether you write down what God has done, place an object on your desk to remind you, or take a picture of something mighty God has accomplished) will help you withstand the next attack. What is your Ebenezer? Take a moment to think through a recent spiritual victory. Can you find a physical representation of that victory? Place it somewhere you can see. Remind yourself of the God who speaks and enemies scatter. Remember the importance of letting go of your idols. As you see your Ebenezer, repent, then entrust yourself to the God who fights on your behalf.

When you're in the midst of overt spiritual attack, sometimes the stress of that can mire you in worry or cause you to forget just how big and capable God is. Next time you face it, remember the acronym PREVAIL.
In the midst of overt attack, I can be sure that God is:

- **P**owerful. He is greater than Satan, greater than any attack. He is higher than the angels. His power created the earth, the sky, the heavens. His Son conquered death.

- **R**edemptive. Because of Jesus Christ's sacrifice on the cross and His subsequent resurrection, He will redeem you. Not only that, but He will take your difficult circumstances and work them out for your good and His glory.

- **E**ternal. God has always existed. He knows your past, present, and future, and discerns your story in its entirety. Therefore, He is able to come alongside you with perfect wisdom in whatever attack you face. He takes in the long view.

- **V**ictorious. In the end, the devil and his demons will be cast into the lake of fire. Today, God has triumphed over sin and death. In light of that, no matter what comes our way as warrior women, we know that ultimately God has the victory.

- **A**vailable. God's availability is closer than our own skin. His

Holy Spirit lives within us, helping us stand firm in our faith against the onslaughts of the evil one.

- **Intelligent.** God is the most intelligent being in the universe. Therefore, He can offer supernatural wisdom as you face the lies of the Enemy.

- **Loyal.** God is a covenant-keeping God. He is utterly loyal to you, bound to you by the blood of His Son Jesus Christ. In that new covenant, God promises to lead you not into temptation, but to give you power to stand against Satan and his hordes, to enable you to walk in victory. He will never leave you, never forsake you.

Concentrating on God's ability to prevail in spiritual warfare is a better tactic than studying Satan's wily ways. We as warrior women must become students of our amazing God, resting once again in His power over every enemy.

———

Mind if I pray for you?

Lord, I pray for my sister who is undergoing overt attack right now. Open her eyes to how big You are and how small the enemy is. Help her not to pay attention to all the commotion Satan causes, but to quiet herself and listen solely to Your still, quiet voice. Deliver her from her enemy, Lord. Speak truth into her heart when she doubts and worries. If she fights on her knees on behalf of a loved one, I pray You would give her specific prayers to pray, and definitive ways to act that will show her loved one how loving, big, and strong You really are. We thank You that You ultimately prevail over the dominion of darkness. And we choose today to believe You see us as warfare rages. You are our very present help in times of distress and we rest our lives in Your capable hands right now. Amen.

Part Four

VICTORY:
We Can Live with Hope When the Beautiful Battle Rages

We've taken a long journey together. We've learned the theological underpinnings of spiritual warfare, defining our Enemy and understanding the power of God against him. We've seen how a warrior woman can live proactively, daily walking with Jesus, confident in her standing before God. We've tackled spiritual warfare as it happens and learned how to react in the moment. I've given you many tools to walk as a warrior woman. But there's more. Life is not merely about this cosmic battle. It's also about living victoriously with joy and confidence despite our sometimes-bent toward sin, the painful circumstances of our lives, or Satan's malicious attacks. Let's end our time together thinking on joy and God's ability to bring victory.

Chapter 21

Overcoming in Community

God displays His wisdom not through you by yourself or
me by myself. He chooses instead to reveal His wisdom
through you and me together as the church.

Mary DeMuth

You will not overcome the Enemy's attacks all by yourself—you need the body of Christ. Why? Because the Christian life is not meant to be lived in isolation. In isolation, we keep secrets so dark they consume us. In isolation, we convince ourselves of things that aren't true. In isolation, we have no balance. In isolation, we grovel in shame.

Recently, I endured an overt spiritual attack while my husband and I walked through a misunderstanding. After a few hours of stewing and not talking to him, I decided that I couldn't live in this controversy without another perspective, so I e-mailed two good friends to see if they were available to talk the next day. By God's sheer grace, Patrick and I worked our way through our misunderstanding. I didn't end up meeting with my friends, but their prayers certainly infused the situation. Please note that I had no intention of going behind Patrick's back—I simply needed prayer and perspective. My own mind started going wonky in the midst of our disagreement, so much so that I briefly entertained the idea of canceling a long-anticipated anniversary date. In isolation, I could've given in to theatrics, canceled the date, and made things painful between us. By inviting two trusted friends into my pain, I was able to stop, rest, and think through the situation logically.

In America we tend to view our Christianity through an individualized lens. It's all about me, my relationship with Jesus, and how I can pull myself up by my bootstraps and live the Christian life. And yet there's so much more. We miss out on God's supernatural provision by neglecting to believe the church is Jesus's body on earth, by not wrestling through our issues in community. Hebrews 10:25 admonishes us: "Let us not neglect our meeting together, as some people do, but encourage one another, especially now that the day of his return is drawing near."

In 1 Peter 2:4-5, Peter writes, "You are coming to Christ, who is the living cornerstone of God's temple. He was rejected by people, but he was chosen by God for great honor. And you are living stones that God is building into his spiritual temple. What's more, you are his holy priests. Through the mediation of Jesus Christ, you offer spiritual sacrifices that please God." Jesus's temple on earth is us, the church. We, together, are His priests. *Together*, the church conquers hell's powers. When Jesus spoke of the dawning of the church, he told Peter, "I will build my church, and all the powers of hell will not conquer it" (Matthew 16:18). The powers of hell will not conquer a holy church, which proves the power believers have in community.

Isolated we fail.

Together we not only stand, but we also advance the kingdom of God.

I never cease to be surprised by the unbreakable connection between community and spiritual warfare. Read Ephesians 3:10-11 carefully. Then read it again, asking God to open your eyes. "God's purpose in all this was to use the church to display his wisdom in its rich variety to all the unseen rulers and authorities in the heavenly places. This was his eternal plan, which he carried out through Christ Jesus our Lord." God displays His wisdom not through you by yourself or me by myself. He chooses instead to reveal His wisdom through you and me together as the church. To whom does He display His attributes? The devil, the angels, both unfallen and fallen. But He does so through the church.

When we lived in France, as I mentioned earlier, our daughter Julia began to hear voices. If Satan wanted to attack us, of course he would directly afflict the one person in our family who had no relationship (yet) with Jesus. And he knew that if he attacked our child, we, the parents, would despair. We did worry. We prayed. We gathered our community around us and prayed. We e-mailed friends back home and they prayed. We shared Jesus with Julia several times.

What transpired shows the beauty and surprise of how God delivers through the body of Christ. Patrick and I had to fly to Lisbon for a leaders' summit, but we worried about what we would do with our kids. We didn't yet have strong enough relationships in France to entrust our children to folks for a week, so we made a plea to our home church. By God's grace and beauty, Cyndi and Nancy decided to sacrifice by coming to France and watching our children while we were away. Both moms with hearts for the nations, we were thrilled to have them. Cyndi also brought along her homeschooled daughter Bethany, then 12 years old.

When they arrived, we pulled them aside and told them what Julia had been experiencing. Sometimes she'd lash out at her siblings. Sometimes she'd wake in the middle of the night, afraid. Sometimes she'd act completely out of character with no explanation.

We left for Lisbon with our hearts heavy. We worried about Julia and how she'd act with Cyndi, Nancy, and Bethany. We prayed. We asked the congregation of leaders to pray. And then we got the best phone message we've ever received.

We'd been in a strategy session all morning with our cell phones off. Patrick turned it on and checked his messages—he had just one. Julia. She said, "Mommy and Daddy, I just wanted to let you know that I invited Jesus into my heart today." I cried when I heard her sweet, quiet voice, saying those important words.

When we arrived home, we learned what had happened. On one particularly taxing day Julia had acted out yet again, so 12-year-old Bethany asked her if she'd like to go to her room to talk. Julia nodded. Bethany shared Jesus with her, letting her know that if she met Jesus, the voices that tormented her would go away. Julia agreed. So Bethany prayed with her to receive Jesus.

When I approached Julia, I had a bit of reticence. What if she still heard voices? What would we do then? Although I believed firmly that the devil couldn't possess her now that she loved Jesus, I knew he could still influence her. So I asked, "Julia, are you still hearing voices?"

"Well," she said, "I am, but it's one voice. And He's telling me to make wise choices."

I let out my breath while tears raced down my cheeks. "That's the Holy Spirit, honey," I told her.

Our daughter's battle involved the body of Christ. God, in His surprising plan, used an American 12-year-old to bring Julia to Himself. His method of deliverance involved community. And for that, our family is forever grateful.

How else can we engage with the body of Christ to gain spiritual victories? By building one of the greatest sources of encouragement for Christian women: our friendships.

Whether we're sensing hormones for the first time in a rush of I-need-chocolate adrenaline or we're flashing red with night sweats, we think about our girlfriends or our lack of meaningful friends. With an increasingly mobile society as our backdrop and a life scheduled to the nanosecond, we seldom take time to develop one of God's beautiful gifts—women's friendship. In that, a few cautions.

Don't neglect your first love.

Unfortunately, when I need help I tend to text a friend rather than hitting my knees and crying out to the Maker of all friendships. Author Dee Brestin expands this notion in *The Friendships of Women*: "As women, our tendency toward dependency on people is our Achilles' heel. We forget that our only security is God, and we trust instead in each other."[1]

I've been smothered by women, and I've smothered others. I now realize that keeping my friendship with Jesus first is the best thing I can do for my friends. I need to run to Jesus, flooding Him with my worries and fears because He is the only One who won't leave me. Psalm 9:10 puts it beautifully: "Those who know your name trust in you, for you, O LORD, do not abandon those who search for you."

A few years ago, I wore out my friend Stacey with constant neediness. Instead of companion, I made her chief counselor and called her whenever I felt tears sting my eyes. In love, she said, "Mary, you need to turn to Jesus first. Only He can heal your heart. I'm happy to be here for you, but I can't be Jesus. Turn to Him." Her words seared my heart—the way words do when they burn truth. It's been a wonderfully excruciating journey to set the phone back down and instead call on Jesus. My strained relationship with Stacey mended after I repented of making her an idol and turned to the jealous God who wanted all my heart.

Be open to surprising friendships.

I've been surprised by the friendships the Lord has placed in my life—more often because they are not the friends I initially thought would become lifelong companions. Like Samuel, I've been taken aback by friends who come wrapped in unusual packages. "The LORD doesn't see things the way you see them. People judge by outward appearance, but the LORD looks at the heart" (1 Samuel 16:7).

God designed the Body of Christ to grow up together.

Heidi, one of my dearest friends, was not someone with whom I initially had much affinity. She enjoyed fixing cars; I fixed gourmet meals. In the initial stages of our friendship, we played a gentle tug-of-war with our personalities. At one point, we separated.

But God had other plans. After nearly ten years of only sporadic communication, Heidi called and wanted to visit our family in Texas. She played with my children as if they were her own. We connected deeply that summer week as we talked about her new friend, Mike. When she went home, Mike became her fiancé. That Christmas, I stood next to her as her only attendant when she said her vows.

Corrie ten Boom said, "Every experience God gives us, every person he puts in our lives is the perfect preparation for a future that only He can see."[2] Today, Heidi is one of my closest friends. She is someone who will drop everything and pray for me.

Seek friends who sanctify.

Although I sometimes wish the sanctification process would occur in a vacuum, I've come to understand that God uses friendships to make us more like Him.

God designed the Body of Christ to grow up together: "He makes the whole body fit together perfectly. As each part does its own special work, it helps the other parts grow, so that the whole body is healthy and growing and full of love" (Ephesians 4:16). How beautiful that Scripture sounds! How hard it is to implement! Especially when some people in Jesus's fold are hard to love.

Mattie phoned and told me she'd be flying to visit me for a week. My calendar was beyond full. Still, I cleared some things and tried to make her stay enjoyable. It was not. Through tears, she told me how selfish I'd been not to spend more time with her. When she got home, she returned all the letters I'd ever sent her and ended our friendship. Although I knew her reaction was a bit extreme, I thought about my selfishness. Echoes of her rebuke stay with me, teaching me the dangers of me-centered living.

The most important friendship lesson we learn is forgiveness. I had to forgive Mattie for sending back my letters, just as she has (hopefully) forgiven me for my selfishness. Not only does God's amazing forgiveness affect eternity—we can now go to heaven because of the gift of His Son on the cross—but it also enables us to forgive those friends who have wounded us.

Having a high view of the body of Christ enriches our friendships—past, present, and future. It empowers us to cling to the God who dares to call us His friend. It helps us anticipate new friends who often come in surprising packages. It opens our eyes to God's friend-shaped sanctification journey.

But even more than that, connecting deeply with people who love Jesus helps us overcome the schemes of the evil one. Jesus promised that He would be present when we gathered. "For where two or three gather together as my followers," Jesus said, "I am there among them" (Matthew 18:20).

And where He is present, we have victory.

—

Mind if I pray for you?

Jesus, You demonstrated just how important our relationships are. You poured life into 12 friends, and they, in turn, turned the world upside down. Help us to see the importance of surrounding ourselves with people who love You. I pray for the dear person reading this book, that You would open up new doors of friendship even today. Help her see not as man sees, but as You see. Open her up to surprising friendships. May You become her very best friend, and may that friendship become the springboard for healthy community. Heal the wounds that friends have inflicted. Help her forgive those who have wronged, and give her the holy courage to confess her sins to her friends and ask forgiveness when necessary. May her life be marked by deep love for Your body, Jesus. Move in and through her to touch many. And use her friends to minister peace and truth to her. Make her a woman of integrity in her relationships, Lord. Amen.

Chapter 22

Mountains and Valleys

*On the mountains I feel blissfully close to God's
presence, only to find myself parched and needy
in the step-by-step plodding of daily life.*

MARY DEMUTH

I'll call her Anne, as in *Anne of Green Gables*—a moody girl prone to bipolar disorder.

Anne's addiction to highs intrigued me at first. Not the sort of drug-induced highs tell-all books exploit. No, these were spiritual highs. She listened for God's whispers, straining to hear. And when He said His piece, she declared His presence in magnanimous language. "God spoke this to me. He told me this. I am forever changed!" She reveled in the rapture, and her elocution of God's spectacular endeavors seemed to stretch the truth.

But when He seemed far or fickle, she fell headlong into despair. She used language like, "Never has there been a more tragic day in my life," or "The devastation I experienced nearly killed me." Prone to theatrics and addicted to life-made-perfect, Anne is an exaggeration of all of us. Of me.

We need humility on the mountains, hope in the valleys. Anne had neither. And if I'm willing to admit it, I'm the same.

Still, I want the mountains. The elation of the climb. The craggy peaks with vistas aplenty. Forgetting that growth and character emerge from the valleys, I addict myself to that which will not grow me up. I believe Satan's subtle lie—that genuine life comes through continually experiencing highs and running far away from anything that smacks of a mountain's underbelly—the dreaded valley.

Mountains are metaphoric of God, His presence. David lifts his eyes to the hills from where his help comes. God resides in Mount Zion. We are told to ascend the mountain of the Lord. We equate God's spontaneous and amazing presence with the climb, the heights, the glory of His presence in thinner air. And indeed, the higher we climb, the closer we come to touching heaven, the nearer we are to tasting eternity. This is part of our pursuit, part of being a passionate Christ-follower.

Yet most of life happens in the ordinariness of the valleys, and this is where we tend to faint. On the mountains we feel blissfully close to God's presence, only to find ourselves parched and needy in the step-by-step plodding of daily life. Is it even possible to taste God in the dreary valleys? Or in the places we sense evil's presence or the temptation to despair?

Yes.

But how?

By understanding the secret of the *bisse* (pronounced "beese").

We spent a week in the Swiss Alps recuperating from our long and difficult years church planting in France. To rejuvenate and touch Jesus afresh, I took plenty of walks up hills, up mountains, along ridges. The vistas replenished me, reminding me of the Pacific Northwest where I spent my childhood. In the mountains I felt alive, close to God's presence. One morning, I took an easy run along a *bisse,* a small canal channeled from the heights to the lower four valleys beneath me. The valleys, quite green, used to be incredibly dry, devoid of water. In the 1400s, laborers spent decades digging shallow and long channels—*bisses*—about two feet deep and two feet wide, from the glaciers above to the valleys below. These *bisses* flowed gently, almost imperceptibly, downhill to supply the valleys with an abundance of clear, fresh water. There are trails along the *bisses* where you can easily hike with families and small children, so gentle their slope, so calming their sound.

Along the *bisse,* the Lord spoke to me. "You must dig in the valleys," He said, "in the ordinariness of life. That's where My presence will flow. To acquire it, you must labor." I thought of those folks in the Middle Ages who labored on behalf of the valleys below, how much sweat and toil it must've taken them to dig and dig and dig. Hardly glamorous work. But in order to harness the pure glacial water, it had to be done.

Here's the sad truth about me: I would rather scale a peak and drink from the glacier on top than dig ditches in the valleys, even though the valley is where I live most of the time, where I cultivate life with Jesus. Why do I experience a parched soul? Because I prefer alleluia-ing in the mountains to digging trenches in the valleys. I despise trials, suspecting them to interrupt the climb, when it's actually the trials on the trails that deepen my experience of God.

David spoke of valleys in the Psalms, including one very famous one called the Valley of the Shadow of Death, where evil lurks. "Even though I walk through the valley of the shadow of death," David writes, "I will fear no evil, for You are with me" (Psalm 23:4 NASB). The very next verse, David writes these amazing words: "You have anointed my head with oil; my cup overflows." An overflowing life happens in the valleys of death! The cup of our outlook can overflow in the midst of trials and temptations and warfare and duties and monotony. If we dare to carve out space for God, digging *bisses* in the valleys, we'll experience the overflowing of His presence even there.

We should not become passive consumers of God, waiting for other diggers to supply us with the waters of His presence.

But so often we settle for consuming mountaintop experiences to the detriment of our souls. Or we'll chase after things we think will satisfy because they seem like an easy way around digging ditches in the valleys.

So much of Western Christianity is passive. We go to church to sample the wares of the pastor. We grade our worship experience as it pertains to our own needs. We hop from place to place, looking to be filled. We buy into Satan's lie that church is about our needs, our wants, our preferences. We are consumers of church rather than active participants. This spills over into our spiritual lives. When we feel parched, we look for a mountain of a program to reorient us. We've abandoned the dogged pursuit of God, trading it for passive spirituality. We simply make ourselves available for others to fill us—to lead us to molehills.

But the folks in the 1400s didn't wait for the water to come to them from behemoth mountains. They dug. They labored. And so should we. If we feel distant from God, devoid of His available presence, it is up to us to pursue the heart of the Almighty, laboring to dig a *bisse* for His presence to flow through. It's not glamorous work; in fact, it's often unseen. We should not become passive consumers of God, waiting for other diggers to supply us with the waters of His presence. We are pilgrims on a journey, pursuing relationship with the One who made us, the One who wants to amply overflow us with the water of His presence—in the valleys.

Ease means others bring mountains to you.

But digging a *bisse* in the valley involves labor and pursuit—and sometimes a mountain glimpse. It's steady, rhythmic digging, not prone to Anne's bipolar mood swings. It's an affront to Satan's tactics, as it connotes a steadiness, a wherewithal, a holy tenacity to endure even when God seems distant.

Isn't that when Satan's lies seem the most delectable? When God appears far away, lofty on a mountain, while we muck it out in the valley? And yet, we are called to grow up. We are called to labor. We are called to love God even when He seems far. Psalm 131 gives us an instructive picture of our walk with God. It's a song about the journey upward toward Jerusalem. David prays, "LORD, my heart is not proud; my eyes are not haughty. I don't concern myself with matters too great or too awesome for me to grasp. Instead, I have calmed and quieted myself, like a weaned child who no longer cries for its mother's milk. Yes, like a weaned child is my soul within me. O Israel, put your hope in the LORD—now and always."

David has learned to grow. He has calmed himself even when things might be scary. And he has grown up. He is no longer a baby, needing the constant care of God. He has been weaned. He has learned to talk himself down. He is not what Paul accuses the Corinthians of being: a baby. "Dear brothers and sisters, when I was with you I couldn't talk to you as I would to spiritual people. I had to talk as though you belonged to this world or as though you were infants in the Christian life" (1 Corinthians 3:1). Though babies are adorable, they are also a host of other things. They are selfish, demanding milk when they're hungry. They're helpless, needing a parent constantly maintaining their needs. They're undiscerning, unable to know the difference between an electrical outlet and a toy. They're immature, unable to articulate their needs except by crying.

Look back over that list. Selfish. Helpless. Undiscerning. Immature. Pray over that list. Ask God to show you where you're a baby. Satan likes nothing more than for warrior women to embody selfishness, only concerning ourselves with what makes us happy or content. He would love us to kick aside our valor and instead insist on being rescued. He rejoices when we lack discernment and run headlong into unwise decisions or sinful behavior. He smiles when we grovel in immaturity.

Satan would love us to kick aside our valor
and instead insist on being rescued.

Growing up, living joyfully and strategically in the valleys, riles Satan. Which is why it's time we grew beyond infancy. This is not glamorous work. In good conscience, I can't write a spiritual warfare book full of hints and tricks about defeating Satan. Why? Because we must settle the deeper issue first. Are we willing to grow up? Are we willing to move beyond basic elemental belief?

What is holding you back from that kind of maturity?

Why bother with growth? Because growing up helps us discern the tactics of the evil one. Paul assures us that if we stay in infancy, we will not overcome Satan's subtle attacks—attacks which usually come through well-meaning people who seem trustworthy. But if we grow up, "we won't be tossed and blown about by every wind of new teaching. We will not be influenced when people try to trick us with lies so clever they sound like the truth" (Ephesians 4:14).

Growing up does not mean becoming a student of Satan's ways, lies, and methods, another reason why I don't elaborate extensively on Satan's activities and mindset in this book. Growing up means thinking rightly about God, even when He's hard to see. Paul further instructs the Corinthian believers, "Brothers, do not be children in your thinking. Be infants in evil, but in your thinking be mature" (1 Corinthians 14:20 ESV). We must grow up in the way we think— beyond selfishness, helplessness, an undiscerning mind, and immaturity. How do we grow? Through sheer, undecorated obedience. Paul boasts about the Roman believers who understood that maturity comes through obeying. "For the report of your obedience has reached to all; therefore I am rejoicing over you, but I want you to be wise in what is good and innocent in what is evil" (Romans 16:19 NASB). Again he confirms the importance of innocence in evil, yet cultivating wisdom in the things of God. And he commends the fame of their obedience.

This idea of growing wise in the ways of God and innocent of evil is not strictly a New Testament idea. Jeremiah warns, "'My people are foolish and do not know me,' says the LORD. 'They are stupid children who have no understanding. They are clever enough at doing wrong, but they have no idea how to do right!'" (Jeremiah 4:22). The prophet ties this idea of growing up to *doing* something: doing what is right.

It's time to stop playing at life. It's time to grow up into righteousness, a long word which simply means "right living." The author of Hebrews assures us, "For someone who lives on milk is still an infant and doesn't know how to do what is right" (Hebrews 5:13).

It's time to stop playing at life. It's time
to grow up into righteousness.

What does this look like as we grow? How can we dig deep in the valleys, grow up, and do what is right? I found the secret as I listened to a report about cowbells. One thing I already knew: Farmers placed cowbells on their cows to keep track of them. I learned this when we vacationed in Switzerland and heard the amazing cacophony of cowbells as bovines grazed on idyllic pastures.

But I didn't know this: Farmers are selective about which cows they adorn with a bell. They choose the smartest, wisest cow because they know the others will follow.

Could it be that God does the same with us? He places cowbells around the necks of those who are smart in the Spirit, who exercise wisdom. He entrusts those of us who grow beyond infancy, who dig in the valleys, with responsibility.

The problem: since we tend to like instant Christianity with instant success and instant holiness (oxymoronic as that is), we want God to place the cowbell around our necks when we're not ready. We want the glory of it without first demonstrating our worthiness for it. God is like the farmer, roaming His eyes across this vast herd of humanity, wanting to bestow His authority and power on those who take their relationship with Him seriously. Who understand that life in the Spirit is often unseen, unapplauded. Who cherish their integrity more than their reputation. Who are wise and kind and loving when no one sees.

Are you ready for that responsibility? Are you ready to wear your big girl pants, to become discerning about the things of God, becoming increasingly innocent of Satan's ways? Will God bestow the cowbell, adorning your neck with His confidence?

It's my sincere prayer that you are ready or are becoming ready. May it be that we are warrior women with strong arms, obedient hearts, tenacious joy. May it be that we are as dismissive about Satan as we are wildly passionate about God Almighty. May it be that we see our labor not in vain, but as a stepping-stone to deeper understanding of God's ways. May it be that we nurture others to grow up, to be strong, to take a stand. May we dig in the valleys, say yes to God, and be entrusted with God's holy cowbell.

Mind if I pray for you?

Lord, we want to be grown-ups. We want to be warrior women who dare to dig in the valleys—for our sakes and the sakes of those we love. Forgive us for our spiritual lethargy. I pray for my sister in Christ, that she would live a life worthy of the cowbell, that she would become a holy woman of influence, of sacrifice, of joy. Give her the gumption to obey You even when it hurts or when no one is looking. She is Your servant. Grant her some mountaintop moments. Help her chronicle and recount those when she walks through the valleys even now. Amen.

Chapter 23

Finding Abundance and Perspective

I came that they may have life, and have it abundantly.

JOHN 10:10 NASB

Six years ago, I left a place of abundance. In Dallas I had deep friend-ships, a lovely home, great kids in great schools, enough money, a life-giving church, significance in my writing work—everything a soul could want. I desperately wanted to be the kind of wife who followed her hus-band wherever he went, that supporting Proverbs 31 wife who sacrificed her dreams for a higher purpose, which, in this case, was church plant-ing in southern France. I wrestled with my tentative soul for a year before we left, trying to deny that I really didn't want to go. But the truth was, I didn't. One month before we left, I let out my worried heart, spilling it out before my surprised husband. I flat-out didn't want to go. As the French say, *pas du tout*. Not at all.

The Lord helped me then. He gave me enough strength to pack up our house, to look with a tiny glimpse of anticipation toward a small villa in Le Rouret, France. I hoped that life would be easier than I feared it would be once we landed, but as you know from my stories throughout the book, stress and difficulties ramped up from the get-go. I lost all my sense of abundance. My life did not overflow.

In France, I felt the very real and oppressive presence of Satan. I could nearly taste his presence. I let it settle into my spirit, pelting my joy. One particularly dark night, as a French believer named Marie placed a blanket over my shoulders, I was reminded afresh that I need not hold on to this spirit of heaviness. She read from Isaiah 61:3. *"L'huile de l'allégresse au lieu du deuil, et pour les vêtir d'habits de louange au lieu d'un esprit abattu"*—"The oil of gladness instead of mourning, the mantle of praise instead of a spirit of fainting" (NASB). At that dark time, I needed some of that oil! I needed to wear that praise mantle.

Through Marie, Jesus offered me glad oil and praise clothes. For a blessed moment, I saw that because Jesus was raised from the dead, I could sing praises. Because He lives, I could shed my mourning, replacing it with tangible joy. It was not easy. The truth is, I'm more apt to live like Puddle-glum from the Chronicles of Narnia, in a perpetual state of sadness—or Eeyore, always wondering why my tail has fallen off again. And yet, the sun shined on both—the glum Marsh-wiggle and the woe-is-me donkey. That day, when Marie spoke words of life over my deflated, defeated soul, I wrote a prayer:

Oh dear, sweet, amazing Jesus. This is what I pray today: Give me Your oil of gladness. Place Your cloak of laughter upon my shoulders because they are weary. Turn my gaze heavenward. Teach me the power and joy of praising You in a land where few do. I'm dreadfully needy, Lord. But You are the lifter of my head. Renew me, Jesus. Renew me. Come. Refresh. Rejuvenate me. Place Your hand upon my head; I want to hear Your whispers of approval, Your words of encouragement. I am ready. Amen.

I wrestled through the remainder of that year, fighting a battle within myself between despair and hope. And often, sad to say, despair won.

The Word

In the swirling pain of France, God spoke one word over me: Abundance. That's it. That's the simple word God gave me on the beach, watching the waves and reading about abundance in the Bible. These verses touched me:

> For the Lord has ransomed Jacob and redeemed him from the hand of him who was stronger than he. They will come and shout for joy on the height of Zion, and they will be radiant over the bounty of the LORD—over the grain and the new wine and the oil, and over the young of the flock and the herd; and their life will be like a watered garden, and they will never languish again. Then the virgin will rejoice in the dance, and the young men and the old, together, for I will turn their mourning into joy and will comfort them and give them joy for their sorrow. I will fill the soul of the priests with

abundance, and My people will be satisfied with My goodness (Jeremiah 31:11-14 NASB).

I look back at my life and see how amazingly God has delivered me from the hand of the enemy. It's true. It's evident. But what I've come to realize is that so much of my transformation, unfortunately, has been birthed from my own initiation, by my own strength. I have decided to change, so I have. And yet, I wonder why at the end of the day I grow terribly weary, lacking the abundance God provides. I wonder why my spiritual battles fail. I don't want to be a person who acts like Jesus in my own insufficient strength. I want Jesus to strengthen me from within because of my weakness. That's where abundance comes.

When we forsake our glory for His.

When we lay down our lives for the sake of others.

When we stop pitying ourselves and instead prostrate ourselves before God.

When we believe in the bigness of God and the smallness of the enemy.

God wants to flood our empty-cupped
lives with laugh-out-loud hope.

We should yearn for abundance. Not our self-manufactured abundance, but His overflowing, river-like abundance that springs deeply from parched souls. We must grow tired of ministering from our lack. We need Jesus. To sit at His feet like Mary instead of puttering around in a Martha-like frenzy.

More than Optimism

Isn't that what we all want when we talk about winning spiritual battles? There is a marked difference between optimism—glass half full—and biblical hope—an overflowing, victorious life. And the difference is Jesus. I've struggled with pessimism my whole life. I've aimed far too low, merely wanting to mimic my husband's effervescent optimism. God wants more for His children. He wants to flood our empty-cupped lives, spilling Himself over and around us, surrounding our capricious souls with surprising love, abounding Spirit-driven strength that defies the enemy, and laugh-out-loud hope. If we are merely optimists, viewing the glass of our lives as half-full, it's not enough. We need more.

This chapter was birthed years ago from a conversation with my husband, Patrick, in the middle of our second year in France, right after God had spoken the word *abundance* to me. "I will go home if you can't be happy here," my husband told me, kindness in his eyes.

Forgetting God's word-of-the-year to me, I retorted, "What does happiness have to do with anything? There are people in the world who are starving. Others are martyred. Who am I to dare to want to be happy? This is my sacrifice to Jesus. No, I'm not happy. Granted. But I am called to endure. To grit my teeth through life."

"That's not living, Mary," Patrick told me. His words stopped my heroic sentences. And all at once, I realized I'd been living my life in Jesus with a poverty mentality—glass all empty, teeth clenched in determination. And in my soul, I realized that Jesus didn't merely want me to move from an empty glass to a full one, but that He wanted to do something entirely different—to spill His infectious presence into my parched life in such a way that I would thrive, not merely survive.

These words are a result of that quest, about God's surprising and practical abundance for everyday women like me, a pilgrim who struggles, who sometimes glimpses snapshots of God's abundance, who longs for more and more and more of Jesus's presence in her ordinary life.

I wrote a poem about this. It captures the journey I take now—the struggle to understand an abundant God who wants to overflow my weary heart, even as the beautiful battle rages.

> I'm a little girl clutching wilted daisies
> wetting my shoes with anguish
> head cast downward to the stony earth
> The King's supposed to pass this way
> I hear the sound of His laughter
> while daisies drop petals like tears
>
> I see His face; I hide my own
> He lifts my chin to sunshine eyes
> and breathes in the bouquet of me
>
> His retreating steps pound my heart
> I feel His abundance still
> And I am holding roses

My prayer is that you'll let Jesus breathe in the bouquet of you, let Him hand you an abundance of roses. I am on this journey with you, still longing for more, still tripping through life, so utterly clod-footed. He calls warrior women to abundance, but the devil woos us to wallow in our perceived deprivation. And he sometimes reorients us to the past so much we can't see forward to a good future.

Unfortunately, I spent a great deal of my Christian walk looking back. Having grown up in a dysfunctional home, I picked through the wreckage of my upbringing, trying to make sense of it all. Now in my forties, I understand the necessity of letting go and moving forward. Still, it's a hard habit to break. Even looking back on spiritual victories stifles my forward momentum.

Who has helped me shift my focus from backwards to forwards? Lot's wife, the Israelites, and the apostle Paul.

Remember Lot's wife.

Lot's wife looked back at Sodom and Gomorrah and became a Morton's salt statue. Scholars say her "looking back" can also be rendered "lagged back" or "returned back." Some suggest she hadn't internalized the faith of her husband and longed more for the comfort and luxurious life she knew in the past. Jesus said our hearts would be where our treasure was. As she looked back, her heart (and her entire body) became one with her treasure.

It's not an easy story to digest, where disobedience and God's judgment are so clearly delineated. In light of this, I've often wondered why Jesus told us to remember Lot's wife (Luke 17:32). In the context of the passage, He's talking about His second coming, how folks would be living their average lives, cooking, eating, merrymaking—oblivious to the fact that the end of the world was around the bend.

Prior to this, Jesus said, "A person out in the field must not return home" (Luke 17:31). This is reminiscent of Jesus's words about the kingdom—that folks shouldn't bury their fathers or look back to their plows because following Him is all about leaving the past behind and going forward with Him in the great adventure.

I embodied Lot's wife when our family moved to France and life became unbearable. My heart latched onto my home culture. I lamented that I'd lost the old, familiar Mary. I pined for who I was in the United

States—stable, dedicated, steadfast. Amid culture shock and other difficulties, I felt like I'd lost the essence of who I was.

It took me two excruciating years of struggle to look forward, to embrace France as our home. Ironically, four months later our family moved back to America.

Israelite me.

I lived those two years in the land of lament when I should've been looking forward with baited expectation! I'd become like the grumbling Israelites, crabby about where God had led me for the sake of His kingdom. I doubted God's provision. I said bitter prayers like, "Why did You take me here, only to be beaten down? Why did You allow so much heartache when we chose to follow You to the ends of the earth?" Nearly reveling in the pain, I let complaint be my language of choice. I pined for Egypt, disdaining the wilderness. It's never easy to admit you're an Israelite, particularly in this context. But I was. Like them, I was guilty of:

- Retooling history to make it more glorious than it was.
- Gulping in fear over the present and the future.
- Failing to believe God would do good things.
- Choosing to live in the glory days.
- Allowing the enemy to speak unhindered words of discouragement.

To this backward-looking nation, Isaiah preached these God-breathed words: "Do not call to mind the former things, or ponder things of the past. Behold, I will do something new, now it will spring forth; will you not be aware of it?" (Isaiah 43:18-19 NASB). The haunting part of that verse is that question. *Will you not be aware of it?* God's about to do amazing things, creating pathways through our wilderness lives and waterways through our parched souls, but if we continue to look back with longing for what was, we could miss the things God is doing today. To pine for the glory years is to give Satan a foothold on your attitude.

Oh, to be like Paul.

The apostle Paul could have reveled in his past life. In Philippians 3, he highlights his amazing spiritual resumé. He tells of his circumcision, his impressive Jewish lineage, his zeal. The old Paul was passionate about following God, so much so that he persecuted a pesky sect called the Way.

Paul's past was perfect—in terms of Judaism, flawless. Does he stay back there, longing for his former legalistic zeal? No. "But whatever things were gain to me," he says, "those things I have counted as loss for the sake of Christ" (Philippians 3:7 NASB). Later in the passage he views his previous life—in this case, his life before knowing Jesus—as dung, because knowing Christ in the present is of much more value.

So much of what God wants to perform in the lives of warrior women involves this movement from legalism to freedom. We applaud our slavery to a rule-based religion because we've become accustomed to the chains. They feel familiar, but taking them off is not. In fear, we remain shackled to the way we did things in our past.

I remember my disillusionment after I graduated from college and started teaching junior high English. For two years, I lamented that I was no longer "making a difference." Back in college I'd memorized Scripture, enjoyed an early-morning quiet time, ministered to many folks, ventured on mission trips. I was Super-Christian! So when I languished in the classroom, crying every day as I came home from school, I worried I had lost my spiritual self.

Little did I know that God used those years of classroom frustration to rebuild me. He showed me that I am much more than what I do for Jesus. He values me, not merely my legalistic output for Him. Yet I fought Him fiercely as He retooled me into a more balanced believer. I forgot Paul's sage words, "Therefore if anyone is in Christ, he is a new creature; the old things passed away; behold, new things have come" (2 Corinthians 5:17 NASB).

In his landmark book *The Rest of God*, author Mark Buchanan summarizes beautifully the importance of Paul's words. "Don't revive what God has removed. Don't gather and piece back together what God smashed and scattered. Don't place yourself in a yoke that God broke and tossed off with His own hands."[1] It is a choice to let go of who you were in the past, embracing what God wants to do today. There is victory in that.

Let the past sleep.

I've pined for the old country and the old me, just like Lot's wife. I've grumbled in the wilderness like the Israelites. I'm learning to walk a tentative, forward-moving faith journey like the apostle Paul. I long to follow Oswald

Chambers's sage advice: "Let the past sleep, but let it sleep in the sweet embrace of Christ, and let us go on into the irresistible future with Him."[2]

Onward and upward we climb toward the freedom-infused life God has for us. Unlike those who look back, we turn our faces forward with holy anticipation of the rivers of His presence spilled over into our lives. Life might've been difficult in the past, or it might've been so good that we spend our energy pining after it. Even so, new adventures with Jesus await us around the bend. Will we not be aware of it?

The Call to Finish Well

My grandmother always loomed over me, lean and sometimes bitter, but when she reached for my hand I knew it would be our last clasp. Her eyes, normally full of fight, held fear. I flew home from that last visit with a burden—to tell her about Jesus once again. So I wrote her a letter, sharing how Jesus had rescued me, forgiven me, healed me. A few weeks later, we talked on the phone. "That letter you wrote," she wheezed. "I read it over and over again." A month later, she died. As I sang "Amazing Grace" over the wet earth holding her coffin, I hoped she'd ended her life well, holding the hand of Jesus on her final journey. But on this earth, I'll never know.

My grandmother's death marked a change in my life—a fiery desire to finish well. To not only live in the moment for Jesus, but to follow Him to the very end of my days. I didn't want folks singing songs over my grave, wondering. From the breath I take today to the last breath I inhale on this earth, I want folks to know I chased after Jesus, that I finished this life well—that I didn't give in to the wily temptations of the devil, that I proactively followed after Jesus.

Who in the Bible started well? And who finished well? What kind of lessons can we glean? Let's look at the stories of two kings: Asa and Manasseh.

King Asa: Started Well

King Asa of Judah had a heart after God. He fired his own grandmother, who worshiped foreign gods. He tore down pagan altars and sacred pillars, and he removed the high places. He strengthened the defenses of his cities, building up an army of 300,000 men. He encouraged Judah to follow God: "And he commanded Judah to seek the LORD God of their fathers and to observe the law and the commandment" (2 Chronicles 14:4 NASB).

Even as a million-strong Ethiopian army threatened Judah, Asa sought the Lord. "LORD, there is no one besides You to help in the battle between the powerful and those who have no strength; so help us, O LORD our God, for we trust in You, and in Your name have come against this multitude. O LORD, You are our God; let not man prevail against You" (2 Chronicles 14:11 NASB).

What happened? God stopped the wars threatening Judah until the thirty-fifth year of Asa's kingship. But something occurred in year 35 that jeopardized the way Asa finished his life. Baasha, the King of Israel, surrounded Judah and prevented trade—a sure sign of invasion. Instead of seeking God as he'd done in the past, Asa decided to take the treasures from the house of the Lord and bribe a pagan king to protect Judah.

God sent Hanani the seer to reprimand Asa. In this context, Hanani uttered his famous line, "For the eyes of the LORD move to and fro throughout the earth that He may strongly support those whose heart is completely His. You have acted foolishly in this. Indeed, from now on you will surely have wars" (2 Chronicles 16:9 NASB).

The phrase for a complete heart here is *levav shalem*, a Hebrew term that means *wholehearted* or *undivided devotion*. Asa, now the owner of a divided heart, did not heed Hanani's advice. Instead, he imprisoned him and began oppressing his own people. At the end of his life, Asa contracted a severe foot disease (probably gout), and still did not seek God, relying instead on foreign physicians.

Asa did not finish well.

King Manasseh: Finished Well

King Manasseh didn't start well. He began his reign at 12. He worshiped the stars. He crafted altars for pagan deities inside the temple. He practiced witchcraft, divination, and sorcery, and regularly consulted mediums and spiritists. He capitulated to Satan's schemes. He misled his people.

God sent the Assyrians to capture Manasseh and bring him to Babylon. Clothed in bronze chains, Manasseh finally cried out to God. He humbled himself before the Lord. When God brought him back to Jerusalem, Manasseh "knew that the LORD was God" (2 Chronicles 33:13 NASB). Manasseh ended his life by tearing down the pagan shrines he'd erected before, obliterating idols and altars. Instead, he sacrificed offerings to God.

Manasseh ended well. Just as we want to.

How can we learn from Kings Asa and Manasseh? How can we start our lives with wholehearted devotion and then finish this life well, completely devoted to God?

Give God the credit when He delivers you.

God delivered Judah from the massive Ethiopian army. Maybe Asa took some of the credit, believing he was responsible for the victory. Maybe his longing for God's glory changed into a delight in his own. Maybe his heart became proud—much like Satan's when he fell from heaven.

Hosea warned, "As they had their pasture, they became satisfied, and being satisfied, their heart became proud; therefore they forgot Me" (Hosea 13:6 NASB).

Manasseh, instead, chose to give God the credit for delivering him from his enemies. He believed God and dedicated himself to serving God the rest of his days. He understood that God deserved all the glory for his deliverance.

Trust God when things are bad.

Unlike Asa, Manasseh's father Hezekiah prayed to God in his illness. Stricken with a terminal disease, Hezekiah begged God for reprieve. He reminded God of his *levav shalem*. God heard Hezekiah's prayer, and chose to heal him, adding another 15 years to his life. No doubt Manasseh knew this story. Perhaps this is why, when led away in captivity, he begged God to rescue him, following the example of his father. Asa, when calamity came in the form of disease, trusted in himself and doctors; in times of turmoil, he turned away from God's strong support.

Journeying with God is a marathon, not a sprint.

Asa followed God many years. It wasn't until year 35 of his reign that he grew weary of seeking God by trusting in his own man-centered shortcut. But the spiritual life is not about shortcuts. It's about putting one foot in front of the other, day after day, week after week. This marathon called walking with God is always laborious—full of sweat and grit and a rugged determination to keep going when things get tough. Oswald Chambers wrote, "God wants you to be entirely His, and it requires paying close attention to keep yourself fit. It also takes a tremendous amount of time. Yet some of us expect to rise above all of our problems, going from one mountaintop experience to another, with only a few minutes' effort."[3] Though Manasseh limped through his first years, he finished by walking step by methodical step.

Even so, remember grace.

No doubt Manasseh understood God's unswerving grace. After opposing God in the most horrific ways, only to be rescued by that same God, Manasseh remained completely changed by grace.

Even Asa experienced God's grace. The people of Judah remembered him as a man devoted to God. When we forget to give God credit, when we stop trusting God when things go sour, when we forget that following God is a marathon, there is still grace. With God's unmerited support, as believers we can have a *levav shalem*—a heart completely devoted to God all the days of our lives.

When I grasp a family member's hand for the last time, I pray they see a Manasseh-like desire to follow God to the end of my days. And when someone sings "Amazing Grace" over my grave, I hope they sing it as a testimony to a life that finished well. I want abundance, freedom from being shackled to the past. I have a feeling you do too. By God's grace, we will live our lives, day by day, for His glory. And when we do, we will rile the enemy and bless the God who made us.

> When we forget to give God credit, when we stop
> trusting God when things go sour, when we forget that
> following God is a marathon, there is still grace.

Mind if I pray for you?

Lord of finishing well, help us to walk in a manner worthy of Your calling. Help us to remember Lot's wife, tethered to her past, so that we don't live in our memories. I pray for my friend reading this chapter, that You would give her a holy yearning for You, for Your ways, for Your voice. May she stand confidently on the truth that You go before her, that You fight for her, that You provide everything she needs. Make her a grateful believer every day of her life. And this week, may she remember You, to praise You for the victories You bring her way. You are amazing, God. Simply amazing. Amen.

Chapter 24

Go Forth!

*Instead of having spiritual ADHD, a woman who
singly pursues Christ bothers and angers Satan.*

Mary DeMuth

O ne morning I woke up with the idea for this chapter swarming my
brain. I immediately opened up the forum on my website and asked
women to share freely which women's tendencies made Satan happy and
which women's traits ticked him off. We'll start with ten Satan loves to see
in us, as those are things we'll need to look for, examine, and eradicate from
our lives. Then we'll explore 20 traits that anger Satan —positive traits we
can cultivate as we live our daily lives.

Satan Loves to See a Woman Who...

1. Lives in resentment.

A resentful woman does a lot of damage to the kingdom of light. Her
unforgiveness prohibits her from reconciliation. It deadens her heart to the
things of God. Resentment over the past, or even what happened today, creates a hardened heart. Her envy over what others possess causes her to lust for
more. Resentment's natural result is bitterness, and bitterness stifles God's
ability to work through a woman snared by its clutches. It prevents life-
nurturing relationships to form, the very relationships meant to grow her.

2. Slanders.

When a woman gossips, Satan applauds. When she slanders, he dances.
Since God created us all in His image, whenever an image-bearer tears

down another image-bearer it breaks His heart. The spewing of the mouth is the cause of most misunderstandings, arguments, breaks in relationship, and heartaches. A woman who chooses to not control her flow of words gives Satan a great gift—the gift of discord and disunity.

3. Coddles selfishness.

A woman who gives in to her selfish bent delights Satan. Why? Because in doing so she opens up her heart for only one person: herself. Her world becomes myopic, centering only on what will bring her delight, to the detriment of others and the hindrance of God's kingdom advancing. A selfish woman seldom thinks beyond herself. She doesn't worry about those who don't yet know Jesus. She doesn't fret over broken relationships enough to repair them. She doesn't care if she hurts others (unless in doing so, it directly hurts her). She doesn't see the downtrodden, the weary, the hurting. She misses out on the opportunity to see Jesus in His distressing disguise.

4. Feeds on her inadequacy.

Satan would rather a woman focus on what she's not than realize her great potential in Jesus. He would prefer she nurse her insecurities, believing God would never use her rather than boldly entrusting herself to the One who created her for greatness. Satan rejoices when a woman believes his onslaught of lies about her worthlessness, knowing that if he can get her to live as if those lies are true, she'll be completely unable to engage in God's work.

5. Gives in to busyness.

Satan is the king of distraction. If he can't lure us away from meaningful kingdom work, our world (his domain) will flood us with so many opportunities we'll work ourselves sick. If a woman is overbusy, she'll neglect her time with God. She'll let her relationships slack. She'll prioritize her to-do list over the Almighty. She'll equate her worth with what she does rather than who she is, so that when circumstances fall apart, she is more likely to do so as well.

6. Shrinks from her calling.

Satan knows that God has uniquely created each of us to serve a useful purpose in God's kingdom and in His body. Satan is happy when a woman sees her calling and then fearfully walks away from it, letting her worry dictate her future rather than her faith in the God who created her for good works.

7. Lusts.

When a woman lusts, Satan smiles. She can lust for all sorts of things—a man who isn't her husband, a house that she doesn't yet have, a skill she envies, money she thinks she needs to feel secure, clothes that will make her look cool, a youthful appearance. When she lusts, she is looking to idols to fill her heart. And anything other than God who fills her heart will lead down many destructive paths: addiction, sin, obsession, and sometimes ruin.

8. Is appearance-focused.

Satan loves it when women fret only about the outside. I'm not simply referring to appearance, though that can become an obsession. I'm referring to how we appear to others, how we manage our reputations. If all we seek to do is decorate the outsides of ourselves and our personalities, we'll never focus on the place God truly wants to change us: our hearts. Satan loves it when we become really pretty Pharisees.

9. Gives in to discouragement.

This world is discouraging. Satan revels in getting a woman to the place where she gives herself over to discouragement, allowing it to determine her mood, perspective, and actions. A woman who finds God's perspective in suffering makes Satan shudder, so he prefers a woman who allows herself to be consumed by life's painful circumstances.

10. Lives for control.

And yet some women in their quest for non-discouraged lives seek to control every aspect of their lives. They think control will eliminate pain. Why would Satan love this? Because control places the woman in charge of her life, not God. It makes her choose safety over risky faith. It teaches her to follow comfort instead of God.

Satan Hates to See a Woman Who...

1. Reads and obeys the Bible.

Not only does she read her Bible, memorize it, and meditate upon it, but she applies it to her everyday life. She learns not by merely reading

Scriptures, but by living according to them. Her obedience to God's Word riles Satan, makes him cringe, because she advances God's kingdom and renews her mind every time she reads it.

2. Admits wrongs.

A woman who is able to say "I was wrong," ticks Satan off. Why? Because when she does so, she opens the door for relationship and slams the door on discord. Satan is all about disunity and broken relationships— anything that might distract a person away from the triune relational God. In her ability to ask for forgiveness, she recognizes her need for Jesus and His radical act of forgiveness on the cross. And whenever the cross is elevated, Satan shrieks. It's his place of greatest defeat.

3. Is single-minded.

Instead of having spiritual ADHD, a woman who singly pursues Christ bothers and angers Satan. She won't let his lies permeate her heart because she's so consumed with Jesus and His opinion of her. She risks. She trusts. She pursues. She is like Mary, sitting at the feet of Jesus, choosing the good part that can't be taken away.

4. Knows who she is in Christ.

Satan does not want warrior women to realize how valued they are in the kingdom of God, how forgiven, how set free, how beautiful. A woman who realizes who she is in Jesus Christ, who knows that she is now adopted into His family, wildly loved by Him, and endowed with spiritual gifts to build up the body of Christ and advance the kingdom of God, is a dangerous woman to the kingdom of darkness.

5. Practices the presence of the Spirit.

A woman who daily walks in the Spirit, being continually aware of His presence within her, is a dangerous woman. She hears. She obeys. She serves. She sacrifices. Whether she is doing dishes or paying taxes, she is walking continually with God, speaking to Him throughout the day, letting Him interrupt her at will.

6. Prays.

Likewise, a woman who communes with God moment-by-moment through prayer becomes so engrossed with God and His voice that she no longer listens to the lies of Satan. And she watches expectantly as God does the miraculous in and through her. She sees how He answers her prayers in a supernatural way, which makes way for praise of God's goodness.

7. Worships.

A woman who applauds God's worth has less time to worry about Satan and his diabolical plan for the world. A woman who worships takes the focus from herself and her daily life and places it instead on the God who created everything. When circumstances threaten to lay her flat, her commitment to worship God anyway becomes her strength.

8. Encourages.

A woman who seeks to give courage to others is a woman Satan does not like. She looks beyond her day to see others, watch them, and then specifically encourage. She revels in strengthening her friends and family with words of affirmation, gifts, prayers, time, and kindhearted e-mails. She senses the depression in others and seeks to alleviate it, becoming a healing balm to those who hurt.

9. Trusts.

Instead of trusting in her own control, a godly woman trusts in God's ability to order her life, others' lives, and the universe. When a warrior woman places her full trust in God, she removes her gaze from her circumstances. She is more apt to have peace and not give in to hasty decisions and frenetic activity. She rests in God's goodness.

10. Practices contentment.

Although she may want more things or different circumstances, when a warrior woman practices contentment, she learns a great secret: Jesus is all she needs. Satan would rather we look everywhere else for our happiness, so he gets particularly angry when we let go of our desire for things in light of being satisfied with what we have right now. And what we have right now is Jesus.

11. Is secure in God.

Insecurity breeds fear. Fear gives way to faithless living. But when a woman finds her security in Christ, she holds a treasure. She finds peace that passes understanding. She realizes that her problems are small and her God is big. She doesn't have to find her security in what she produces, how she looks, or who she knows. Fame doesn't entice. Superficial beauty doesn't woo. Acclaim pales. Which is why Satan doesn't like a secure woman.

12. Focuses on the heart.

Unlike a Pharisee who only worries about externals and reputation, a woman who angers Satan is a woman who focuses on her heart. She asks God to search her, to change her. She is happy to engage with others in community because in that she'll find more ways to grow. She understands that her weakness isn't something to despise or cover up, but a perfect place for God to display His strength.

13. Has a heart for the lost.

Satan wants people shackled to his kingdom for eternity, so when a warrior woman harbors a heart for the lost, he hangs his head. He knows God delights in using a woman like that to bring others into His kingdom. She understands the paradox of dirty hands and a clean heart—hands that long to dirty themselves in the lives of others while maintaining a clean, passionate heart.

14. Follows her calling.

A warrior woman who realizes her potential in God's kingdom is one who weakens Satan's hold on her. She discerns what God is saying in the story of her life. She takes seriously how God has created her, what call He's placed on her life. Though she might be afraid, she fully embraces the task God has entrusted to her. Like the parable of the talents, she takes what God has given her and then invests it in the kingdom, seeing fruit 100 times her investment. In that passionate pursuit, she, by the power of the Holy Spirit, advances the kingdom of God.

15. Is wise with money.

Satan delights when we live shackled to debt and the fear of lacking money. He shudders when we remember that God owns all our money, our possessions, our talents. When we give of our resources freely, when we spend wisely and don't overspend, when we tithe to God as a sign of our dependence, we help fund God's kingdom work. This does not please Satan, who would rather have us ensnared by poor money choices.

16. Refuses to listen to Satan's lies.

We all hear those accusations—about our worth, our lack of beauty, our incapability. The question is: what do we do with them? Listen? Coddle? Believe? Act on them? A woman who ticks off Satan is a woman who chooses to take those thoughts captive, who hears, then rebukes what she hears, who knows God's Word so well she is able to talk back with truth.

17. Is sexually pure.

A woman who understands that her body is God's temple and protects it as such really bothers Satan. A woman who has been violated sexually but seeks to get healing from her Creator through counseling, prayer, and authentic relationships, is a woman who can then help other women who struggle with sex. A woman who dares to keep her mind clean by avoiding licentious TV, magazines, and books is a woman who has mastered her heart. She knows the truth of Psalm 101:3: "I will refuse to look at anything vile and vulgar. I hate all who deal crookedly; I will have nothing to do with them." A woman who dares to be honest with her spouse when she's tempted to entrust her heart to another man is a woman who walks in freedom and light.

18. Knows and offers forgiveness.

All women have regrets. Satan's ploy is to magnify those regrets so that women forget the radical forgiveness of Christ. But a woman who makes Satan shudder is a woman who believes in her forgiveness. In light of knowing the length of how far God went to secure her forgiveness, she, as a sinner saved by grace, offers it freely to others.

19. Finds joy amid suffering.

All of us can suffer poorly. But a woman who makes Satan mad is a woman who finds joy in the midst of suffering. She finds peace in chaos. She praises in the storms. She remembers who God is whether she's walking in the valleys of pain or the mountaintops of elation. She stands out because of this. She becomes a woman of influence, the type of woman non-Christians see and become attracted to. She becomes like Jesus: irresistible.

20. Is tenacious.

A woman whom Satan despises is a woman who keeps going despite the pain of life. She tenaciously takes the next step, then the next, then the next. She does not lose sight of the goal. Like Paul, she presses "on to reach the end of the race and receive the heavenly prize for which God, through Christ Jesus, is calling us" (Philippians 3:14.) She perseveres. She stays true to God, even when He seems distant. She does the right thing even when others question her. She entrusts her reputation to Christ instead of the fickle words of others. Even if it means no earthly reward, she chooses to do the right thing, say the right thing, believe the right things. She is unshakable, unswerving. And she obeys her Master with joy.

My prayer is that you are the type of woman Satan hates, that you're actively following after Jesus in every area of your life. My prayer is that this book has served to open your eyes to the battle raging around you, that you clearly understand the importance of living for God's kingdom. My prayer is that you've seen God bigger than you've perceived Him before, that you're more attuned to His beauty. And more than anything, it's my prayer that you'll walk away from this book knowing you are wildly loved by Jesus. In light of that, may you be the sort of woman who takes seriously the calling on your life—to love God, to love others. May you become wholly enraptured by the story God has written about you and through you. And may you dance and sing and revel as you take the next step in your adventurous story. Godspeed!

—

Mind if I pray for you one last time?

Dear, sweet Jesus, it's been a privilege to walk alongside my sister in Christ through the pages of this book. Stir her heart to fear You, to reveal You, to give You glory in every aspect of her life. May her life shake the kingdom of darkness in this beautiful battle. May she no longer settle for less, but give her a holy heart, pursuing and following after You. Show her You love her in tangible, her-shaped ways this week. Open her eyes to the battle raging around her. Let her not be afraid, but firm and persistent. Help her be faithful in small things, humble in big things, and altogether rejoicing along the way. I pray she becomes a warrior woman after Your heart, Lord. Use her beautifully even today. Amen.

Notes

Part One Introduction—Foundations

1. J. R. Vassar, "Spiritual Warfare" (sermon, Apostles Church, New York, August 16, 2009).

Chapter 1—Our Story

1. Augustine, *Confessions,* trans. Henry Chadwick (New York: Oxford University Press, 1991), 3.

Chapter 2—Satan's Story

1. C. S. Lewis, *The Screwtape Letters: Letters from a Senior to a Junior Devil* (New York: Harper-Collins, 2005), 3.
2. Scott Horrell, "Angels Elect and Evil: The Christian in Spiritual Warfare." Photocopy from the class *Angelology, Anthropology and Sin*, Dallas Theological Seminary.
3. Sydney H.T. Page, *Powers of Evil: A Biblical Study of Satan and Demons* (Grand Rapids, MI: Baker Academic, 1994), 296.
4. Lewis, *Screwtape Letters*, vii.
5. Malcolm Thomas, conversation with author, October 2010.
6. Timothy M. Warner, *Spiritual Warfare: Victory over the Power of This Dark World* (Wheaton, IL: Crossway, 1991), 18.

Chapter 3—The Right Story

1. Joni Eareckson Tada, *When God Weeps: Why Our Sufferings Matter to the Almighty* (Grand Rapids, MI: Zondervan, 2000), 202.
2. Oswald Chambers, *My Utmost for His Highest*, ed. James Reimann (Grand Rapids, MI: Discovery House Publishers, 1992), November 11.
3. Eugene H. Peterson, *The Message* (Colorado Springs: NavPress, 1993), 839-40.
4. Tada, *When God Weeps*, 107-8.
5. Dietrich Bonhoeffer, *The Cost of Discipleship* (London: SCM Press, 1948/2001), 44.

Chapter 4—Living the Right Story

1. Lewis, *Screwtape Letters*, vii.
2. Neil T. Anderson, *The Bondage Breaker: Overcoming Negative Thoughts, Irrational Feelings, Habitual Sins* (Eugene, OR: Harvest House Publishers, 2000), 254.

Chapter 5 So What's the Story, Exactly?

1. J. R. Vassar, "Spiritual Warfare, Part Two" (sermon, Apostles Church, New York, NY, August 23, 2009).

2. Sandra Glahn, e-mail message to author, November 9, 2010.

3. Frederick Buechner, *Beyond Words: Daily Readings in the ABC's of Faith* (New York: HarperCollins, 2004), 27.

Chapter 6—Breathing Prayer

1. Andrée Seu, "Oxygen for Prayer Life," *World Magazine*. November 24, 2010, http://online.world mag.com/2010/11/24/oxygen-for-prayer-life.

2. John Dawson, quoted in: Pete Greig and Dave Roberts, *Red Moon Rising: How 24/7 Prayer Is Awakening a Generation* (Orlando, FL: Relevant Books, 2005), 67.

3. Henry J. M. Nouwen, *The Way of the Heart* (London: Darton, Longman and Todd, 1999), 60.

4. Juan Carlos Ortiz, *Disciple: A Handbook for New Believers* (Lake Mary, FL: Strang Communications, 1975), 73-74.

5. *ESV Study Bible* (Wheaton, IL: Crossway Bibles, 2008), 1855.

6. Visit http://healingrooms.com to learn more about this ministry.

7. Brandilyn Collins, "Psalm for Sickness," *Forensics and Faith* (blog), November 13, 2009, http://forensicsandfaith.blogspot.com/2009/11/psalm-for-sickness.html.

8. C. H. Spurgeon, *Spurgeon on Prayer and Spiritual Warfare* (New Kensington, PA: Whitaker House, 1998), 47.

9. Greig and Roberts, *Red Moon Rising*, 62-63.

10. Jack Deere, *Surprised by the Voice of God* (Grand Rapids, MI: Zondervan Publishing House, 1996), 319.

11. This story is also recounted in: Mark Herringshaw and Jennifer Schuchmann, *Nine Ways God Always Speaks* (Carol Stream, IL: Tyndale, 2009), 74-75.

Chapter 7—Loving Truth

1. Mark Buchanan, *Spiritual Rhythm: Being with Jesus Every Season of Your Soul* (Grand Rapids, MI: Zondervan, 2010), 231.

Chapter 8—Practicing Risk

1. Helen Keller, *The Open Door* (New York: Doubleday, 1957), n.p.

2. Lewis, *The Screwtape Letters*, 40.

3. John Ortberg, *If You Want to Walk on Water, You've Got to Get Out of the Boat* (Grand Rapids, MI: Zondervan, 2001), 16.

Chapter 9—Slaying Idols

1. Tim Keller, *Counterfeit Gods: The Empty Promises of Money, Sex, and Power, and the Only Hope That Matters* (New York: Dutton Adult, 2009), 165-66.

2. Richard J. Foster, "The Marks of Spiritual Power," in *The Contemporaries Meet the Classics on the Holy Spirit*, comp. Randall Harris (West Monroe, LA: Howard Publishing, 2004), 33.

Chapter 10—Worshiping God

1. Sam Storms, *Pleasures Evermore: The Life-Changing Power of Enjoying God* (Colorado Springs: NavPress, 2000), 47.

2. Mark Buchanan, *The Rest of God: Restoring Your Soul by Restoring Sabbath* (Nashville, TN: Thomas Nelson, 2006), 24.

Chapter 11—Living the Bible

1. Jack Deere, *Surprised by the Voice of God: How God Speaks Today Through Prophecies, Dreams, and Visions* (Grand Rapids, MI: Zondervan, 1996), 257.

2. Damian Decker, July 30, 2010, comment on "The ESV Study Bible: Customer Reviews," *Amazon*, http://www.amazon.com/The-ESV-Study-Bible/product-reviews/1433502410/ref=cm_cr_dp_hist_1?ie=UTF8&showViewpoints=0&filterBy=addOneStar.

3. Michael Card, Liner Notes, *Poiema,* compact disc, 1994.

4. Ken Gire, *Windows of the Soul* (Grand Rapids, MI: Zondervan, 1996), 17.

5. For an extensive, yet stimulating, discussion of Bible study methods, see: Howard G. Hendricks and William D. Hendricks, *Living by the Book: The Art and Science of Reading the Bible* (Chicago, IL: Moody Publishers, 2007).

Chapter 12—Embracing Rest

1. Buchanan, *The Rest of God*, 83.

2. Richard A. Swenson, *Margin: How to Create the Emotional, Physical, Financial, and Time Reserves You Need* (Colorado Springs, CO: NavPress, 1992), 91-92.

3. Buchanan, *The Rest of God*, 130.

Chapter 13—Chasing Healing

1. Buchanan, *The Rest of God*, 198.

2. Walter Wangerin, *The Book of the Dun Cow* (New York: Harper Collins, 1978), 71-73.

3. L. B. Cowman, *Streams in the Desert* (Grand Rapids, MI: Zondervan, 1997), 254-55.

4. Lewis B. Smedes, *Forgive and Forget: Healing the Hurts We Don't Deserve* (New York: HarperCollins, 1996), 79.

Chapter 14—When Fear Rushes In

1. John Piper, *The Misery of Job and the Mercy of God* (Wheaton, IL: Crossway Books, 2002), n.p.

Chapter 16—When Your Mind Attacks

1. Chambers, *My Utmost for His Highest,* June 1.

2. Ibid.

3. Ibid.

Chapter 17—When Your Family Faces a Battle

1. Marjorie Thompson, *Family the Forming Center* (Nashville: Upper Room Books, 1996), 25.

2. Joseph A. Califano, Jr., *Accompanying Statement: The Importance of Family Dinners VI* (New York: The National Center on Addiction and Substance Abuse at Columbia University, September 2010), i-ii.

3. Judy Douglass, "The Gift of a Prodigal," *Weekly Refill Blog, FullFill Magazine,* May 17, 2010, http://fullfillmagazine.blogspot.com/2010/05/gift-of-prodigal.html.

4. Hannah Hurnard, *Hinds' Feet on High Places* (Wheaton, IL: Tyndale, 1993), 137.

5. Ibid.

6. Judy Douglass, "Prayer for a Prodigal," adapted from: Philip G. Kayser and Mark Bubek, "Christian Parents of Rebellious Children," in *Prayers for Spiritual Warfare* (Omaha, NE: Biblical Blueprints, 2009), 14.

Chapter 18—When Sin and Addictions Threaten

1. Jerry Rankin, *Spiritual Warfare: The Battle for God's Glory* (Nashville, TN: Broadman and Holman, 2009), 57.

2. Roy Hession and Revel Hession, *We Would See Jesus: Discovering God's Provision for You in Christ* (Fort Worthington, PA: CLC Publications, 2005), 60.

3. Rankin, *Spiritual Warfare*, 31.

Chapter 20—When Overt Attack Assails You

1. Michael Pocock, quoted in Laura MacCorkle, "Taking a Closer Look: The Devil, Demons and Possession," *Crosswalk*, January 22, 2011, http://www.crosswalk.com/movies/11644585/.

Chapter 21—Overcoming in Community

1. Dee Brestin, *The Friendships of Women: The Beauty and Power of God's Plan for Us* (Colorado Springs: Chariot Victor Publishing, 1997), 160.

2. Corrie ten Boom, *The Hiding Place* (Ada, MI: Chosen Books, 2006), 12.

Chapter 23—Finding Abundance and Perspective

1. Buchanan, *The Rest of God*, 89.

2. Chambers, *My Utmost for His Highest*, February 18.

3. Chambers, *My Utmost for His Highest*, April 15.

Mary E. DeMuth is an author and speaker who loves to help people live uncaged lives. Author of 12 books, including parenting books, Southern fiction, and a memoir entitled *Thin Places*, Mary speaks around the country and the world. She lives in Texas with her husband and three children.

Other Books by Mary E. DeMuth

You Can Raise Courageous and Confident Kids

Author and mother of three Mary DeMuth has a passion to help families experience authentic, life-changing relationships with God. With biblical wisdom and encouragement, she reveals effective, simple ways for parents to create a safe haven for kids to explore their worlds while strengthening their kids' confidence and faith.

Ordinary Mom, Extraordinary God

Stay-at-home mom Mary DeMuth offers a devotional aimed at the deeper issues of the heart and one that will provide a soothing respite amid chaos. Think of it as Oswald Chambers meets Busy Housewife.

150 Quick Questions to Get Your Kids Talking

Mary DeMuth was tired of family dialogue based only on schedules, chores, or bedtime negotiations. Inspired by Jesus's meaningful interactions with others, Mary shaped this great resource to help parents develop discussion skills, nurture relational talks with kids, and create connected families.

More Great Reading from Harvest House Publishers

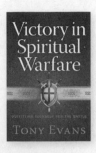

Victory in Spiritual Warfare:
Outfitting Yourself for the Battle

Dr. Tony Evans unveils a simple yet radical truth: every struggle and conflict faced in the physical realm has its root in the spiritual realm. With passion and clarity, Dr. Evans demystifies spiritual warfare so that readers can tackle challenges as they find strength in prayer and sufficiency in Christ.

The Bondage Breaker: Overcoming Negative
Thoughts, Irrational Feelings, Habitual Sins

Neil T. Anderson's bestselling *The Bondage Breaker* guides those bound by any sin to embrace the promise of Christ to win the spiritual battles for them.

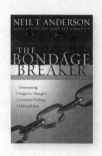

"I'm Not Good Enough"...and Other
Lies Women Tell Themselves

Sharon Jaynes looks at the common lies women tell themselves and shows them how they can replace those lies with Truth. Her book is a handy reference tool that will help women renew their minds and think God's thoughts rather than be swayed by the enemy's deceptions.

Why Do I Say "Yes" When I Need to Say "No"?
Escaping the Trap of Temptation

Readers discover tools to recognize Satan's guises and disguises, find God's "avenues of escape," develop a strong sense of purpose, and gain control over temptation so they can experience the abundant life God promises.